The Wild Rose

Also by Martín Prechtel:

The Wild Rose

*S*tories of My Horses: Volume II

Written and Illustrated by
Martín Prechtel

North Star Press of St. Cloud

Library of Congress CIP data available upon request.

First Edition
ISBN: 978-1-68201-124-9

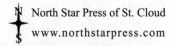 North Star Press of St. Cloud
www.northstarpress.com

Printed in Canada.

Cover painting: *Rewa Dreaming*, by Martín Prechtel.
All text and interior line drawings by Martín Prechtel.
Cover design and interior layout by Liz Dwyer of North Star Press.

Type set in Times New Roman, headings set in Brioso, and Brioso Semibold Italic.

Table of Contents

Notice

All three volumes of the *Stories of My Horses* are meant as an overdue love letter and tribute to all the horses of my life and my beloved New Mexico for the spiritual nourishment and down-to-earth vitality that like a beautiful blanket has kept me warm and hopeful through the cold cynical blizzard of modernity's compromised sense of wonder.

While every adventure, misadventure, and episode found in these books took place precisely where and how they are described, I have taken the liberty of assigning alternative names for most but not all of the humans in my eternal faith that even mean people can change for the better, but also to protect the sweeter kind from any retribution from those that won't change and to respect the privacy of the shy. None of the horse's names have been changed so they can be remembered again by those who knew them.

Disclaimer

Neither the Publisher nor the Author accepts any liability for any mishaps, accidents, or any damages to people, property, or animals occurring from anyone who after reading the *Stories of My Horses* is erroneously led to act on any of the opinions expressed herein as advice of any type or who foolishly decides that they should try to re-enact any of the episodes described in these books in their own lives!

A Dedication

Because the undeniable presence of Pueblo people's early expertise with the old magnificent breed of horse on which their European oppressors arrived has been consciously and unfairly diminished, dismissed, or completely written out of the record of horse history by Euro-American academics, all three books of this series *Stories of My Horses*, are dedicated to the Tewa, Tiwa, Towa, Ashiwi, and especially the Keres speaking villages of the area now called New Mexico. These Pueblo people were indisputably the very first North American First Nation tribes to ever ride, drive, own, and raise horses. Despite four and a half centuries of colonial oppression, it was the original Native Pueblo people's continued proficiency with, reverence for, and adoption of the old Spanish *Mesta*-raised horses into the heart of their spiritual lives that actually converted these unique horses right out from under their own would-be religious converters, turning the colonialist's animals into the very different and fine Native horses they became. Either directly or indirectly it was from these Pueblo herds that *all* the great Native horse cultures—of the Plains, Prairies, and Northwest, of the entire American and Canadian west—received their first "indigified horses" upon whose backs their renowned mobility sky rocketed into the prominence their memory still maintains in the history of the North American Native West.

Introduction

Every Backyard Rose Has a Wild Heart

This series, *The Stories of My Horses*, is not just a compendium of imaginative romantic narratives written to casually entertain the horse loving public.

As romantically remembered as they might seem to be, they are actually straightforward historical accounts of what happens when a life-loving fool like me, a native of that beautiful land-locked, cultural island called Northern New Mexico, who in the latter half of the 20th century, decides he must live his everyday life in direct defiance of the soul shrinking threat of modernity's earth-wrecking ugliness and mediocre existence, by keeping some modicum of the bright shine and outrageous living passion of our real souls alive by flying free and beautiful on the backs of flesh and blood horses over a live unpeopled, unmanicured land.

None of these horses or what happened with them were conjured out of my head, they just seeped into my life like

1

water into a spring, for I knew every one of them personally and lived the life described herein. One of these horses, as of this writing, though very old, still graces our corrals, alongside his great-granddaughters and sons, by the Ojo Caliente creek.

They really did dance with bands in parades, one really had a mouse for a suitor, another bravely fought and killed a mailbox, all of them bucked, one was born in a snowdrift, another under ice, another sliced to the teeth with tin and was sutured up with his own tail hair, they really did save lives, they really lived, loved, died and did all those things written here in these three books, but never at a safe distance, never at arm's length. I was always on top of them singing when they danced, there when we bucked, got rolled on, kicked, or run away with. I was the one who doctored their illnesses, wept for their deaths, made their saddles, and a billion other things we did together and was in turn infused with veritable life when their courage, speed, beauty, sense of humor, weird quirks, and liveliness forced me, through my love for them, to jettison all spiritual laziness, thereby understanding the Holiness in Nature by their natures, despite my young angry self.

No, I didn't want these stories to divert the reader's mind *away* from life but to cause them to get away from the screen, out the door and *into* life.

I wanted these stories to inspire the same courage in you that these little powerful horses have always given me, so you could again find your little-kid smile and the bright eyes of the very young, as if seeing the natural, vital world for the first time, and thereby make the brilliance of your own more original soul find a way to shine out of the prison walls of modernity's shallow choices of inorganic self-designation, to shine out of the cynical myopia of the age where *nothing is good enough*. The *Stories of My Horses* are intended to bust you out of that complacent-citified-cybermaimed-settler-brain we were handed and tendered as reality; to ride again beautifully your own story-horses, not away from life but directly into life, where the freedom of being well right where you nobly stand, becomes the delicious motive for getting up in the morning.

There was a time, and in some small pockets it is still that time, where no matter how tough or weird life seemed to get, certain cultures and people still had lives with enough room to make mistakes, enough time to strengthen their souls and work out their troubles, lives with permission enough to ingenuously shine, where people weren't ashamed of their *bright eyes and sweet smiles*.

Let's face it, even the toughest boring curmudgeon, or the quietest forgotten child, or the most pessimistic environmentalist, or the most self-righteous, cynical, low-vocabulary millennial hipster may feel they are too sophisticated or embarrassed to admit it, but very deep down, like all people who love the world's animals, plants and people, their hearts want a world where they could live exuberantly romantic, a world lyrically expressed, unabashedly unhip and filled with the seriously tangible deliciousness of a heroic soul who struggles magically to antidote the one-size-fits all dead rhythm-drone of modernity's long promised delivery of the *brave new world*.

I say it's alright to be a romantic, it's alright to be heroic, but never in service to hate or success over other humans. For life is not about function or about *getting there*, it's only the beauty of how you go that really matters. Getting *there* doesn't matter but creating a time of hope and real life that you will never see, by the way you go towards it, does matter.

If loving the small details of the natural world, the details of the small farm, loving the fascinating details of the small home of a truly big thinker, loving the complex symphony of the smallest birds, or to have the courage to keep alive the beauty of a deeply lived small existence without causing suffering to land or animals, or by loving the differences in the beauty of people's skins, languages, music and food and thought ways is being naïvely romantic, then yes I'm a romantic.

I'll admit I'm a romantic and heroic. But to be honest, it's not my fault: it's the fault of all the horses I've ever known. For horses since forever, real horses I mean, have always been romantic, noble and heroic by definition of their very existence, and to be with them well, you too have to develop a soul that corresponds!

In my romantic struggle for beauty in an unromantic mechanical age, my horses, simply by how they were, and how we looked, and how we were together, although no more than a tiny broadside against the ghost ship of mediocrity of this crazy age was some kind of victory just by the fact that we still existed. Horses inspire courage against hopeless odds just by their courage and beauty.

To describe this funny micro-struggle of mine, I figured that one simple two-hundred-and-fifty-page book would suffice. I designated this book *The Mare and the Mouse* and proceeded to lay out the tales of the mad antics of all the horses I began to buy, supple and resell during the 1980's while seeking life and refuge in the mountains of New Mexico after returning from those beautiful, but tragically terminated days in the Mayan highlands of Guatemala.

Not only did I underestimate the number of horses I'd actually owned and ridden, but I grossly underestimated the number of wild episodes we were involved in until two hundred and fifty pages became more than a thousand, with me still plowing ahead! I had to break them into thirds and thus the trilogy *Stories of My Horses* was born.

Where *The Mare and the Mouse* leaves off *The Wild Rose* immediately takes up: at the point in time where I ceased buying and suppling grade horses, and was now only interested in gathering up a small herd of the very old New Mexico/Spanish originated, Native American finessed and land-raced descendants of the same horses upon whose backs I rode as a child, whose rare presence had unexpectedly reappeared from their assumed extinction, all to my great delight.

At that time we were still camped up on the Glorieta Creek, at the base of those same Pine, Fir, Juniper covered cliffs at eight thousand feet at the southernmost reach of the North American Rockies, surrounded by wild Roses...

Chapter 1

The Guardian Horse of
the Water Monster Springs

All along the edges of the lives we led inside the mountains of our exile, the modern world of course prevailed. Though we could just barely hear the rumble of its never satisfied, half-awake, mad rush to everywhere and nowhere coming in on the breeze from the interstate a mile off, we paid it little mind.

From where our tents, cabins and corrals sat in the forested canyons, we just continued to grow our old-time native blue corn, eat our home-grown chile, steep our teas from plants the wild hills behind us allowed our hands to take, and with water hauled up to the camp from the clear eddies in the creek we bathed inside our mountain steam bath.

To this day highland Guatemala's Mayan Indians love the venerable institution of the *touj*: their version of the steam bath. Though the fixed, rectangular, oven-like, low timber and wood building to which they were accustomed was not quite feasible where we now made our home, we continued this traditional way of bathing, but in a style that was new to us. To keep alive a lot of *old country* traditions, we had to absorb a lot of old local Native ways of doing similar things, which made it all seem fresh.

From our Native friends and clients, especially those from the Diné area who continued to call on us, we learned to build, bathe, and keep from dying of winter cold in sweat houses of a more Apache-Navajo design.

Becenti, besides being the commissioner of New Mexico's McKinley County and one of my most dedicated clients, was also a medicine man—a traditional Navajo *Hatali*. As both a peer and a friend, it was he, with his family, who directed our little clan how to adapt and construct a Diné style sweat house, which served the purpose of a Tzutujil *touj* very well. When overworked and feeling *undone* we would all pile into the hot vapors and slowly sweat ourselves back to life. But when I'd gone too deep and too far in my doctoring of the people, I applied to him for assistance, as well as he did me. In the form of various shorter Navajo curing ceremonials which I had Becenti sing over me, he would bring me back into *Hozhro*.

For those rituals with which I doctored his sons, daughters, wife, grandchildren and in-laws, as well as the ceremonies he administered for me and mine, the presence of clear, unfrightened, untamed, magical water was always central and the first thing we both had to gather. In some cases this could be Rainwater, or even melted Hail, Snow or Sleet. But both of our traditions felt that the life-giving spirit resident in natural water was *frightened* out of the water by metallic storage tanks and plumbing making it de-natured. Such *scared* water could not heal the sick, but itself needed doctoring as much as a sick person to make it *natural* again.

On the other hand, water from a natural spring was considered powerfully endowed with the direct substance of the Holy Beings in Nature. From some springs male water trickled, while others held pools of female water, in some springs both male and female water bubbled up. Though distinct and separate in language, tribe, landscape and ritual theory, the procedure and ceremonial etiquette of how one should receive and carry water away from such springs had so many practically identical customs that Becenti and I would sometimes economize and gather our ceremonial waters together, either driving or riding horseback with our respective offerings to specific wild, untapped springs.

There we both conversed directly with the bubbling water, each in our own language, reiterating the mythological history to the Deity form residing within. We both agreed, as well, that it was no good to talk third person about somebody if they're standing right in front of you as if they were absent. And since the water of the bubbling spring didn't only house a God, the water actually *was* the God or Goddess, He or She was very present and therefore we spoke directly to the Holy Water.

In a dry, mysterious place like New Mexico, it almost goes without saying that the presence of springs are special to everyone, not just Natives. But because the ceremonies of life-maintenance we did in the present came from a time before the European interruption, some Natives knew more about the memory and whereabouts of springs that had once existed, long before anybody's time, some of which could no longer be seen. Those who made the maps today didn't know about these.

Most beautiful of all were those caved-in ancient springs which originally bubbled out of the land into kiva-like rooms sunk into the earth around them—sacred subterranean chambers whose floors were pools. Here, much older cultures had maintained their sophisticated rituals right in the water inside the ground. These places were still considered inhabited by the water's spirit though no water could be seen, having dried up, and the walls in ruins.

The mystic reality we'd all been told was that when these original people had moved or disappeared, the presence of the water went with them. However the memories of these places are still remembered by today's Native ritual societies, who even though the water was gone, the Holy water bowl and medicine preparation in the ceremonies that necessitated the memory of that particular spiritual spring's water presence could be now supplied by melting snow or rainwater that naturally collected in the precincts of the residual jumble of these old tumbled-in water temples.

Mr. Becenti, because of his ritual education, had spoken many times of an *eastern* spring that lay somewhere in the area surrounding our camp. It belonged to a Towa people affiliated with the powerful Pecos Pueblo one hundred and fifty years previous, before they were forced to emigrate to Jemez Pueblo, a Pueblo traditionally allied with certain clans of Navajo people. Becenti still knew what the spring spiritually signified in the ritual geography of the long story from which the ceremonies he wielded derived their procedure to heal. And I knew exactly where that spring lay, for it was still alive and bubbling and very much in everyday use both by Natives and non-natives. To that very same spring, more than any other, I regularly took my offerings to pray for the health of our family and my clients. An old stone Pueblo shrine was still alive there, hidden in the bristly undergrowth of wild raspberries, above and behind a small cave mouth out of which tinkling water flowed into a stone rimmed pool in front. But old Spanish speaking families living in remote hillside villages thereabouts also relied on this spring for all their drinking water. They called it the Ojo Sarco.

Becenti and I concurred that water from this spring should be the one I should use this time in the *doings* to restore his wife's ancient mother, who, because of Navajo custom, Becenti himself was not allowed to doctor. Her family had brought her to our camp after she'd rolled out of a truck and was pretty bruised up. What she wanted of me was to divine the spiritual reason behind her mishap, find out what trespass they had committed, causing some God or Force, maybe Lightning or a Bear or the Snakes or whomsoever it might have been, to cause her to be hurt by an insulted Earth. She wanted a ceremony that would inspire the Holy cause of her mishap to *personally* come spiritually to my ritual and restore the woman and to become friendly with her destiny again. Native healing relies on realigning an entire situation: the history and sequence of the cause of distress. It was not simple-minded and mechanical like modern medicine.

No one is young enough to go unhurt when rolling out of trucks when a door unexpectedly flies open while driving down the highway, but this lady was very old, way too old to be rolling out of moving vehicles. She was pretty beat up, but she was not frail. And for all that, she was unconcerned about her bruised body, she knew that would heal on its own. What she wanted was a way to restore the *Hozhro* again, the good-happy-everybody-doing-well kind of being, so accidents like this would cease!

Tough people like this woman are not only born from their mothers that way, but the lives they lead are their real mothers, from whose vicissitudes and necessity a resilient body and vision of life are kneaded into their being as they mature. The way of life she'd always known made her vital and pliable, and her strength, like many other women of her day, is what made them patient enough to be grateful for the lives they'd been dealt. One third of her was created by her people's lifestyle, another third of her came from the people she was born to, and one third of her tenacity came from the rugged land itself, whose supernatural ordinances made her who she was.

The Diné Navajos have many permutations of a large array of beautiful ceremonies that are prescribed to realign goodness in the event of various mishaps or sicknesses. Very logically her people thought she should have had a traditional Diné *Inaji* ceremony sung over her, but this old lady had her own ideas and insisted that Martín and his rituals were what she wanted to put things right with the *Hozhro*. This *bimasani* always mystified me with the friendship we enjoyed and the complete faith she had with my half-breed origins and my tribal medicine from faraway. It was she who had named Zajlani, my mare, the year past during their last visit.

In the meantime Zajlani had dropped a beautiful, solid seal-bay colored colt some three months previous, and whenever I rode out on his mama in the unpeopled land he just ran right alongside us. This was the old method of training a young horse the world over: because all animals learn most everything they know, both good and bad, from their mamas. If Mom could be ridden or driven and baby comes along participating in every motion, baby learns very quickly how to do everything that Mama does, and it's not long before the little horse is saddled or harnessed and being ridden or driven.

Accidentally bred through a fairly conducive rubber band fence, Zajlani had arrived to our mountains already pregnant. Nobody mentioned she might have had a foal in her belly when they sold her to us, but to our great delight, one morning there he was, a big knobby-kneed bay colt loudly suckling his patient mother's udders. The colt was beautiful, Zajlani had plenty of milk, all was fine. I guess that was the beginning of my horse breeding days even though I don't think I realized it yet.

◆ ◆ ◆

The morning of our pilgrimage to the spring, this good-looking colt ran circles around us as Becenti and I rode up into the mountains. Becenti was an open-country man from livestock herding Navajos who knew how to ride really well; he was a great companion. Once we were out of earshot of the camp, out in the woods and within the earshot of the Gods who live only in the wild, Becenti started singing, a lot like I always did.

A retired member of the Navajo Mounted Police, Becenti rode very erect, a little bit like a cavalry soldier, while I, the half-breed, rode more like a *crazy Native*. We laughed a lot about it. With the colt running circles around us, we jogged up and over the ridge behind the camp and then down and past the Pecos River and up the opposite slopes to an almost hidden cañoncito whose narrow sides were covered in Oaks, Firs, and Wild Raspberry bushes. After opening a side gate and passing around a cattle guard into BLM land, we found our way temporarily blocked by a band of thirty golden-colored heifer cows and their calves who just stood and stared at us.

Just as I was about to shoo them off our trail to let us by, an out-of-breath old fellow on foot, with a big, antique .44 revolver in his belt dropped out of the surrounding woods and walking briskly up to where we pulled up, accosted me in not too friendly a fashion:

"Who the hell do you think you are? You think you're something, eh?"

"Well sir, my mother told me I was a human being, and if that's something I guess you're right."

"Well, did your mama tell you *you* could go on other people's land without asking first?"

Becenti was about to respond, but I signaled him to hold off a minute.

Like myself, Becenti knew by the style of fencing through which we'd just ridden that technically we were on public land open to us all, but it wasn't prudent to challenge this old-time Spanish man's ancestral claim to land. Land that his family no doubt still considered communally deeded to them by an old Spanish land grant for their village, but out of which they'd no doubt been illegally divested. The notorious political chicanery of American corruption in the 1920's and before had done the same to so many others, and on this old issue so much bad blood and unresolved grief still sat fresh in people's hearts statewide.

Though I'd never met him, I was pretty sure who this old guy might be, so I took a long shot.

"Those are pretty nice looking cows you got there. They're all golden, eh? Are they all yours?"

Becenti looked down at his saddle horn grinning quietly to himself.

His pistol pulling mighty heavy on the pants of such a skinny guy, the old man grunted, sneered, pushed his hat back, then looking grim started winding up to speak when I acted on a hunch:

"Mr. Maestas, can I ask you a question?"

"Why'd you call me Mr. Maestas, I don't know *you*?"

"Isn't that your name? Pedro Maestas, the man from up the canyon whose son is a plumber, and whose family's been here a long time, and whose family is famous for their golden cows, who sometimes milks them, and the milk is really good for ice cream?"

Startled and not sure which way to head, he looked off at Becenti who was suppressing his grin, eyes bugged out, still staring hard at his saddle horn.

"Yeah. That's me, who told you that anyway?" still sounding pissed off.

"What do you mean? Everybody knows you."

Silence, the smell of cows, Zajlani's colt whinnied out his cute, gravelly little sound. More silence. Only then did I speak.

"Look Mr. Maestas, can I ask you a question?"

Our horses were getting pretty antsy, pawing the ground and increasingly difficult to keep still.

"Okay, what you want to ask?"

"Is it alright if Mr. Becenti and I, with our horses, cross over your land here to get up to the old Ojo Sarco on the side of the mesa there? We came to get some spring water."

All of the sudden smiling and petting my horse, Pedro laughed:

"Sure, why not, don't be crazy, you don't have to ask! When you guys are done come on over to the house and have some coffee." It was all a normal New Mexico "how d'ya do?". I'd grown up with a whole generation of beautiful heartbroken people whose nobility just needed you to recognize the legitimacy of their presence. I really wasn't any different.

Whistling and yelling, we helped Mr. Maestas drive his cows where he directed, up the trail to the ridge top, way past where we should have cut off. Then we turned our horses around and headed back down towards the spring, waving to the friendly old fellow on our way down.

Grinning like a little kid, Becenti leaned over to me from the saddle as we descended, "you know this land doesn't belong to him."

I laughed and replied, "Yeah, but it used to, and you Navajos probably think it all still belongs to you!" And continuing our joke as we arrived to the spring: "One thing I do know is this land sure as hell doesn't belong to me, it belongs to the Holies."

"Hasho. Hasho." Becenti concurred laughing.

The entrance to the spring always looked different every time I went there. There were still remote mountain families with houses glued to the sides of slopes who counted on this spring's water for all their drinking and cooking. People were always adjusting or even hiding its approach to keep the water clean. Today, we found it had been fenced with cedar branches, wired to keep cows and elks from loitering in the water and fouling the little pool in front of the cave from where the clear water gently rippled out. But someone had the good thought to dig some little rivulets lined with stones to allow a small amount of water to run out from under the little fence to fill some shallow mint-lined side pools where any animal could drink to their heart's desire, but be less inspired to topple the fence trying to get into the clean water.

We tied our horses to some scrub oaks behind the cave and after climbing up to the shrine cleverly hidden in the brush, we made our prayers there and left our offerings. I pulled out the little clay pot from my saddle bags we'd brought along to fetch the sacred water. Then pushing off our boots, rolling up our pants, we crouched down and sort of half crawling, waded into the little cave.

At the back, on a rock ledge, I balanced the empty pot so it would slowly fill up with water from the little drips raining down from the stalactites on the ceiling of the grotto. This was the Male Water which always falls vertically down. Such water came from the Sun himself and was just what we'd hoped for. Female Water was that clear, delicious liquid singing up from the Earth's rocky floor.

This cave's pool was known to Natives as the Water Monster Springs. Like tiny dragons, newts with their frilly gills flitted around, these were the water monster's babies. Becenti caught one and dropped him into the pot with a turquoise bead as a gift. He'd come home with us to witness our *doings* and I'd bring him back and release him here again in a couple of days. When we began our singing, the cave echoed and thudded so powerfully with the song that the pool rippled in rings from the audial force. When Becenti's songs were over, he drank deeply from the pot, then passed the pot to me and I did the same. Then replacing the pot, we let her fill all the way up while together we sang my songs. Both our songs were our prayers and the water filled up with them. We concentrated and sang hard, trying to ignore the loud rumble and ruckus of horse squealing and hoof-beat thunder rolling over our heads in the grassy glade above the cave.

Once we'd come to the end of our prayer singing, surmising that our horses might have gotten loose, we ran out to take a look. While our animals were still dutifully picketed and tied, a little butter-colored gelding, with a long neck like an eel, was rearing and gnashing his teeth and violently charging Zajlani's colt who I'd left grazing free, trying to drive him off and away from his mother, like stallions do to breed their mamas. The strange thing of it was this obnoxious assailant was not a stallion, but a fat and intrepid gelding with shiny dappled sides, a big hard head with a short skunk mane and a long tail. Zajlani, though tied, had already taken a lot of fur and a flap of skin off the intruder's chest with her own furious mule kicks.

Becenti whispered: "Look at that crazy horse, he's got the same face as your colt!"

I looked and he was right. They had the same expressive jaw lines and eye set. Becenti tapped my arm and pointed with his lips at the gelding. "If you could catch that horse, you and I could make some money."

I turned and stared at him detecting some ancient eager delight, which I took to be that of an old-time Navajo horse thief. "What d'ya mean, he probably belongs to somebody?"

"Ya maybe, but that horse is the Horse of the Sun. Check him out. He could outrun an Antelope, he's bound to be fast."

"No way! Look at that his neck," I said, "it's like a snake, and his butt's all jacked up like a redneck truck, it's a full head higher than his withers."

"Exactly! That's just what makes him fast!"

"I thought the Horse of the Sun was an Abalone Horse (a Roan Paint)?"

"Oh yeah, some people say that, but only in the summer. This is a Winter Sun's Horse, he's very fast, that's why winter days are so short, because he runs his race so much faster!"

"Ah ha," I said in wonder, for I'd never heard that part.

"I wonder whose horse he is? He's probably not wild because he's up here all by himself, plus he's gelded, just pretending to be a stallion." Then grinning Becenti said, "maybe his owner would sell him to you and then we could race him on the big Rez!"

But we were on a bigger mission and there was no one to ask about him. We headed home.

Cradling the pottery jar, we took turns singing as we ferried the water and the Water Monster Baby gently back to our camp. The ceremony coursed to its height and after another day of feasting, a day of resting, riding and joking, our Táa Diné friends packed up and drove away west to their homes. Grandma felt better and life went on.

Chapter 2

A Round Horse in a Square Hole

Sometimes even the wind has to catch her breath, for now and again the sound of the wind politely held off, resting from her loud project of sieving winter out of the mountain springtime air, using the delicious smelling end-buds of Firs, Pines and Junipers as a colander.

During those lulls, you could hear the wet clicks and gurgling trickles of the remaining shade-sheltered snow patches melting in the sun; the lacy winter ice that still clung to the edges of the potholes that peppered those big raspy capstone tongues that paved the flat tops of our fossil packed sandstone cliffs melting into cliff top pools.

This shy, rock-wetting sound was the favorite of animals listening everywhere: those still underground and those already emerged, for the collective din of all those tiny dribbling voices from a couple miles of creekside cliffs meant we must congratulate one another on having survived yet another cold winter up in the highlands of New Mexico.

Dammed by the edgerock, these cliff-top pools would eventually overflow, the cold water careening off the cliffs to hang in long strings of droplets so evenly spaced as to create screens of glass pearls that seemed to stand still, like beads in a curtained entrance to the little cliffside caves and ledges.

But at the base rock, onto which these waterfalls crashed from their fifty-foot free fall, the curtains exploded into a fog of mist from whose violence the frail Pasque Flowers, sheltered by the over-hanging boulder bottoms from where they peeked, just missed being thrummed to death.

All the plants, birds, bugs, mammals, rocks and a few humans (the reptiles were still all sensibly asleep) knew, though all these tiny melting sounds throughout the mountains gave birth to a short-lived annual spring rendezvous of waterfalls and great stone walls of seeping water, that Her generous moistening of our otherwise much drier world was in reality Her pushing as hard as she might to get as far away from us as she could, rushing her water into any local stream, and from there on to a proper river, rolling frantically down, down, in white water currents to her Mother the sea, negotiating a thousand tricky miles of dams and irrigation projects farther to the south to get there.

Our winters in the mountains were nothing less than an annual re-enthronement of the royalty of what little remained of the Pleistocene, who still alive at the edges of its past, now only ruled in a single season, but who faithfully left the throne to Spring, who took our ice-age snow melt too quickly away from the arms of the land back into the rising oceans.

But the aroma of last year's rotting leaves, dead creatures, earth, and stone exposed by the melt of the mountain springtime no doubt smelled in some small way no different than it must have, the first time it ever happened, after a hundred millennia of glacial ice finally thawed into the cyclic seasons of our day. What an aroma that must have been! And in its new annual miniature form, this smell in our late spring still released into the air so many of those original life-giving-post-Pleistocene-snow-melt ions that it could reboot the body and soul of every plant, animal, and person that had ever been allowed to sniff it, or drink its electric trickles rolling over the eaves of the cave edges.

This smell was an old smell that made all things new again. A smell whose inhaling firmly bucked off all the B.S. of every tail-chasing, mind-wasting entropic winter preoccupation to which the modern person's mental claws so desperately cling to keep from losing their place in the checkout line at civilization's insane shopping-mall-existence and silly cyber-assisted parade to anywhere besides the sanity of Nature.

This smell cleared the mind of impossibility and cleaned the soul of desperation, and gave the body organs bravery enough to live on another year in a mortal world.

The imaginations of our natural souls gently herded out of winter's quiet abbreviation of living by this mind-reaming smell of springtime's creaking-thaw, were once again whipped back to life, and like water dribbling through the purple lichen-covered stones, could again dream some outrageous, unlikely plant-like notions complete with roots, fruit and a hope of culture beyond our own.

But...

Not today...!

For at that very moment—like all my horses who suddenly exploded, crashing against the corral fencing, looking for any way out—my own dreamy core jumped out of its annual springtime reverie, flushing like a covey of startled quail.

The entire land jumped when the roar of a shiny Blazer rolled into our mountain camp. Like a monster maneuvering too fast between the trees and my blinking soul, its horn blared away even after the Blazer had stopped, and its engine stilled not thirty feet from where I'd been sniffing spring and listening to the water heading to the sea.

The synthetic stink of a car just switched off, the creaks and pings of an engine trying to cool took over the air, under the still-fading echoes of the horn off the canyon cliff, until a lady's voice began to bugle from the driver's window, "Hello, hello, hello," launching another kind of echo over the receding sound of their entrance.

"Hello, hello, are you Martín?"

I descended the cliffside, ambling sideways down the rocks, and before I could answer, a middle-aged woman popped from behind the wheel, grabbed a walker from the backseat and rushed to meet a rather roly-poly gentleman spilling his generous self out of the passenger side.

His door swung wide open in the sun and before he'd even properly plugged himself into his walking device, and before his feet had met the rugged mountain ground, he too commenced bellowing as loud as he was big in what was intended, I'm sure, to be a friendly, well-rehearsed blaring introduction:

"Hello sir. We've come to buy that tough little Spanish Barb gelding you're trying to sell that's short enough for a man like me to mount, and strong enough to carry my weight, and that can go the distance."

What looked to be ten, one-hundred-dollar bills fluttered in his right hand all the while he sang this well-rehearsed refrain:

"And here's a thousand dollars, so we can buy that little horse right away and get this all settled before some accursed idiot gets a hold of him before I do, like the last time."

Growing up in my family, and with proud Pueblo Natives, "money flashers" like this were invariably assumed to be Texans, and such flashing of money was pretty much considered an insult to the more gradual back and forth trading to which we were more accustomed. Though always humored, none of us were ever impressed, no matter how economically hard-pressed any of us might have been. Anyway, I was still full of the delicious smells of spring on the mountain, and for my soul, I did what we always did. I laughed.

"Looky here, I've got a picture of the horse I'm looking for right here," and with his walker propped against the Blazer door he deftly slid a pretty fancy photo album off his dashboard (he was a photographer it seems) and managed to pull a large photo from it and push it into my hands.

I hadn't even spoken yet. Not one word!

"Now, this guy here is exactly the kind of animal we want to buy. The lady at the stables said if anyone had another horse like this, it would probably be you."

Walking out of the deep shade of the trees into the light where I could see more clearly, there to my great astonishment, for all the world to see, was a picture of none other than that very same bothersome, little, buckskin Indian pony from the Water Monster Springs who had been dive-bombing my Zajlani and her colt! I couldn't believe it.

But in this picture, he was captured in a big square photo, frozen and unmoving, not wild and scary, with no vicious whinny, his forelock combed, standing very calmly, all squared up in a square fenced pen, squarely mounted by a pretty square looking little fellow sitting in a tiny English saddle, with a *proper* riding helmet strapped on his square little chin, holding the reins very squarely in his gloved fists, one of which gripped an English riding crop! How peculiar! I had to chuckle.

Still laughing in wonder, I turned my head to read my horses off on the hill: they were still tense, but quietly lined up together, acutely assessing the proceedings from a safe distance.

Natives laugh about everything.

Some people didn't understand Indians when they laughed, not recognizing it as the audial flowering on the tree of a joyful soul, for their own chuckles were the swing of a sword, the fling of a stone, the firing of a social bullet intending to mock or make another small. So where I grew up, Natives learned not to laugh around whites and to fear a white man's mocking laughter. Because of that, a lot of whites thought Natives were stonefaced.

I unfortunately never learned the custom of hiding my glee and laughed at all irony in the delight that something bigger than people was at work in the world.

Fortunately these two didn't notice much of anything besides their own narrow trajectory.

They'd ask me a question and forget to listen for my response, and as soon as I'd begin to make one, they'd interrupt with more questions, which of course made me laugh even more.

The horses and I concluded these frantic people were a couple of privately endowed Dust Devils, who after three pots of coffee each, couldn't slow down, and spent their entire existence spinning and raising dust in search of interesting people and meaningful situations! They couldn't stand still long enough to take in anything I was trying to convey, like the fact I had no horses for sale, hadn't sold a horse in two years, and wasn't raising Barbs to sell them, but just had them so they existed once again.

"You are Martín, aren't you? The lady at the stables said Martín would have just the horses we were looking for. This one they had there, the one in the picture was already sold out from under us, and she said if anyone had one just like him it would be Martín. Are you Martín?"

"Yes, I'm Martín, but I'm not selling…"

"You're not selling old Spanish horses for endurance rides? The lady at the stables said she knew you and you were selling them, that's why we're here," said the lady of the Blazer, sounding slightly pissed.

"What lady is this?" I asked, wondering who would be sending these kinds of impatient, big-city, whirlwind types to my camp. I couldn't guess.

After pressing a fancy business card into my left palm with his puffy pale fingers, Mr. and Mrs. Whirlwind from Arizona crawled back into their Blazer, lit the engine, handed me the photo to keep and yelling over the motor, the fellow made clear:

"If any horse like this one crosses your path, no matter who owns 'em, please give us a ring, we'll pay you a finder's fee, I'm serious." And just like they whirled in, they whirled out, honking when they hit the asphalt, already running.

"Randy and Manny Lochmier, Action Photographers," read the card. Dust Devil people. Obnoxious but affable. The horses were still bunched up and watched for a long time, just to make sure they were really gone.

Chapter 3

Your Waiter Today Will Be...

Besides it not being any of my business whatsoever, it was also beneath my natural born dignity and totally out of character for me to be calling up the people at the stables that the Whirlwind People had mentioned to find out why they were sending people out into my mountains to buy tough Barb horses, when they knew very well, those I had, I wasn't selling.

What was it to me, that I should be such a busybody as to call them up to ascertain if indeed the butter-colored horse in that photo was the same wild horse at the Water Monster's Springs? What difference did any of it make, that I should need them to tell me how such an incorrigibly rude feral Mesta style Indian pony had come to be a resident equine photo prop in their *proper* Dutch-door, stall-type stables, all tamed up and genteel?

Why should I care who bought that mysterious horse *out from under* Randy and Manny Lochmier (the Whirlwind People)? Especially since I hated talking on telephones at all, on top of which, most horse people drove me nuts no matter how we spoke.

But...

I phoned them anyway!

The people at the stables laughed when I called, having taken bets whether I would or not. The horse in the photo had *not* been sold at all. They were just boarding him for a Ms. Estacionero who still owned him, and that he was *still* very much for sale, and why didn't I just please come by and have a look at the little horse, which is why they'd sent the Dust Devil people up to my camp, to pique my interest. The stable people figured it would be unlikely that I would not come down out of my canyons to at least get a look at a horse like this.

Ms. Estacionero, they said, had made up the story about the horse having been sold to get the action photographers off her back, because she didn't like their *mainstream vibe*, despite the fact that they'd been willing to pay double the asking price (all to the great eyeball-rolling of the stable owners).

This little horse in their stable and in the photo *was* the Guardian of the Water Monster Spring. After escaping from Ms. Estacionero's land partner's pasture just east of the Pecos river, he ran further back into the mountains, and when he found the Ojo Sarco hillside springs (the Water Monster Spring), like some mountain outlaw, he installed himself there and began boldly assaulting anyone who came to fetch the precious water. For over a year he ruled that mountainside.

Strangely, Ms. Estacionero didn't know where he'd ended up, figuring he was just gone, and never seriously searched for him. Most of these tough mountain people would have shot and killed that horse in a second with no qualms, and no one knows why they didn't. Instead Mr. Maestas called the local brand inspector who darted the horse and eventually located his rightful mistress and returned him to her with a waived fine (that's what nice livestock inspectors do).

Knowing she could never handle his wildness, and that he'd refuse to be a pasture ornament and would just jump out again, Ms. Estacionero made the decision to sell him. So, she boarded him at these stables, offered to pay them to train him for riding and put him up for sale through newspaper ads and posters.

For six months, a string of interested parties came in to see him at these stables, and not a few of these made good offers to buy the horse, but she refused every one of them! When questioned, she said the horse told her she should wait for just the *right* party to show up and take him, 'cause she was a New Age Healer and by channeling the horse's spirit he would let her know.

Meanwhile, the feed and lodging bill had continued to mount unpaid, and after eight months the stables were pressing Ms. Estacionero to sell him to pay what she owed them, so they started looking for buyers too.

The afternoon I was to come see the little horse at these stables, another man was there to do the same. A tall young fellow in a small felt cowboy hat leaned against the round pen holding a magazine-like publication with the page open to a specific spot, waiting for them to bring out the butter-colored little Indian pony.

I just vaguely recollected that this kid was the little brother of the woman who'd sold me my Barb mare, Zajlani. We shook hands and waited together.

At the stables, because he was unique and a bit weird, this little horse had become a kind of mascot, a favorite of all the workers and everybody called him Sunny. Compared to all the other gigantic, thin-skinned Hanoverians, Trakehners, Quarter horses, Thoroughbreds and a few smaller Arabs, he was basically a large mouse, and though they considered him to be a pony, he was bigger in soul than all the others.

But when they brought him out, Sunny was definitely the same little yellow gelding from the Water Monster Springs, for you could see it in his form, color and the expression on his face, but the actual *horsality* of the animal I'd met up in the hills was not anywhere in sight. *That* horse was hidden somewhere else.

The year before with Becenti, at the Water Monster Spring, it had taken us an entire hour to get out of range of this little Indian pony's gnashing teeth and striking hooves, and to drive him off my mare without cracking our ancient pottery jar filled with the precious water, and a salamander. We had to stick to the ritual rules which stipulated that once we had the water in hand, the return pilgrimage could not be ruined by any swearing or any thinking with bad thoughts in them; for the cure one hoped to effect by means of the ritual meant the water had to arrive home with us bearing in our hearts the same condition of goodness we hoped to affect! But like a seven-hundred-and-fifty-pound-dive-bombing-mosquito, this gelding, for a half a mile, had given us no peace, thoroughly testing our capacity to *keep a good thought*! We kept the faith, arrived home with the jar, and the sturdy old lady got well. Meanwhile that crazy little horse had run back to his spring and was all but forgotten.

And here he was again. But now, when they walked him out of his stall, already saddled and bridled just like he was in the Dust Devil people's fancy photo, Sunny stood square, and like a three-month-old foal following his handler in perfect obedience, whinnied in a dainty little wispy trill, ever so charming. Wow. What a hambone. Such shameless acting.

It was just as if, while peacefully walking out on the mountain trails with your lover, both of you were unexpectedly assaulted by an armed thug who kept trying to beat you up to have his way with your sweetheart. A ruffian who won't give up, with whom you have a running battle all the way out of the hills before he flees. Then later, when you and your rattled partner decide to be seated in a pleasant restaurant to relax and calm down, find out that your waiter is none other than this same pushy ne'er-do-well, on his best behavior, and doing a marvelous job of serving your amuse-bouche and wine!

It really was that odd.

But not for long:

For to further demonstrate Sunny's reported w*onderful disposition and capacity under saddle*, Bill, the trainer at the stables, mounted Sunny, and very convincingly rode him in a couple of circles and then into their fancy *punchbowl*-style round training pen.

And that's where the waiter spilled the tray.

We watched through the slats as Bill took Sunny around the circle a couple of times. Then all of a sudden, stiff-legging it, Sunny came to an unsolicited stop. When urged forward, the little horse reared straight up in the air, then jumped out like a Jackrabbit, did another circuit at a wild gallop, jerked back and started crow-hopping around in every direction, grunting in the cutest way. His rider started yelling commands right along with the horse's grunting, until frustrated by the lack of compliance, he pulled hard on the reins to stop him, which only exacerbated the extravagance of the ride. For Sunny was prepared and cleverly dropped down onto his knees intending to catapult his rider off forward, but luckily his rider ably side-stepped out of the saddle and scrambled off, out of harm's way, and watched as the horse ran off, really bucking and kicking and raising a lot of dust. After climbing out of the pen and the dust, once Bill stopped choking and caught his breath, he pushed back his goggles and said very soberly:

"Guys, Sunny's never done any of that before." Then smiling, "I guess it was in the honor of you fellows!"

I tried very hard not to laugh, but when I failed, we all had a big long laugh about such a thoroughly inspired demonstration of a well-mannered horse who was still kicking up his heels, bucking in circles, triumphantly screaming and raising dust in that wooden bowl. Bill really was a pretty good sport, but everybody knows *never* and *always* are two words banned from the vocabulary when talking about horses.

"Well, Bill," the tall Rich Kid said, "I think I'll have to pass on this one," and then went inside the office to chat with the proprietors.

For my part though, I was much relieved.

Strangely enough, it was much better this way. For after such an honest and energetic exhibition of what a powerful, uncomprehended little horse could do, I could clearly see how agile, smart, and vital he was, how meticulous his footing was, how steady, and though clever and pretty conniving, he still had a durability and a good sense of humor. Plus, he looked too much like a Mesta horse of some kind for me to ignore.

I remembered Becenti's endorsement of the speed of such an animal, and his personal corroboration of the shape and style of such a beast as being of the original Winter Sun, an Indian/Mesta horse, albeit very slight and antelope-like; not so much like the rhino-lipped horses of my youth.

He was an old style Barb to the last detail. I asked Bill if I could halter Sunny and just walk around together with him for a little while. Though grinning and a bit mystified, he let me. This horse and I walked and talked together up and down the straight roadway in front of the facility, back and forth until Sunny stopped sweating and his heartbeat finally calmed.

Sunny and I pulled off the road when the Rich Kid, driving an old yellow Suburban, tried to get past us as he was exiting the stables.

Stopping, with the engine idling, he motioned me to his window as he searched for a page in the publication he'd been clutching all along.

It was good to notice that Sunny was at home with cars and engines, so much so that when I came up to this boy's window, Sunny's head was next to mine looking at the book right with me.

"You know who this horse really is don't you?"

"What do you mean?" I ingenuously asked. Who else is a horse but himself standing right next to you?

"Look," he replied holding up his open page. And there in one of four black and white horse photos, stood an adolescent looking Sunny, whose lengthy caption said his name was Amarillento, foaled in Northern Cheyene Reservation, Montana, June 19, 1978.

"When I saw his picture on the feed store for-sale poster, I thought he might be Amarillento. Do you remember my sister, the one that sold you your little mare?" (Zajlani)

"Yeah, sure."

"Well, when I was seven or eight, she had big cow about this little horse when he was a stud colt sneaking in and mounting her prize mare without my sister's say so, and had him instantly thrown down and gelded on the spot. She gave him to a friend of hers from massage school who took him out to the mountains so everyone would forget about him."

"Well, that's interesting," I said mildly lying.

"That mare got pregnant by this very horse you're walking around with here, before my sister cut off his nuts. This mare eventually gave birth to a beautiful buckskin stallion. Now that stallion is really good looking and he's our main stallion. He is Amarillento's son. Do you know what that means?"

"That your sister is really embarrassed?" I said.

"No, she doesn't even know Sunny here exists or that he is Amarillento returned."

"What does it mean then?" I asked.

"That the foal *your* mare dropped last year" (Zajlani's colt, the one that ran circles around Becenti and the one this horse here had been hassling at the springs), "is the son of that same stallion of that unplanned breeding. This makes your little colt the grandson of this horse Amarillento!"

Amarillento was smiling. The Guardian of the Water Monster Springs was the grandfather of Zajlani's colt, and he was standing here triumphantly grinning.

This time I didn't lie.

"Wow, that really is amazing."

So I bought Amarillento, and I bought him just for the stable fees, for Ms. Estacionero said that Amarillento finally told her I was the one! Though I have to admit I was already pretty much set on buying him when he was still Sunny, the Horse of the Sun, the Guardian of the Water Monster Springs, before he turned out to be Amarillento, my colt's grandpa!

They really did have the same charming face.

Chapter 4

Amarillento

Amarillento was the definition of a naughty little horse.

He always made trouble wherever there was some to make, and almost always got away with it, because of his tiny, gawky-looking self and very cute face from which no one would suspect any scheming. Whatever mischief he'd been up to, by the time any human was watching, he was always standing in just the right spot, at just the right time, to exonerate him from all guilt, whinnying with his wispy high pitch, friendly voice.

Like the bored, little, genius-school-kid in the lunch line who keeps tickling the ears of the slow-brained brute, three kids in front, with a long skinny invisible wire with a chicken feather glued to the tip, until the bully boiling over turns around and slugs the innocent kid behind him, while the guilty party just stands there in his misted horn-rims looking like an ineffectual beat-down nerd, Amarillento was the horse who would sneak out, unlatch all the corrals at night, let every other horse out, then lock himself back into his own corral, looking like he'd been the only one behaving while everybody accused someone else! He was brilliant and too easily bored.

You had to keep him working or he'd be at it again.

When riding Amarillento, you had to remember you were mounted on some giant, mischievous, shiny, dappled, butter-colored weasel whose body was just the short rear detail of his long snaky neck, with which he whanged his very hard, pretty head around like a sledgehammer on a spring, capable of knocking cold anybody trying to mount, or already in the saddle, or even just standing next to him that wasn't ready to duck to avoid his lethal cephalic thump. He was so cute he faked everybody out.

Our first ride was basically a jujitsu match. Not the kind where anybody gets in a move, but the kind where every move is countered by both contestants. He was checking me out to see if I was worthy of his lordship's effort to carry me across this flowering earth. Like an abandoned street teenager, he was testing me out to see if he could trust my friendship after so many years of betrayal and neglect, to see if I would still stand by him after trying to kill me.

In the American West there are a lot of people who routinely use a tiedown in an attempt to discourage the tossing of their horse's head, but this usually makes it so the horse pushes even more against the restraint and never stops tossing the head and getting behind the bit.

Amarillento had definitely had his head tied down and been ridden on all kinds of martingales and so forth.

But today, I just bridled him and saddled him with no breast collar and ducked when he whanged back at my head with his head as I mounted. Having survived that, when I urged him forward he decided he'd quickly turn his head and bite my left knee, but I lifted both legs, put one on each side of his funny, angry neck, and then turned him left and right with my boot soles behind his eyes.

He was so admiring of this that he thought he might drop to his knees, lift his bottom and get me off by rolling forward in a somersault. Instead of countering that, I encouraged it, and never letting go of the reins, I slid down and off his neck and out of the way before he rolled beautifully over and forward with me watching by his side. Very embarrassed that he'd tossed himself upside down on the ground and not me, Amarillento righted himself, and stood there shaking his mane out pretending like none of it had actually happened!

So I proceeded to mount again, to which he thought he might sidle off to the *lance side* planning to whang his head back at me if I tried to pull him in, instead I picked up his hind leg and held it so he couldn't put it down, when he tried to kick me with it I grabbed his front fetlock and dumped him again, right onto his even more embarrassed side.

I then sat down on his ribcage and started singing my favorite blessing song. Amarillento lay there under me sighing and brooding, snorting dust off the ground. But I knew he was still cooking something up under the guise of seeking sympathy.

When we decided he might again stand, I was already in the saddle before he had all fours on the ground, and this infuriated him so much he reared up very violently, intending to roll over backwards and finish me off. Once again I was lucky to step off and let him do it. We did it again, and again.

After his fourth rear-up after remounting, I deliberately pulled his head to the right all the way to my knee and kept it there until he finally rolled down into the sand sideways, with my left leg locked underneath him.

I talked calmly to him, holding him down, still on top, knowing how many people are grievously maimed when, after being pinned under a horse, as the horse begins to rise, they sometimes put a foot through the downed rider.

Horses love musical language, so in a couple of Native tongues I said: "Now wouldn't you rather be ridden by someone who is comfortable with your funny old quirks, and who thinks you're as handsome as they come, and who would want you to carry him and his people like the Horse of the Sun carries the Sun, and a rider that knows when you die as an old, old horse, you will reincarnate as the Horse of the Sun?

"You must realize horses have a hard lot and don't always get so many chances with good people. So let's both take this one and fight the idea that rich people are the only ones to have a right to say what's a good horse or not. And that the land and the indigenous capacity to live in that land can make it so a lot of good people and old-time horses like yourself can be ridden once again?

"What do you say young Amarillento?" (He was nine then.)

When talking to horses, one has to be lyrical and romantic. It helps both of you to keep your soul intact. But with horses it's also best to be a little realistic too, so I threw in the colophon that must always be there:

"Otherwise, I really do like the taste of horsemeat and you, sir, have a lovely sweet smell!" Which was true: he always made me hungry whenever I got on him, 'cause he smelled so edible.

Giving him a minute to think it out, I slowly released his head and let him rise, intending to make him get to his feet with me on his back, still in the saddle. He had a hard time achieving that because of course he barely weighed seven hundred pounds, if that, but finally together we did it.

Then... he let us ride relatively calmly back to the edge of our camp, where I dismounted, put him up and fed him. That was our first ride!

After prevailing in our first *karate match* ride, without losing either my temper or any ground, this strangely shaped, sleek, little, yellow gelding with golden dapples decided I was good enough to ride his back and we became sidekicks, not sweethearts, but brothers of a kind, comrades in doing inspired, unexpected things, even outlandish horse-things together. Not like some thoughtless unruly self-serving outlaws, but more like noble robber-barons who together stole nothing but people's hearts.

For Amarillento, as tiny as he was, would never allow himself to be ignored, not because he was friendly or cuddly, 'cause he wasn't, but because he shone with a kind of dignity whose haughtiness was never easy, and had to be met by a certain candor of equal royal disdain or he wouldn't let you in. Though he was never in your face, and often hard to catch, he was always inconvenient, very brave, extremely capable and consistently scheming for some practical joke. He deceived everybody because he was so small. He even looked big at a distance!

Both horses and people either loved him or hated him, with no one in between, except myself, who laughing, felt both ways when he pulled some caper that would take three days to repair.

Tougher than steel, he had ironically never been discovered for what he really was, for not suspecting it, no one had ever ridden him to capacity. Perhaps he had a shape no modern person could understand, besides which, technically in modern terms he was *just a pony*.

People restrict horses to stereotyped forms, which are just like their projected forms for people, into which very few horses and no people actually fit. In their attempt to breed horses to fit the rigid official mold, in looks and bearing, if you took a really good look, after just a few generations to achieve this *breed standard*, some other very vital horse-thing was always lost in the process. Mongols and ancient Scythians and other expert horse cultures have revered at least forty different body types in their horses. Only a couple of these are even recognized, much less accepted, as legitimate by Euro-Americans today. What should horses be built like? Like themselves, who else? No different than people, who— once they are forced to conform to cultural bias—lose both spiritual and physical imagination, and their general health and vitality.

To me, he was beautiful and a unique, gigantic being in a tiny body. Amarillento was definitely the epitome of the fairytale horse: a powerful and magical animal hidden in a body shape which modern people disregarded as small, ugly, and unrideable. Just exactly like the folktale hero's horse with the old-time look, who in the story ends up saving the underdog hero, and from whom the people suspect no greatness, seeing only an ugly horse and a low-born fool. They nonetheless beat the established code at its own game, together saving the Queen of the kingdom by becoming beautiful together when both horse and hero establish a forgotten way of seeing.

Even by ancient Euro-Asian thought, Amarillento's build was not ugly, but built to truly fly, just like Becenti's traditional Diné vision of this little horse.

His bottom was jacked up high, which gave him huge thrust, his neck as long as the rest of him, at the end of which his big cute head was hammered, his eyes luxurious and beguiling: he was definitely always leaning forward and built to run.

But by any rule of horse physics, Amarillento was *not* built to stop! As hard as he himself might have wanted it, he could hardly ever figure out how to come out of a hard run. So he just kept running!

On our second *ride*, I ran him, or I should say I let him run, for I don't think anyone had ever allowed him to go all out, probably out of fear, for when he did, he did so in a way so fast, and with such agility, that because he was so light, as a rider you had to be just as able and active as he was, to slide with his motion, leaning, laying down, straightening back up, then dropping your body to his side, done all in split seconds, then holding flush to his neck with your head, then back up and dancing along lightly in the stirrups so he could do his old-time Indian war-horse best. It was all a constant shifting to balance yourself, a very athletic dance. Together we learned to do all this fast enough, but our first run was not so tidy.

That day, for some intuition, the saddle I strapped on him was not one of my fancy home-built saddles, but Shindai's old trap, which didn't actually fit as well as it should have.

As I took him out, prancing, Amarillento really did remind me a lot of a huge weasel crossed on a bat, for when I let him out, he was so agile, wheeling up and down and around, so sure footed that he viciously ate up the air we sped through. That first run together was so precarious that after a mile, a piece of saddle was left behind every hundred yards. My left stirrup was the first thing to go, caught on a staub, on a corner we were rounding that we took too tight. Seeing it coming, I pulled up my leg just in time as we were going the speed of light. The sweat leathers were ripped completely off the saddle tree, only to be outdone by the snapping of the rear girth billet a minute later, after it too caught on some other projecting branch as we came around the hill before the straight-away down to our camp.

Just like the slick-weasel-dragon he was, the little horse grunted lustily at every four beats. We ran so fast and maneuvered so hard that his extreme extending and contracting caused the single girth to start slipping, until the saddle listed so dangerously to the right that the entire saddle finally rolled under the horse!

I leapt up just as my right foot left the one remaining stirrup, which went flying off wildly through the air as it was hooked by yet another dead protruding branch and ripped completely off and away from us. The upside down saddle, now blown totally free of its mounting tumbled into the dust, over which obstacle Amarillento expertly jerked up and over, leaping completely free as if he were a bird flying over some discarded junked chair tossed onto the trail!

The miracle is that with one hand firmly knotted onto his withers mane and the other on the reins, he was still upright, and I still mounted, both of us still moving crazy-wild even after the saddle had been jettisoned. Mindless of the rude ruckus our homecoming caused at Purdy's, where the derisive hoots and catcalls of a very big cowboy with a split nose, who'd seen this maneuver, swore out at us, while he unsuccessfully tried to calm his own gigantic Quarter horse upon whom he sat all be-chapped and tacked up, bucking away, 'cause his horse thought he might join us in a run and his rider wouldn't let him, we just rolled on by.

But the trouble remaining was how to get this little yellow horse to slow into a stop! Some people might think we were not running, but bolting, but that was not the case, for the little horse sincerely would have instantly stopped if asked to, and to the ground both of us would've crashed. He'd been made so hard mouthed by his previous riders, and due to his jacked-up butt, peculiar weasel neck and light build, he'd crash into a pile if you didn't know how to take him into a landing. He desperately looked to his rider to guide him in, just like a fighter pilot guides a fighter to the narrow landing deck of an aircraft carrier. The same things that made him faster and more agile than a Sharpshin Hawk made it so he couldn't simply come to a stop. Like a fighter, we could have benefitted from an elastic catch rope stretched across the end of the runway!

Many Mongol and Kazakh epics still talk about famous horse races where the winning horses couldn't stop, but had to be caught by out-riders ready with *catching poles*, who after snagging the racer's necks, slowly turn them in giant spirals to ease down their dedicated trajectory to a slower, cooling speed where the horses could finally come on in.

This was definitely the case with Amarillento. But there were never any catch ropes or out-riders.

After running hard, it would take me at least five minutes to very gradually get him down enough, turned enough, and slowed enough so he wouldn't washout and crash, but finally come down out of the sky into a sensible canter, then a trot, and then to walk cool.

No one, especially myself, could believe or fully remember exactly how I'd survived such a mad-mile-ride after losing the entire saddle, piece by piece, and still stayed on. It all made for a lot of jealousy and rib-poking-hilarity in the neighborhood.

Later that day, me walking and Amarillento being lead, we retraced our ride to pick up the pieces. I found a stirrup dangling six feet above ground from a tree branch, a sweat leather ripped and flopped forty feet off the trail, another rigging ring tossed into the dust, and another stirrup and buckle strap dropped very carefully over a Chamisa bush, and the saddle itself, the tree cracked right through the arch of the swells, tossed and trampled. It made for a strange, rolled up bundle of parts. I tied it all up with a rope and packed it back up onto the horse's back, and leading him by the halter, hauled it all home.

It was as if the saddle had exploded, for there were three major components we never recovered. A little startling. But this weird ride had a magical purging effect. It was a kind of ritual sacrifice: by outdistancing the generational unhappiness that had haunted the little horse, the crazy ride had magically removed his bad luck and the stigma of inadequacy. Through all the dust, and the narrow peephole of survival, during which our focus took all the attention, only later did reality's tread become apparent. From that day on a brand new Amarillento commenced.

This really had been Amarillento's first time totally open and alive and moving with all he had with someone he now trusted on his back. I was down a saddle but, like a 12th century knight and horse coming in from a successful joust, we were thankful to be still standing and smiling, proud of our splintered gear and romantic bravado in service to the beauty of full living. It was stupid and silly to some, but for Amarillento it was the establishing of his nobility as a champion for having outrun hell's sad menu of mediocrity.

For me the whole phenomena was great: Amarillento the weasel horse, who, like a streak of light, was always in two places at once. He was brave and willing. Really fast. And funny. And for the rest of his life, hell for both of us to stop.

Chapter 5

Out of Harm's Way

Except for trying to stop at a full gallop, little Amarillento's agility and responsiveness to the quirt handle was so stupendous that after a fashion I didn't even need to touch him with it. With the whip dangling, a simple wrist or arm motion would suffice!

All of this came in very handy one afternoon when the horse-rich, split-nosed cowboy bingeing-it-up with Conrad for a couple of weeks decided he'd had enough of my horseback euphoria, and my irritating-little-horse-zooming past him out front of Purdy's. He set out to deflate the fun we were obviously flaunting just to make him feel *less of a man*. Out of an unimaginative need for vicious entertainment that had to somehow pierce the thick, quarrel-prone cloud of daily whiskey-driven hangovers he lived through to get back to the comfort of his cure, this man who supplied all the film companies with equines for *herd scenes* and who owned at least three to four hundred horses for the purpose, felt the need to knock me down a few pegs.

If you absolutely just had to ride by Purdy's, it was always about *getting past* Purdy's. When Conrad and his *cowboy* friends were drinking, I always felt like a little kid in an old Scandinavian fairy tale trying to tiptoe past a den of dull-brained, man-eating ogres, hoping we could get past without being seen, so as not to rouse their loutish bluster from its torpor. That afternoon Amarillento was carrying me along at his famously quiet fast-walk past Purdy's and we were almost back in the woods and out of view when Harmon, who'd been sitting hidden on his horse laying in wait for us, challenged me, popping suddenly out of the Sabina trees to block the trail.

"Hey, aren't you ashamed to ride a horse that small and ugly in plain view? You should be carrying him."

I thought just to ride past him, but he maneuvered his horse onto the narrow part of the trail at the corner of Purdy's jackleg, before the drop-off down toward the creek, so we couldn't get by.

"How you doing Harm?" that's what Conrad called him. His name was Harmon.

"What's that crap you got on that rathorse's head anyway?" Harmon was always very charming. Togged out in his *Marlboro* duds: his red shirt, calico scarf, a slick leather vest with snaps (I hate snaps), fancy inlaid spurs, an expensive appropriately beat up vintage Stetson, a cigarette in his rough hands, batwings chaps, and sitting on top of a great, old Wade saddle, strapped onto a handsome, sweet-faced, sleek Quarter horse with his tiny head, four socks and short tail, who stood at least sixteen hands tall, to match Harmon's six foot, six inches; Harmon was dressed for battle.

"You don't like my silver bridle? I just made it for this little guy. He won't go anywhere without it." Which was true, Amarillento had gotten pretty attached to it, but it was probably not a good thing to say.

When I was young some Pueblo people had horses that still wore those old-time, solid-silver bridles of that wonderful Diné 19th century construction. They were so highly regarded as elegant heirlooms and a powerful statement of tribal majesty, that as a kid I'd promised my amused Mother that when I grew up, as soon as I could afford to, I would become a silversmith and start hammering out silver bridles just such as these, reviving the long forgotten custom back to life for every horse I was planning on owning.

As it turned out, I did become a silversmith, and this actually became a reality, Amarillento's bridle being the very first one I had made. They were a bit tricky to build because you had to fit them to the specific face and eye position of each horse, and being solid silver, they were expensive to make and quite heavy, but once set with a few very good turquoises, they were worth more than three or four trained horses on the market.

"Okay wise guy, you think your little blanket-ass horse is pretty fast?" Harm always raved about Indians, Blacks, and Mexicans, and I always felt honored that he lined me up with at least two out of three of his pet hatreds, even though I was blonder than he was.

"How about, lets you and me race?" Harm challenged.

"Okay, sounds good, where to sir?"

"I didn't mean today." Harmon started back peddling...

"What d'ya mean? When did you have in mind?"

"I want to see how you do on a real racetrack, like in Galisteo or Santa Fe."

"Racetrack? Who the hell needs a racetrack to race? That's flat and just going round in idiotic ovals, there's no glory in that. Come on Harmon, let's you and me let our horses run full-out for real. How about from here, where we stand, to the top of Rowe Mesa over there and back right here?"

"That's gotta be ten miles round trip!"

"Right, you said you wanted to race didn't you? It wasn't me that brought it up."

"Okay" Harmon said, "from here to the bottom of the mesa and back, not to the top. I don't have time." By which he meant he had to get back to his drinking.

"What are you gonna bet?" I said.

"Whatever you want, you shit, 'cause you're gonna lose."

"Alright, ten thousand dollars." I said just to try him out.

"You don't have ten thousand dollars!" which was very true. But he did.

"Okay, I'll bet my silver bridle against your horse."

"Done."

Harmon laughed. Not much of a bet for a guy with three hundred horses, but I took the bet.

Harmon yelled for Conrad to come out of his den to start us off. He emerged grinning at the novelty of gigantic Harmon on his powerful, red gelding racing my little five foot, six inches on my 13.3 hand, yellow Mesta in an Indian silver bridle and saddle. Agreeing to drop his hat to set us off per accepted Southwestern tradition, Purdy said, "Okay Harm, now you two shake hands and all bets are sealed."

When Harmon leaned over to shake my out-stretched hand, he veered off in a flash and slipped his giant, calloused hand beneath Amarillento's bridle, behind his ears, and, in a well-practiced maneuver, lifted the headstall off in a deft jerk that popped the chin strap, and in one motion succeeded in removing the entire bridle off the little horse's head, after which he swung it around and whomped Amarillento's butt with the entire force of the bit and silver in an effort to get him running wild and bucking with me stranded in the saddle with no means to steer or stop him.

Ever since I'd stopped using the bridle and reins to signal and steer, Amarillento had become increasingly loyal and would only move when I asked him to, if I were in the saddle, plus he'd been trained to not move forward when whomped in the rear, only if tapped on the withers. So, he just stood there, ears back, irritated but stationary, acting like nothing at all had happened but ready for the race to begin!

A little stunned that his prank had fizzled, Harmon held my fancy silver bridle dangling from his fist like a dead snake. The reins, though, were still looped to the duckbill saddle horn of my fancy, silvered-up, homemade saddle with the big box stirrups, and thinking up another mischief, Harmon overlooked that I still had the reins, and when he attempted an old schoolboy prank (one I'd grown up dodging), and moved to kick the stirrup off my right foot, I put my quirt to

Amarillento's neck who very nicely obeyed and spun around 180° to face my disbelieving cowboy opponent, whose practiced meanness wasn't working. With no target, his intended boot-kick flew wild and knocked Harm off balance, almost dropping him to the ground. In the second it took him to right himself, I had already slipped the shaft of my quirt into my bridle's silver browband and touched my Yellow Boy's withers, who jumped out, responding in a perfect medieval jousting charge, blowing us past Harmon. The sheer torque of the little horse's great power ripped the jeweled leather bridle from Harmon's grip, popping it right back into my lap!

Sometimes short and fast is best.

Spinning back around, facing the mesa towards which we said we'd race, I spent a second to wrap the reins and bridle around my waist fastening it like a chunky belt, then yelled to Purdy to drop the hat and start the race.

Too dumbfounded by our strange recovery, Conrad was grinning and didn't hear what he was being asked to do.

"Come on Harmon," I whined "Let's race like we said."

"Aren't you going to get that bridle back on?" Harmon said, working the pain out of his hand.

"Nah, it's just there for looks. We don't need it. Come on, let's run. Okay Purdy, dang it, drop your hat," I yelled again.

And he did.

And off we shot straight south, Harmon moving his big animal to knock us off the first leg of the old, rutted, wagon trail, which wasn't very wide, bouncing us like a beach ball to the side.

But Amarillento was very competitive, and whoever got close, he shot out faster. As a matter of fact, he only ran as fast as needed to be first, always staying within range, always out in front, but close enough to see any horse coming on. He always ran plenty fast no matter what, but would surge into lightspeed if any other horse started closing in.

We really needed rain, so our dust was thick. The little, yellow, weasel-horse who loved to run made the most of it by finally kicking-in at about quarter-of-a-mile and really started running well. I looked back, which is always the wrong thing to do in a race. But I did so anyway, and all I could see was another trail of dust streaking up behind us a hundred yards back.

When we'd finally got ourselves beneath the Interstate, over the rail tracks and onto the three-mile, pot-holed, dirt straightaway, up the beautiful red clay incline through the thick forest of large Piñon nut trees that *tee'd out* at the base of the Mesa, where we had agreed to turn around and run back the way we'd come, we almost collided with Harmon's horse, just now coming up at us from the opposite direction, his stirrups thunking, the reins trimmed short and dragging, but without Harmon in the saddle!

Amarillento arched his neck in fury that we had to slow down to catch Harm's riderless horse, making it even harder to grab the big, wound-up animal. But that horse was tired, and leading him behind Amarillento, we were forced to move at a slow trot back the way we'd come bolting, searching for some sign of Harmon, down or standing, but there were no humans anywhere. I hoped something bad hadn't happened to Harm.

With Amarillento's precious silver bridle still belted around my waist, safe and sound, Amarillento smiling, his sweat dried off and a little calmer now, both of us covered in a crust of red clay from the dust, we came into Purdy's, with Harmon's horse in tow, head down and tired. Already half-drunk, the bottle between them, half-empty and perched on the ground, Conrad and Harmon in little chairs leaned back against the shed.

Riding up to the two of them, I offered what was left of his horse's reins to Harmon.

Disgusted, he motioned me away, and in a not too kindly tone asked, "Aren't you taking the horse?" since technically I had won the bet, I guess.

"No, I don't really like Quarter horses that much, though your horse here is pretty cute, and I can tell he's attached to you, and I'd hate to break up a friendship. Plus, I can feed five of my *rathorses*, as you call them, on what it costs to feed one of these behemoths. Me and my Indian pony here just love any opportunity to rationalize a good run!!"

Then Purdy blurted out, his cigarette smoke muffling the message a bit, "That horse isn't even his, it belongs to his daughter!"

I laughed and shook my head, imagining what it must be like to be Harmon Siegler's kid. Meanwhile, both of them drinking and smoking, their chairs cocked back, were looking at me with scared eyes, like I was some small, dangerous thing, kind of like Juniper did with the singing mouse.

"You know, if you really would like a silver bridle like

this one here you tried to lift, I could make you one to fit one of your own animals, but I'd need a thousand down for the materials and so forth, and we could trade out on the balance."

"Go back to hell, I'm keeping my distance from the likes of you, you're in league with some kind of bad medicine."

"Why do you say such a thing, just 'cause I didn't let you kill us? Come on, be a good sport. Weren't you the one who said 'Let's Race'?"

"You faked me out. How was I supposed to know you had a trick horse? Where'd you find him anyway, in the circus?"

"He's not a trick horse, you just hate us 'cause we're both little and fast. Look, his mouth was all ruined by someone before he came to us, and he took to that old-style quirt-riding like a pro, so I just put a bridle on him to let him know we're starting for the day and we're done when I take it off." I tried to explain what none of these fellows really cared about.

"And how the hell was I supposed to know that?" Harm yelled, reaching for his bottle. He bared his teeth and sneered, smoke coming out of the nostrils of his big, split nose.

"What difference does that make? Do you expect any unsuspecting passers-by to just lay down like a dead cow and let you beat on them? What happened to *you* anyway, how come your daughter's horse dutifully ran the race with your saddle while you're over here partying?"

Always ready to make someone feel bad, Purdy stood up, stepped quietly behind the seated Harmon and grinning, started motioning with his fingers to indicate that his friend had tumbled out of the saddle and had to walk back, while

Mr. Harmon Siegler explained his version: "I had to take a leak, and since I knew I could catch up and beat you, when I dismounted, Springles here pulled the reins out of my hand as I was zipping-up and took after you like a streak. I decided to walk back."

"I could hear him swearing a mile away!" Purdy added.

"Weren't you worried about recovering your horse?" I had to ask.

Harmon turned his head to the side and yelled back into Conrad's house, "Lacy, this guy's finally back with your horse."

"Springles! You're back!" And up and out of the cabin, a strong looking teenage girl with waist length hair the color of an Afghan dog ran up and took the reins I proffered and hugged my waist. "Daddy said he'd sent you out to find my horse when he ran off. Thank you very much for finding him and bringing him home." Looking pretty expert, and talking all the way, she pulled her big, tired horse to a rail, tied him up and commenced unsaddling him.

"You want a drink?" Harmon asked, holding up the bottle and grinning.

Purdy had disappeared.

"Maybe some other time, but thanks." My mother had always said I should be courteous to my enemies.

In a way almost imperceptible, as if it were my mind pushing him, I managed to turn my impatient, butter-colored gelding with a little shiver of my wrist, and into the breeze Amarillento and I scampered home, out of the ogre's lair, and happy to be out of Harm's way.

Chapter 6

Hard to Lose for Winning

Walking around downtown Santa Fe, I came across a long art gallery window, where in between a big, framed painting signed by the newest star-painter in the Native American Art scene, and a picture of a yuppie couple in their big-city linens, seated, enjoying small food and big wine in an expensive restaurant up the road, there hung a truly exquisite handwoven Diné saddle blanket of just the right size and thickness to stick out from the saddle skirting for a flashy ride.

No doubt knowing her creation would probably end up hanging on a rich person's wall as an adornment and not on a horse, the weaver had nonetheless woven a totally usable saddle blanket of handspun angora and churro wool, to original old-time riding specifications, whose tribal standards demanded both traditional beauty and personal ingenuity.

All three: the painting, the dinner in town, and the rug were being exhibited as prizes to be awarded to the winners of a friendly, benefit horse race, running nine miles on the old dirt road that connected Highway 14 to the beautiful, little village of Galisteo, southeast of Santa Fe.

The saddle blanket was the second place prize, the painting first, and the night on the town third. Rated according to retail *value* in the Santa Fe art gallery prices of 1989: the blanket was valued at twelve hundred dollars, the painting at three thousand dollars, and the night at the Bistro three hundred and fifty dollars.

Each person entering the race had to *donate* one hundred and fifty dollars to enter. Sponsored by the Indian Artist who painted the first prize painting, the race was intended to gather funds to pay the rent for a well-loved local charity that fed and sheltered homeless families, whose facility was being threatened with eviction.

Having no idea what a race like that would actually look like, but having finally become an artist of some moderate renown everywhere except where I lived, I had enough cash to enter the race, but not enough to really rationalize spending that much on such a gorgeous horse rug.

Amarillento loved running, loved competition, and I loved being carried along by him, for together we had developed a whole other method of cueing that was all our own. At least that's what I thought, until a few years later it was shown to me that what we were doing was a variation of how many central plains Natives, old Scythians, and North African nomad Berbers had trained their horses and themselves to ride.

His mouth had suffered so much abuse by previous would-be riders that his bars were insensitive and calloused and no type of bit caused any reliable response. So, with a fancy bridle on his head and cool reins draped to the horn for looks, I used other methods to indicate our starts and changes: with no heels, and using only my toes above his forearm, I *pointed* him gently into rights or lefts. With a fancy antler-handled quirt with long soft lashes, I signaled the degree of speed between his ears by simply laying the quirt with the lashes hanging over his forehead. For a gait change, I'd slap my right wooden box stirrup with my quirt, making a mellow cracking sound, then placing the quirt between his ears, push forward or back, just like a volume lever on a soundboard, to signal the *degree* of speed in any gait. To slow his speed, I'd pull the quirt back, to speed up I pushed forward, to start I used my thighs, to turn, I used either toe.

And then to stop?

Well, that was another subject all together! But we got to the point to where no slaps or hardly any visible signals were required for all the rest. All I had to do was just barely lean toward a signal and this butter-colored, crazy-boy horse would sense it and maneuver effortlessly left, right, slow, fast, trot, canter, walk, in and out of my every message. It was slick and he was fast and I knew I could enter that race and win, which was the problem. Because... I wanted the second prize. The painting was lovely, but I couldn't really rationalize it, for though I was an artist and painted, silver smithed, and made medicine for a living, the way we lived, we didn't really have any walls on which to hang art!

I sold off all the art I painted, and we still lived in a camp with tents, tipis, and one single-roomed cabin, all very fancy mind you, for what it was, but the cabin walls were covered with beautiful wall-bags and clothing and Indigenous weaving of our own, no room for paintings.

If I entered that race, I would want to win second prize, not first, and with Amarillento that would be pretty much impossible. This was no boast, but a luxurious reality born from the fact that Amarillento would never really run super fast unless challenged by another horse and rider. If another horse was fast, Amarillento was *always* faster. Every time. Plus, he never tired. He was holy hell to stop, but he never tired. We could run for thirty miles. Slow down, trot for nine miles, walk for one, then run for another fifteen miles, and though by then I was beat, he just got more and more revved up!

His main delight, for me, was the fact you could get him to go different speeds in all his gaits. He could be made to canter in slow motion at a speed that was slower than his prodigiously fast walk, or made to trot at an unbelievably rapid twenty-one miles an hour without ever tiring.

I dug out my grandfather's train-watch again and began timing the little, weasel horse.

We could walk at nine miles an hour, or a more reasonable three or four miles an hour, or trot at a gentle three miles an hour, or nine miles an hour, or twenty-one miles an hour. He could canter in place, or at six or seven miles an hour, or thirty miles an hour, and in a full-out gallop, he went at least forty-five miles an hour, and I swear faster if someone that fast was on his heels.

Nobody could believe me until they'd seen it! But stopping... that was another matter, so for the most part we avoided stopping until absolutely necessary!

Like all the old trucks people drove in my early days, most of which had what you'd call a very limited braking system, where only one or two wheels had functioning brake lines that hadn't been kinked off, or no brakes at all, you just learned to *gear down* to stop.

And driving was always a communal effort. Like flying an old army aircorp fighter, you needed a pilot at the wheel who knew all the ropes, and co-pilot in the passenger seat to help get you started and stopped, who had to jump in and out, to put in and pull out the blocks on the brakeless wheels!

Just to get started, one had to remember that in those times, at least five vehicles, usually all trucks (there weren't really many cars), all shared one battery! This meant you had to remove the battery from somebody else's rig, and install it into yours, to get started. Sometimes it took five people to get a truck going because, of course, nine times out of ten the battery was dead or had been borrowed from a tractor and didn't have enough punch to crank the truck engine.

This meant you had to start the truck by rolling it up to a certain speed with three or four guys pushing, and with the ignition on and the clutch in and in gear, *popping* the clutch at the proper point, upon which the engine would turn, give out a spark and fire up. But of course, if you didn't have any brakes, and you were in gear, you had to put the clutch back in, take it out of gear, and have your *co-pilot* jump out and block the tires with the log he kept in the cab floor so it wouldn't roll back or forward while you revved up the engine to charge the battery!

But if the battery was already charged, often the solenoid was so bad somebody had to be under the engine with a screwdriver to cross-circuit the solenoid, while the driver pumping not *too* much fuel, started the truck, trying not to run over his buddy underneath.

This compounded with the fact, that due to the general chronic cash shortages, and the lack of trained mechanics, a lot of truck ignitions wouldn't crank with a key because it had been lost, and the ignition had been side-wired to a button. So you had to pump the gas with your right foot, pop the clutch with the left, push the start button with your left hand, and pretend to both shift and steer with your right hand, which sometimes meant your co-pilot did the shifting on your command, because driving that type of truck required at least three hands. God forbid you had one of those trucks with a starter button on the floor, which you had to hold down with your left foot while simultaneously depressing the clutch with the same foot, push the starter button on the dashboard with your left hand, keep your right foot on the gas, and your right hand on the wheel!

But, in a truck like that, once you got going and moving towards wherever it was you hoped to be getting, you had to make sure to *never* turn off the engine till you came home, 'cause you might not get started again. This was especially difficult and dicey when gassing up on the flat.

To roll to a stop at a stoplight in a crowded town with no brakes, without stalling the truck in traffic, was the exclusive domain of certain master drivers of derelict vehicles.

To do this, the driver began to gear down way ahead, continually slowing until you were at the place you had to stop. Then barely moving, at your signal, your co-pilot jumped out of the passenger-side with his brick or log, and threw it in front of the nearest tire, and if the truck had slowed enough, it would bump up against the block and stop. While the driver had the clutch in, and the engine revving, your co-pilot remained outside, passenger door open, standing in a kind of quarterback stance, waiting for the light to change, at which point he kicked out the block, picked it up, and ran for the truck, which was already in gear and moving forward, leapt into the seat with his block held like a football, and pulling the door shut, away we went to the next stoplight!

To drive these crazy trucks you had to have five things that actually did work: a clutch, a transmission, a religion with a responsive God, a good friend and, of course, a horn. For if you finally got heading homeward in one piece after dodging a million possible disasters, it was considered good manners to honk your horn like hell as you got close to home, to signal everybody in the neighborhood that you were nearby, brakeless and dangerous, and coming in for a landing, so they could clear the field you were heading toward of all little kids, dogs and livestock, and any precious items you might have to swerve to miss, or miss if you ran over them!

If you and your helper got home safe and sound, it was always evidence that God loved you, and a rite of initiation, whose relief was a kind of religious ecstasy. Wonder and gratitude filled one's soul for having survived civilization's hand-me-down technological disasters just to get home with the flour, coffee, lard, salt, sugar, and life. These trucks made life so vital and precious. If you were lucky to have a hill handy, you parked on it so you could pop the clutch next time without a five man crew by letting it roll forwards, but you had to block the tires when you parked so the truck didn't spontaneously start rolling and hurt somebody.

◆ ◆ ◆

Well, trying to stop Amarillento was a lot like stopping one of those old trucks: for to stop him after a hard run, you had to keep gradually gearing down so he wouldn't stumble, and instead of a horn, he would scream and whinny at the top of his lungs, then I'd start turning him in a wide circle, spiraling round an imagined middle until he came to a stop! It was good policy to imagine him as one of those trucks that had only one wheel with a functioning brake, where if you pushed the brake pedal while you were up to speed, you would flip the truck head over heels. Our circular *landing pattern* usually saved us from washing out.

Luckily Amarillento didn't need a push, or to pop his clutch to get him going, because he was always ready to move out at any speed or gait from a stand still. If you just leaned slightly forward, and gave him the proper signal, he would be roaring at forty miles per hour in a couple of seconds, from a standstill.

I'd never raced with non-Indians on non-Indian horses, and while I had no taste for any aspect of the phenomenon of commercial horse racing, I did love the exhilaration of running together with horses, just like all horses do, for horses do love running together. But then again, they like standing still together too.

Every night I strategized myself to sleep thinking how we might contrive to come running in just slow enough to win second place on a horse who was always first! Though still uncertain as to how I could pull it off, in the end, I did sign up for the race.

In one of those cloudless, paradisiacal, balmy days of early autumn, with no flies, not too hot and not too cold, we headed for the race, my old red Ford dragging the little white horse trailer that I got in a trade for one of my silver bridles. When we got there, Amarillento and I were forced to park a long way down the road behind some forty or fifty other rigs of people and their mounts signed up for the race, who arrived there early.

After saddling, we walked down to the knot of some sixty saddled, unmounted horses waiting, with their riders still on the ground, as the officials running the race, and the police who barricaded the road, read out the whys and wherefores of the race.

Some of the horses, excited to be in a herd, were crow hopping, while others squealed, one had to be taken off a ways by his owner to calm him down, but to no avail.

The judges were dividing everyone up into groups, presumably according to assumed ability, so as to allow the *slow ones* a handicap by being released first.

There were seven Paso Finos, twenty Arabians, a couple of Thoroughbreds, and at least three hunters, a dozen grade ranch horses, a whole phalanx of Quarter horses, and a really big Hanoverian/Percheron belonging to the very generously built artist sponsoring the event.

No one was to mount until their group was called, and the officials were busy doling out our *number vests* to pull over our heads, I got number forty-eight.

When the judge came by, he jokingly asked me if my dinky horse could actually carry me, convinced that my silver saddle and bridle weighed more than the horse, and would I like to head off before the first group to give us a head start?

I said the third group would suit me, and writing down our name and number he shook his head and kept on with the rest.

Just then, a hand came up over Mari's mane, and then a face, and then a voice, which turned out to be big English Annie, here to ride her buckskin Barb for the cause, which she had there in tow. Her horse stood a full hand taller than Amarillento.

"So, Martín, this is the notorious little Amarillento. Is he here to run the race? Do you think he'll do it; have you ever run a race before? This is my first. I'm so excited."

Everybody except the artist and myself had little weightless Styrofoam saddles.

Except for the artist and me, who both wore broad brimmed hats with *barba quejos*, one half of the riders wore baseball caps, the other half riding helmets and goggles, stretch pants, polo shirts, boots and crop with little water bottles and extendable straws strapped to special attachments below the cantle.

Snapping on her English helmet Annie said, "I've been meaning to get a hold of you Martín. Remember the stallion you were so keen to buy? Well, I thought maybe you might be interested to know his brother is for sale, and he is still a full stallion, and he is a medicine-hat paint."

Our group had just been called, the first two groups were already off and running.

"Is that right?" I chirped as we both mounted and turned our geldings to the startup line.

"Where is this stallion for sale?" hoping she would say Albuquerque or somewhere close.

"Oh, he's over there with those horses in Iowa, from where the family has been hauling horses all these years. The horse's name is Blue Medicine. Later on I can get you more contact information if you want?"

"Thank you ever so kindly ma'am, I'd like that very much."

And the little gun popped and off they went. Annie meandered into the ranks of fifteen horses spewing rocks, thudding off and away, some of them sideways, others heading on down the gravel road at a pretty nice clip.

I held Amarillento back, who'd been furious when the other two groups disappeared into the dust and he wasn't with them. But now he was practically running in place as our group moved off. The officials yelled for me to go, laughing like we were some inexperienced backwater hicks, unaware that we were purposefully holding back.

Then I let him go.

He jumped out like a Greyhound, or more like a Leopard, with his two feet stretched out forward and pulling his hind legs up past the fronts, pushing back like a cat. He could extend more than his own body length.

We overtook the third group in three jackrabbit leaps, even before I signaled for him to run.

The crush of horses was so thick that we couldn't get past their butts, so we jumped off the dirt road onto the strip of roadside prairie, where dodging Rabbit Brush and trees of Cholla Cactus, we passed the spitting stones and jumped back onto the dirt road, but I lost our number on a tree in the process.

Amarillento would have slowed down, now that he was ahead of our *third* group, but thankfully he caught sight of the dust clouds of groups two and one up ahead, so I let him rip.

He coursed along at a graceful thirty-eight miles per hour or so, screaming at the top of his fierce little lungs. Then I let him all out.

We caught the second group at about two miles out, some of whom were winded and just walking alongside the road catching their breath till they could get back in the race. Some seven or eight were still going, but considerably slower. There was not quite enough room to get past them courteously, so as we approached, Amarillento, in a normal wild-herd motion, but rather ungallant move, bit one of the running Arabians square on the rump, and when she budged, he wedged his determined shape-shifting self between her and a Thoroughbred, and gunning it, thrust past them all like a Hummingbird out-distancing a flock of Ravens.

Again, he would've hung out right in front of group two if group one hadn't been in sight a quarter mile away.

We'd gone probably three or four miles, so I asked him to just trot fast. He was furious for being asked to slow down. We trotted hard at about twenty miles per hour for a couple of minutes to catch our wind, and by then we'd pretty much caught up to group one.

So I let him run again. Group one was strung out in a long column to the left, so we passed them courteously on the right as the road curved to the left and rose up a couple hundred feet.

After passing these horses, I remembered I wanted to come in second, and now I was first. Or was I? For up on the horizon a puff of staccato dust rose up and over the hill. Amarillento knew it too and didn't want to slow. Thinking maybe there were more riders up ahead, we ran again and caught up to a man heading hard into the breeze with goggles and helmet, riding a dappled, blue-roan Arabian who was really going at it.

I yelled at him as we pulled up alongside, to ask if anyone was ahead of him, but he just gave me a dirty look, wouldn't talk, and just whipped his pony harder.

So, we ran very pleasantly side by side for a mile or so, Amarillento just a couple of feet ahead, until this rider also started to drop behind.

I couldn't tell if there were still some more ahead of us or not, so we ran as hard as I could get the little yellow weasel to go, but he knew for sure what I surmised: we were now in the lead.

So...

I signaled him to slow down into a fast trot with which we curved down the last hills into the adobe town of Galisteo, past the old adobe church, past the highway and past the store. (He could trot amazingly well down hills!)

The judges of the receiving end were still inside the store drinking pop, and shooting the breeze, and hadn't even set up or marked the finish line yet!

I circled Amarillento around and around looking for it, to avoid crossing the line. Finally, a lady judge appeared loaded down with sodas, and a clipboard, and other official looking stuff.

"Sir, you'd better move that horse out of the way, because in about fifteen minutes sixty horses are going to come rushing down here trying to be first in a race; we can't have you making yourself an obstacle, it could be dangerous for both you and them."

The rest of the judges had shown up and would not believe I was part of that very race, for nobody could've got here that fast. Plus, I'd lost my number in the trees while passing.

Amarillento was sweaty and mad that he couldn't get going again, so... I rode back onto the road and headed straight back where we'd come in from, at a fast trot!

After a mile and a half, the fellow on the Arabian, who had been joined by three other riders were coming straight at us, so I rode past them going the opposite direction until we ran into six more riders. We just kept on going back the way we came.

After we'd run into and past some fifteen weary horses and riders, I turned Amarillento around and ran alongside the same horses we'd just met coming the other way. Now Amarillento would want to get ahead again, and we ran the race a second time.

I kept reminding myself that it was the rug, the second place prize, not the painting we were after, but we ran past everybody again. Here we were again closing in on that same grumpy guy, number ten, with the Arabian, running out front, having gotten a second wind. I tried to keep Mari right alongside him, while under his goggles that fellow kept gnashing his teeth and giving us dirty looks.

Only about quarter of a mile now from the finish line, where the judges were finally ready with their cameras and the prizes on easels all set up, in front.

I couldn't stop Amarillento from running right past number ten and staying just a head in front of him. In that formation, we came gently thundering past the chapel, and just about twenty feet from the chalked finish line, which I'd already crossed fifteen minutes earlier, I signaled Amarillento—that brave, fast, little, magic Indian horse—to go from a fast canter to a trot, which gave the Arabian a six inch lead, and we were successfully declared the winners of second place! We'd done it. Second place. I couldn't believe I'd pulled it off!

It took almost an hour for all the horses to come in, the artist pulling in at the rear.

The judges wouldn't believe me that I had not just joined the run somewhere between here and there, close by, until the starting officials drove up and confirmed my entry. Then they scared me by trying to award me first place, but I had already taken possession of my new rug and wouldn't let it go.

I'd given up hoping for praises or admiration for having won twice, but my little horse needed it, so I walked him dry and cool, praised him till he was sleek and ready for another race, and went to shake everybody's hand.

When I tried to shake his hand, the first place winner turned out to be a grumpy lady, not a grumpy man, who still just gave me a tired, dirty look and wouldn't shake this heathen's hand. Annie did shake my hand. And the artist, who came in third from last, couldn't stop laughing when he heard what happened, his belly bouncing when he shook both my hand and his head. I ate lunch in the Galisteo store, then unlike the rest, because I'd neglected to arrange for someone to fetch my truck and trailer around from where we started, I cantered back the nine miles we'd just come in on. Sitting comfortably on my new blanket, smiling and in love with the fall and the clear high desert air, surveying the open land off to the west where I'd grown up, all the while pondering what it might take to get a blue-eyed, Abalone stallion back into his homeland from Iowa.

Chapter 7

The Horse Raid:
Jesus Rescues a Heathen and a Blue-eyed Barb from Hog Heaven Hell

In an old yellow Suburban, dragging an empty twenty-foot, repainted, Prussian blue stock trailer, we left Santa Fe in the morning, heading east, on a mission to buy the Poster Horse's youngest brother: the painted, fierce, blue-eyed stallion Blue Medicine, bring him back to my camp and thereby release him from the grips of some Iowa hog farmers, where he'd been held for almost eight years. This clattering rig, and the rich boy at the wheel, both belonged to the Owners. He was one of their children, and the same fellow who'd showed me Amarillento's photo.

We rolled around the base of the Southern Rockies, past Rivera, past Tecolote, past Las Vegas, New Mexico, and Wagon Mound dropping onto the grassy plains of northeastern New Mexico, pushing hard against the morning sun.

Some three and a half cloudy hours from home, one hour from Oklahoma, as we neared Clayton, the kid and I, like horses, spooked, jumping out of our seats as the rig suddenly started sliding over a foot-deep bed of solid flowing hail. Pulling our hearts back into our chests, it dawned on us what loomed up in our path: for strewn across the highway, and everywhere alongside, cars upside down, still spinning, and wreckage from smashed barns, houses and dead cattle, lay everywhere; some sliding down the highway with us in that sheet of flooding hail that was now our road, forcing us to calculate our motion while violently fishtailing and skating about with no traction over the hidden asphalt.

A large toppled water tower had rolled sideways, square into the middle of the white road, rocking back and forth like an immense drunken toad, floating in the river of pebbled ice, on a collision course with our truck and trailer. In the flash flood of iceballs there was no stopping without us jack-knifing and flipping over. In some old, unthinking, instinctive reaction, from the passenger seat, I instantly knocked the kid back, grabbed the wheel and jammed it in the opposing direction from where he'd been white-knuckling us, straight into the tower. Hoping to purposely cause trailer and truck to spin around like a couple of clock dials to avoid colliding with the tower, when the trailer started to fishtail, I forcefully rolled the steering wheel opposite again. Then kicking the boy's feet off the peddles, with no brakes or acceleration, and out of gear, we glided elegantly in a slow-galactic-motion, successfully sliding one hundred and eighty degrees on the bed of ice marbles, right around the errant tower. With the clutch still down, I now jammed it into third until we were past the Toad, at which point, after I gently lifted my clutch-foot and gradually pressed the gas with my right, we watched without breathing as we swung again forward, still in slow motion, to miraculously reach the dry pavement on the opposite end of the storm.

After officially exchanging seats with the Rich Kid, as the driver, I just kept us heading east out of Clayton, New Mexico, where it was all dark with clouds, but dry and eerily still as if nothing at all had happened!

Some five miles out, the flashing lights of first responders started floating in from Texas, who stopped us to hear what we thought had happened. We heard from them more than we ourselves knew of the extent of what exactly had transpired: that a tornado had apparently flattened a number of ranches and part of Clayton, and had just dissipated to the south. But, still shaking from the adrenalin, we told them what we knew: we'd miraculously come through its immediate aftermath of hail, and never stopped driving! They rolled their eyeballs in disbelief.

Another two miles off to the east, when we had just started to breathe again, it was as if a wet, dripping, wool blanket ten miles wide had been dropped over the entire land.

It was tornado season on the plains, and like the buffalos of old who used to own these flats, twister storms were coming upon us in herds.

It didn't take a minute for the temperature to rise. When the air grew smotheringly thick, and the stormy smell of macerated grasses and sages, just as if they had been trampled by a billion stampeding buffalo at the edge of the storm, came in on us abruptly, we pushed our little unstable rig as hard as we dared to scramble out from under the imminent storm. But it was like trying to push a bark beetle through a bucket of hot tar.

Craning my head out of the window, I periodically scanned the sky to get a clearer view. The little kid in me, the one so in love with Nature's bigger life, was stunned by the beauty of the dramatic roiling and boiling of the sudden herds of clouds, so beautiful in their own powerful way, that I neglected at first to react in fear. But when a funnel cloud emerged at the corner of my eye, dropping from the churning matrix of clouds, spindling sideways and suspended high up and just to the north of us, lengthening out like a bending worm, fat on one end, I came to my senses. "Here comes another one."

Though it threatened constantly to do so, that tornado never quite touched the earth. Like a spindle of thread in reverse, it unspun its yarn back into fluff, the twister unwinding itself back into the clouds. Two other twisters in the next half an hour did the same thing: started to come, then didn't. One of them, like a snake, disappeared back into an unseen hole from the middle of his coil, where he unwound himself back up into God's lap. Tense and wide-eyed, both of us like little kids kept leaning forward, as if that would help us go faster. We kept on plowing east just as fast as that clattering, old, yellow suburban could manage.

It was a lot we had to brave just to pick up a horse, that crazy paint stallion, the Barb brother of the Poster Horse, in some small town in the southwestern corner of Iowa, in some hog-farming family's back yard. But the tornadoes would seem like nothing when it was over.

What had been a vague indulgence to my romantic soul, now took on the form of a mental certainty: that what we were doing had that heightened quality of the constant caution and distinct smell of urgency I'd heard tell in stories of old-time Native American horse stealing raids! After all, weren't we headed directly into what the Natives I grew up with always considered *enemy territory*? But this raid of mine was *not* a raid to steal anything, much less a horse, or hurt anybody doing it, but a type of inverted foray meant to unkill and buy back a horse taken from our lands, and give him back his life by entering mine. I aggrandized our driving to Iowa as some quiet heroic expedition to begin healing the West by coming to *rematriate* Blue Medicine back into the New Mexico mother land he'd been born to.

Old Blue was a New Mexico horse of the oldest blood: bred, born, and descended from Native horse herds for over 500 years. All these episodes that happened on the trip, everything I had to do and go through, all the area we had to cover, all the storms we had to navigate, or the cultural bias and racism I would have to negotiate and bear, all of it was nothing more than a part of an ancient pattern. For one could easily recognize it was all a spiritual test. Some old-time people said that all the troubles and trials on such a raid not only made the horses they would gather back to New Mexico that much more precious, but would be a trial to assess the resolve of one's passion and love for the animals, to see if one deserved to *own* one.

All horses have spirits. But there are different kinds of horses with different kinds of spirits. If they are old-time horses, like Blue's ancestors, their spirits always test their would-be owners to see if these suitors to the throne of their saddles are worthy to sit on their backs. These horses didn't need *me* to rescue them. They wanted someone to bring them home. They needed me to grow into someone who was truly at home and worth knowing, someone capable of a mystic togetherness that developed from a mutual admiration of each other's tenacious natures. Without exception, every single one of these types of horses, over the years, really did test my adroitness and dedication in the most bizarre and comical ways. At first, until I really understood, the greatest mystery for me was that no matter what I had to do or where I had to go, in every case, I could not just show up with money, simply lay it down and purchase an advertised horse. Unlike the rest of the civilized world, who bought the same horses as if they were just new cars on a lot, I had to dance through so many hoops just to get that far.

If I hadn't known better, there were times when I could have sworn that somewhere hidden from the view of people of my *ilk*, a secret cabal of angry ghosts: the souls of Indian-hating-settlers from the past were meeting, furious that any of the goodness of Native peoples or their horses the settlers' historical presence had wrecked, should be resurrected. Ghosts who were dead-set-against any of the old, beautiful Indian Mesta Barbs slowly drifting back into the possession of people like myself, who more resembled and were sympathetic to the original Spanish and Native American owners, in whose hands the horses' magical natures could come back into view.

For it seemed every time I tried to buy, trade for, or earn one of these horses, so many strange, untoward, and weirdly unlikely situations and detours would develop out of the blue as to make a person wonder. Was it just silly superstition to think such a thing? Still it was uncanny, constant, and sometimes completely off the wall.

The truth be told, these horses themselves were physically and spiritually magical to magical people, but in the hands of those who had no magic at all, their substance literally evaporated, and a dull beast stood there in his place. And on that day I was headed into the land of the descendants of those same ghosts: the land of no magic, where I knew I must keep my own magic and my soul hidden from view, firmly armored and camouflaged behind as much middle-American normalness I could muster!

Even today, I find it hard to believe the gauntlet of unexpected and unnecessary trip-ups I had to endure to buy this particular horse. A horse I had already fully agreed to buy over the phone, with cash, for an amount I had ready. Once I'd made the deal, so many obstacles had instantly presented themselves before I even left home, and those were only the vague beginnings of what was in the path to come. It was as if invisible boulders and logs were being dropped in my every path to stop me. It was only the spirit of Blue Medicine himself, watching out for me, and summoning me in my dreams, that gave me the adroitness to outdo the power of someone or something else that wanted to stop me.

An hour before sunset and temporarily away from the twisters, we were now under clear Oklahoma skies, pulling an empty, useful-looking, freshly repainted, Persian blue, twenty foot, tag-along stock trailer, trying to stay in front of the storms coming out of the west, hoping to get into Kansas before dark.

The entire trip, the yellow Suburban would choke and struggle slightly on all the hills, but thankfully between the eastern plains of New Mexico, north through the Cherokee strip to Elkhart, east along the Platte and crossing to Concordia, into the southeastern corner of Nebraska and then into Iowa, there were only very few legitimate hills.

Instead, from the flatness of that region's once natural, life-rich, endless prairie, there now rose the infamous nightmare of shoreless seas of surveyed squares filled with uncreative, zombie corn and soybeans, one size, one height, one type, punctuated by the deep, sad smell of hundred-acre feed lots every five miles, where cattle, cursed to being bulked-up on the same enslaved corn and soy beans, crowded beak to bottom in the misery of their days, till packed in trains and trucks, they were shipped to facilities where unceremoniously stunned to death, skinned, gutted, hung, frozen, sliced, and packaged, they were shipped again, to be dispersed into the bloodstreams of suburban America. This reality always startled a romantic New Mexican like me—who was still accustomed to plenty of room for every creature: open-range cattle, home-butchered meat, home-milked goats, and every family and their horses grazing free—who saw this supposed agricultural *miracle* as nothing but an accursed living nightmare, a way of life no different than the strangled, crowded, unfeeling lives people led in their cubicles in cities, where like life in the feedlots and GMO corn fields, the people had lost the glory of what is meant to live lyrically, as if they couldn't change it, and thought that's just how it was supposed to be! The animals and plants they ate had no more lives than the people who ate them. At least that's the way it looked from where we camped. A lot of the people in cities disagree, but that's just 'cause they don't know any better. We couldn't blame their ignorance, especially when you look at the horrors the adoption of trashy city-life has wreaked upon what used to be *country life*, where people with lots of land now live with just as limited an imagination.

The spirits of a million vital Buffalo—not statistical victims in a coffee-table book or a vague guilty memory in the American psyche, but real, woolly, grass-eating Gods, with wind Gods and Gods of the plains Grizzly, Gods of Wolves and Prairie Dogs and Prairie Chickens and Ferrets—all joined in together, their souls rumbling wild and irreverent, right inside and underneath the whole damned place, and especially beneath the tight skin of the strange human denizens of these flat unnatural travesties, settler descendants whose claim that this stark, bank-owned, corporate, agricultural hypocrisy was a *human* triumph over Nature and a good Christian reality, unaware that they were no-more respected by the system they supported anymore than they respected Nature. A system that just regarded these people as easily manipulated crumbs left over from their struggling immigrant ancestors, who themselves were culturally dismantled by the older version of the same *system*, and now their descendants, reduced by chemicals and big box stores, were sucked dry by the very mediocre lives they pursued. They were not my enemy because I hated them, but because they designated what I was to be the enemy of who they wanted me to appear to be. I was something they thought they'd already conquered.

Miraculously, still here unchanged after millennia, and a century and a half of disastrous land use, still resting in every untilled creekside and bosque creek bottom, were those Sandhill Cranes, who no doubt were the souls of all the Original People of these flat paradises, Natives of a myriad lifestyles whose bodies, rich cultures, and homes had been intentionally and rudely tractored back into this very land, and whose presence was virtually written out of the agri-conqueror's mental landscape, but whose voices and magic were still loud in the throats of the great herds of those tall, big-winged birds who continue to migrate in and out, nest, make babies, leave, and always return. The Indigenous Soul is still there, nomadically pulsing inside the motions of all the migratory life, moving in and out of this flattened settler travesty.

Mosqueros too, the Scissor-tailed Flycatchers: they had lived through it all as well. They knew the real story.

As we chugged by on the highway, they fluttered like feathered hammers thrown up from every tenth fence post, summersaulting after bugs, their fifteen-inch-long tails snipping, shivering and flashing in the light, devouring into their surprising whiteness large suicidal herds of flying beetles, who traditionally sought to end their adult form in exactly such a way. Especially the late Junebugs, who had all schemed together, ever since they were larval grubs, to make sure their adult deaths were such a noble event, instead of being mechanically strained from the air on highways to become just another minor component of the stiff waffles of dried radiator bugs cooking on the grills of every summer truck and car heading in both directions!

Even delicate White Kites and more sturdy Aplomado Falcons hovered and stooped for Grasshoppers and Prairie Warblers, driven by the tinkling jazz of every mile's Meadowlark, whose newest mimicked lick and original compositions were dopplered down by the moderate speed that Rich Kid's mother's homely, yellow Suburban could manage as we kept rolling, our trailer loud and empty, toward southern Iowa's Hog Heaven Hell.

It was my turn to drive again while the kid dozed, as I took the rig north through Kansas. The summer air was boggy and balmy and smelled of a hint of ripening sand plums. Some places at nightfall made the air rise thick and moist, delicious with a kind of lusty, rank musk, and in those places lightening bugs took over the night, blinking in every vale, the frogs and tree crickets deafening.

Under an overpass in Nebraska I pulled over and parked, where we snored till dawn.

In the morning, for some unfathomed reason, the wealthy kid, again at the wheel, preferred the endless criss-crossing of small connecting roads, instead of the quicker highways, making certain it took us half a day what would've been two hours, until we finally crisscrossed right square into the southwestern corner of black-soil Iowa. While feeding on my home breakfast of dry meat, coffee and atole, and the rich boy had his home sandwich, I began to notice with contemptuous Southwestern glee that after an hour of driving in Iowa I hadn't spied even one rock. No boulders, no stony cliffs, no pebbles, just endless black soil and rolling hills of crops. No rocks!

Then at a crossroads in a tiny town, all of a sudden there was a boulder! A big sedimentary, squarish chunk of red sandstone, about four feet by four feet, sitting in the inclined-hill front yard of a dark-white-painted clapboard farmstead house. One rock. This has never seemed peculiar to anyone else, but in New Mexico we know where we are and who we are by the rocks, of which there are infinite varieties and properties. One rock! How unbelievable! I figured it must be a famous rock. And it was.

When we finally bumped down the lane about whose whereabouts the Rich Kid was mysteriously well educated, at whose bottom the commercial hog farm where the horse named Blue Medicine was supposed to be held captive, the evening light was diffused, and the air as soggy as the deep black earth of Iowa. These people had a spread that was covered in grottos, hogs, and shoats. Their house was a drywall mansion, a bubble of Midwestern suburban normality, complete with a lawn with not one dandelion, plastic flamingos, and a concrete strand of sidewalk with ruffled lawn edging leading to their aluminum storm door. Convincingly fenced off from the actual pig farm, which radiated out on every side, the house looked a little like a temporary visitor from the city. Towers with tanks, marimbas of silos, and the frightful aroma of fifteen kinds of nasty disinfectants, chemical soaps and spray-on vitamins, hormones, antibiotics and antihelminthics in large trailers and spray tanks, mixed with the overtone of generations of spilled diesel, made the redolent, actual hog-smell that permeated the entire county a genuine relief for its *real* animal stench, and almost an antidote for all the synthetic smells it had to poke through. The whole symphony of smells roosted so viscously in our nostrils that its presence would refuse to abdicate its olfactory throne for days, even after we'd escaped this strange land.

But for now we were here!

They knew we were coming towards evening, so after we pulled up, like good rural New Mexicans, we stayed in the cab hoping for some style of welcome from the people, either somebody waving or barking dogs. But none was forthcoming.

Looking about, I didn't see any horses.

Their air conditioner was rumbling and the turbine spun on the steep metal roof, pumping out the hot summer air within.

Then after about five minutes someone started peeking from the drapes.

Two adolescent girls, one in red shorts and tennis shoes, the other in a long, faded denim skirt and Mary Janes, both with makeup and long, thin, blond hair to the waist, sidled out the aluminum door. Textbooks clutched to their torsos, they barely looked at us in the truck, their serious gazes fixed on the ground as they bristled past us at a brisk walk.

"Tell Dottie you'll be spending the night," a lady's voice bugled from the house, "I'll call her and let you girls know when to come back, we have to be at church by three tomorrow."

Neither girl acknowledged the message and very soldierly marched off.

From the house emerged a middle-aged lady with a very pale face, dyed black straight hair, black pants and Mary Janes, who turned out to be the voice we'd heard. Standing next to the truck and looking us over, up and down, in a kind of sideways fashion, her fierce eyes pretended to be fixed on the girls disappearing around the hog buildings.

"Which one of you is the one come to see the horse?" she asked in a not quite friendly tone.

No hi. No, I'm such and so, and you are? Nothing.

"I'm the one you talked to on the phone ma'am," I said as I pushed my arm out the window, thinking to shake hands.

Pretending she hadn't seen it, she looked away.

"I talked to both of you on the phone, which one of you is the one that came to look at the horse?"

Looking at the Rich Kid, I wondered what they had talked about if only one of us was, "come to see the horse?"

"That would be me ma'am, I've come to buy your medicine-hat paint stallion: Blue Medicine." I spoke in the most cheerful tone I could muster through my exhaustion and the distinct feeling of some undisclosed weirdness between her and the Rich Kid.

"Well, he's a gelding now. We castrated him a month ago; I told your friend here about that."

What?! I screamed in my mind. Richie here knew the last Pueblo Reservation Abalone Stallion had been gelded and didn't tell me? He let me come this far without ever mentioning it? I thought I might blow, but without losing a beat I didn't flinch or blink. I was raised in the Pueblo, and decided I'd better pull more firmly into myself. After all, this confirmed I was on a horse raid: alone. The kid was a part of the old story, where a supposed friend betrays the other on the raid. This was enemy territory for sure. I quickly rearranged my assumptions, changed my vision of the mental terrain, and making my mind think to fit the situation, put off expressing what I felt till a more convenient time.

With too much unspoken space in a conversation the Rich Kid got nervous, and no doubt having rehearsed the moment of my extreme disappointment, started talking.

"He got to be too much trouble, he was getting temperamental and dangerous," the kid explained, as if he'd been in on it.

"Yes, and they bred him to a neighboring white mare last year in hopes he'd make a nice painted foal, but the foal was born all pink and died from lethal white syndrome in less than three days."

I'd bought this horse over the phone as a stallion; they had no right to cut him without discussing it with me first. I was really ready to blow now, but experienced enough to instantly reassess my situation to find some useful thought that might recover at least some small bit of the intended goodness from this now bizarre and depressingly changed situation.

Realizing I was being conveniently exploited, having been *allowed* to come on the kid's horse-gathering expedition, to the place they never let anybody know about, because he needed an extra hand getting his horses; somebody who had a way with animals who he didn't have to pay, who could double as a *driver*! Oh yeah! Which is why he didn't tell me this stallion I'd been dreaming about was no longer a stallion, when he already knew, to make sure I'd come along. Had they been in on the gelding because they didn't want anybody getting breeding stock except themselves? Then why not just buy Blue and keep him? They already had his brother, who wasn't, for some reason, making babies. I was heartbroken and angry. I'd fought hard to get here, to gather the funds, to come into enemy territory, all for what! And the breeding excuse? Everybody knows you don't breed for color. Colors belong to the Holy. Even so, everybody knows to get a paint from a paint you certainly can't breed a blue-eyed one to a white mare, that's sure to fail!

There were so many things wrong with all of this; it was a real blow, but I stood silent for a while to let the vapors of outrage and rottenness gas off a bit. It really *was* a horse raid. So… I unlocked my jaws and as cheerful as I could manage,

I spoke: "Well, where is this Mr. Blue Medicine anyway, the medicine-hat, Barb *gelding*? Can I take a look?"

"What d'ya mean?" the lady hissed. "He's standing right there in front of you!" And laughing, she pointed into the very pen against which I was leaning. I'd been staring straight at him and had not seen him!

Mystified, but instantly focusing where she was pointing, there he was, the object of all my months of dreaming, and three months of scheming, there he was: head down, almost leaning against the massive, tall holding pen of steel reinforced two-by-fifteen-inch wooden planks, looking all the world to me...

Well...

Like a giant pig!

He was standing right where she said he was, and like a chameleon, he found a way to utterly blend in with these people's environment. He was being a big pig with the color of the pen, the color of the ground, the color of this lady's mood, the color of everything in this place, the color of no color. He was the color of Blah!

He was wider than he was long, super, super fat, a horse that should've weighed nine hundred pounds who'd been inflated to seventeen hundred pounds! His sorrel spots and majestic snow white background were all filled in with a pig manure glaze, the color of blah.

Once my eyes adjusted to the local blah, I could see that he was mooning us! He was hiding in the general blah, and in no mood to be seen. With his big, beautiful Barb head looking small, attached to a couch of a body, with a three inch, depressed crease that ran down his spine, the medicine-hat horse I'd come to buy, the horse in all the pictures, I realized in a flash, was not actually one hundred percent here in Iowa. The horse I'd been dreaming about all these months, whose grandpa was a horse of my romantic Reservation-roaming-time, was only partly here in this corral. His husk of camouflage was here. Blue Medicine, the horse three years previous sent to the Dakota people for the first revival of Black Elk's Horse Dance was not here. The rest of him, whose reunion with him would equal a whole, real horse, that piece was residing safely in some far away wilder place, and that piece could still hear my thoughts as I stood amazed, staring at his pig-poop-colored disguise here in Hog Heaven Hell.

While I thought these thoughts, this blah-colored husk of a horse heard my mind, he turned his head and stared at me, then with his whole pig-poop body shaking, he fiercely and sadly screamed a wild horse whinny that convinced me he might still be worth taking home. His bright blue eyes glared fixedly out of the blah, and I knew wherever his soul was rightfully hiding, the whole Blue Horse could be found again, though not in that body, but running him by remote. His soul was somewhere else. Like an ancient mythic ogre or a wild dream animal, he'd sent his soul to some secret place for safe keeping for the grudge he bore these people, so they would never get a hold of the real him. I smiled and he screamed some more. We knew each other right then.

When I commenced to climb the piggy smelling fence of this fortress-like livestock containment pen to get a closer look at this pony, the lady spoke in an almost friendly chirp, "I'd be careful buddy, if I were you, he's not very tame any more, very unpredictable. I'm sure you don't want to buy him any more do you? You really have to watch out, my husband uses an iron gate to push him into a corner to get a halter on him."

"What have you been feeding this fellow?" I blurted, trying to hide my poisonous contempt at his incredible overweight condition: beads of grease just oozed out of his mucky hide. But my amazement at the horse's incredible survivability of a condition that would have foundered, lamed, and killed any other animal, made me know now that I was definitely on a horse raid, a strange modern raid where even to honestly buy a horse you had to do something stealthy, like mentally excavate a real horse out of miles of discordant blubber, to get a vision of what he really looked like.

"I think Riley's been giving him wheat germ, bran, and pig cubes."

A diet of fattening by-products for a commercial, feed-lot pig or cow, but sure death for a normal horse.

"No grass?"

"We don't have any open pasture that we could catch him on if he got loose."

"I mean, grass hay."

"No, hay's hard to come by here, we feed him cubes and blocks."

Very bad. Very odd. Very…

"He's never foundered?"

"No, we feed him very well."

"Yes." I spoke, trying to hide my disgusted wonderment. "It doesn't look like he's missed too many meals."

I closed my eyes and tried to see this pony's mother in the dry, majestic mountains west of Valencia, New Mexico, north of Ladron Mountain, where he was born. I'd seen his papa, who was still alive, but also hidden with other strange people somewhere far away to the north. I tried to magically *see* where we might find this Blue Medicine's original form, his souls. But I couldn't yet determine this. He'd hidden himself well.

But even so, and even with cut off testicles, here in his accursed breeding failure with pigs and blah, Blue sent me a vision, where I could shamanically see him whole and grand and all mine.

"He looks good to me. I'll buy him," I said, and climbed back out of the pen.

The Rich Kid raised his eyebrows as the husband of the house joined us.

"Not so fast, mister, you have to talk to me about Christ first."

At first I thought he was joking, but he was dead serious.

In a blah colored zip suit, slightly stooped, this tired man with a moustache had ambled up, rising somewhere from the main spoke of Iowa pig alleys, smelling of chemicals, like one would in a place like this.

His wife started to explain:

"This is the guy wants to buy Blue Medicine."

We were all still standing in the farm road, and with nobody inviting us in to sit, the Rich Kid, a little imperious from nervousness, spoke authoritatively:

"Folks, I gotta meeting at your neighbor's house to talk some business, can this guy stay here for the night? I'll pick him up in the morning, if that's alright with you guys?"

He didn't ask me.

I took my guitar everywhere I went, so's I could sing and play if I got lonely. The Rich Kid swung it out of his mother's rig while I pulled the rest of my gear to the dark Iowan ground, and then he drove away.

Looking at me like an unwanted foreign exchange student, Riley grumbled: "Alright. Well, I guess you'd better come in." And in we went, with me dragging all my gear.

Seating me down on a little wooden stool, Riley sat opposite and Mona got us some kind of cold, sugary drink with hardly any flavor I could detect, except sugar and chlorinated water.

"My name is Riley Dirigible and this is my wife Mona." I shook his hand and told him my name, in the middle of which he interrupted:

"Why do you want to buy this horse anyway. I'm sure they told you he's been gelded and he's not a stallion anymore. He's not been very friendly since then and we can hardly get a saddle on him anymore. We had him cut because he got too dangerous."

Like always, and in the tradition of my Native-born, talkative New Mexican upbringing, and my even more talkative Irish and obstinate Cree ancestors, I commenced to guide my tongue into a story. A story about horses I'd known on the Reservation and the way we had lived and how I'd found the Poster Horse and wanted to re-find a way to make more of those horses, horses built on that old-time frame that was practically extinct and how I loved those horses, how I'd searched and tried and how finally Mona and Riley Dirigible had the last medicine-hat straight from the people and horses of my birth, ...at which junction in my tale Riley interrupted me:

"Stop, stop! That's not what we asked you, guy! Listen now: we asked why do you want to buy *this* horse?" Riley, looking mighty worn, like he had better things to get to than listen to my liquid romantic banter, thought what I had to say was incomprehensible and irrelevant and calculated just to make him feel dumb. What I of course didn't understand was: he didn't *want* to understand. We were two different breeds.

"Well, sir," I replied, "if this horse is one of those horses, even though you fixed him so he can't make any more, at least he's one more of his kind that's already been made and he's just what I'm after."

"Don't be a fool; he can't be handled; he's wild and worthless; his mind cannot be trained. Mona took him in to fix him up as a foal when he wrecked his hind foot on the neighbor's spike harrow. The horse's mother was killed in a mudslide over where your friend went, and her foal was still suckling, so we took him in. We both fed him and fixed him up, but he grew up to become the ugly, ungrateful monster you see out in that paddock. I want to send him in for slaughter."

The tone, of course, meaning that if they couldn't *dominate* this once beautiful, powerful horse, then how could what they took to be an unencumbered freewheeling half-breed like me do what they could not?

There was so much wrong with all of this, but I dared not illustrate it to them. For they were too emotionally frail and culturally narrow to hold a horse this deep, so they designated him as ungrateful and dangerous and rationed him like a pig. That Blue Medicine was still even alive, after being fed like a hog for slaughter, meant something powerfully vital still lived on in all eight years of him.

"Look, we even fed him to get him to a *real* horse size, 'cause the only reason these Indian horses are so short is because the Indians starved and stunted their horses for so many generations, but even for all our effort he's still under fifteen hands."

Blue was at least 14.3, a full hand taller than all his seven siblings and all his ancestors. This was as big as any Spanish Indian Mesta horse could get, or should. They are small and good. These people got Blue big, but they wanted him bigger and dumber, and to turn him into a horse that looked like an Old West horse, but who acted like a doormat horse of the modern age. They wanted the appearance, but not the heavy-duty reality.

"Well, that's awfully nice of you," I lied, "but I'll take the chance, give him a good life; maybe something good will happen."

"Listen guy, you're not taking him unless I say it's alright; you understand?"

This place of smelly chemicals, impregnated-unhappy-pig-smelling-land-of-blah with weird, harsh people who hated the Indian in the Indian horse, people who wanted to *cure* the stallion of his old-timeness made it seem to me like I'd landed into some strange chamber of Hell, where they tortured and flattened imagination with mediocrity. Then out of nowhere, in a kind of shrill emphatic voice, Riley Dirigible, staring at the floor, says to me: "Son, we refuse to sell this horse to anyone who isn't a Christian. Do you believe in Jesus Christ? Do you believe he alone can save a person like you from eternal damnation in Hell?"

Now it was confirmed! Blue and I had both been dropped into Hell, so I spoke in a totally honest way. "I sure as hell hope so and pray he does!"

Seeing as Blue Medicine was stuck here in Hell, which had turned his bright beauty to blah, and I in my horse raid had come to pick him up, and get him out of the Hog Heaven Hell into Horse Dream Heaven, I wondered if even Jesus *could* get us both out of this pig hole! But I thought I'd give it a try.

At that point, though I was pretty hungry and really drained, I was awake enough to realize this was the main movement of the symphony of this *horse raid*, and that the Rich Kid, knowing exactly what was looming and really no friend at all, had abandoned me to my fate, where I was stuck in a house, where I appeared to its owners like Atilla the Hun must've appeared to Pope Gregory. After all, they'd even sent their daughters away, because like Blue, I looked dangerous, like a *barbarian* visiting from the hinterlands of America's frontier somewhere, a heathen who had some untamed power who needed converting, reducing and *castrating*, like the horse they could no longer handle, the horse I was trying to buy.

So, I started doing what I did best: I started talking. And I talked some more, and talked even more, and more and more, and all about Jesus!

"Well sir," I began, "in college I actually translated the entire book of *John* from Greek into English," which was true.

"That don't make any difference," he admonished, "it's already been translated."

"Yes, I understand your assumption Riley, but though the Bible's been translated into hundreds of tongues, it's always better to study the original book you run your life by in its original language, because a lot of cool things about your man Jesus get horribly twisted and maimed in translation. And you see, because of course, not every language can express what another language does and no part of either testament was ever written in English or French, because none of those languages existed yet when the Bible came together, and Jesus himself didn't speak any of the New Testament languages anyway, including Greek, there are a lot of simple ideas that simply do not transfer all that simply. So, let me tell you about *Luminas*, *Logos,* and *Pneuma*, which don't translate simply as the *light*, *word,* or the *spirit*. When each testament, each of which was written in a kind of eastern Mediterranean Greek of the era…" and on and on I went until I got to the three Magi, not Kings, and about Mary giving birth in a cave not a manger, and spent an hour on Jesus himself, and went onto horses in the Bible, which are supposedly only mentioned in apocalyptic visions of *Zacharias* in the old testament, but that people have mis-translated Jesus' Palm Sunday horse into a donkey, and about the Jews and the Torah, and the badly misunderstood translations of the colors of horses in the Bible, and on and on I went, for over three hours, with no interruptions, when Mona Dirigible stopped me about midnight, to see if I'd like to eat something.

Riley was pretty quiet. Deep down he probably could tell I was still a heathen, but he couldn't begin to prove it. He was right of course. When Mrs. Dirigible brought out a big white plastic soup bowl of what they called *chile* with a side of saltine crackers and a cup of coffee, once I tasted it I knew then and there that this was another trial of Hell: Iowa chili. While Texas chili is terrible stuff, it's still a distinct substance and tastes like something Texans would like, some of it's even edible. New Mexican chili is never made with ground meat and it has a *lot* of taste, like New Mexicans! But Iowa chili tasted blah. It was hell. But I ate it gratefully, knowing all food is sacred and its presence not always a given. One should never disgrace bad food or slaves, just the history that leads up to that kind of food and the slavers, who keep slaves.

Then I talked more about Jesus being a God of the wisdom of love, not a God of correctness, not a God of rightness or righteousness, but a God of forgiveness, mercy and generosity, and how more often than not, these very teachings caused jealousy and envy in those whose love had been lost, and they, unable to grieve, turned their sorrow into hatred, and therefore those that taught love and forgiveness were neither loved nor forgiven, but punished by the haters and people who changed the rules to make it look like they were *right*, instead of weak, envious people who thought those that loved were trying to make them look bad by endorsing an open-mind, and how this all caused Jesus to get himself crucified for his pains, and so on, until the more I talked the more I began to feel bad for these people who were not the authors of the Hell they loyally sustained, but were themselves mired in the muck of that narrow definition of life that doubled for Hell as far as I was concerned. I could no longer see these judgmental settlers as enemies, but as victims of my real enemy, even though I knew they would always do their level best to make sure *their* God knew they held me to be demonic and unclean. Their own Jesus somehow startled them, especially pouring unexpectedly out of the mouth of an obvious heathen, half-breed the likes of me!

But I wanted that horse, so I kept talking…

Like a pair of dark ghosts, my interrogators faced me only as shadows; hiding their expressions in their silhouettes against the blinding white light of the room-wide wall of pig meat freezers, in front of whose humming fluorescent lighting they were seated. Holding my fetishes in my pocket and keeping my mind fixed on the horse, in great faith, I forged ahead, keeping up a relentless Prechtelian-Irish-Indian stream of worded-knowledge, blessings, and unlaughed-at little jokes, until 1:00am, when one of the shadows interrupted me, speaking in the voice of Riley Dirigible.

"So, you say you're interested in buying Blue Medicine, is that correct?"

Wow, did this mean I'd passed inspection?

"Yes sir, that is why I came all the way to Iowa to see you."

"Okay, good," Riley said, sounding reasonable for once. And then talking like a patronizing, mid-western father to a teenage daughter trying to buy a new car, his shadow cocked its head and said parent-like: "And just how do you propose to pay for this horse?"

"Well sir, I've always been partial to using the currency of the land."

"What's that supposed to mean?"

"I mean, you were selling this horse as a stallion for one thousand American dollars, right?"

"Right."

"And now that he's no longer a stallion, I'm only willing to pay eight hundred dollars, in American cash, right now, for him."

"We aren't able to allow any payment plans."

From my silver-covered shoulder bag I retracted a stack of twenty fifty-dollar bills, held together with a rubber band, and counting out 16 bills, I laid them out on the little table off of which I'd been eating that dreadful chili.

"This is the kind of money I brought to buy your horse with."

He snatched up the fanned out pile and counted them.

"When do you want to load him?"

"When that young guy comes back in the morning I figure should be just fine. But I'd like a bill of sale and registration papers, please."

This must have been some kind of secret signal, for as soon as my words hit the air, both silhouettes jumped up off their stools and hustled off out of the freezer room in opposite directions.

I was alone and exhausted; my head swirling with too much Jesus, pig disinfectant and squinting in the fluorescent light of the giant wall-length, pig-meat cooler. It really was Hell.

The chili had been the worst torture of this particular hell. True, it had meat in it, ground pig meat, whose fat was swimming on top, barely melted on the tepid brew in which it floated. It had only salt and no real spices, no discernable vegetable matter and definitely no chile of any description. Well, all right, maybe an onion and a single baseball tomato had been boiled in the water with flour and a flavor packet in some distant historical time, but on the whole it was barely warm, tasteless and cooked to death. Only second to the coffee, which had also been boiled in the same bygone age, probably at the same time as the onion and tomato, but was nonetheless so un-coffee-like, thin, stingy and unhappy-a-brew as to almost pass for burnt water, but not quite that dynamic. The saltines, on the other hand, were imported from a town and at least had some paste and salt and though too few and pitiful they saved the whole thing.

All and all the trials of this Christian Hog Hell were both subtle and extreme: some mildly trying, others extraordinarily weird. But just as I began to even suggest to myself that maybe I'd survived the gauntlet of most of whatever hell they were planning to throw at me, in fluttered Mona, brandishing a bill of sale in one hand and horse registry transfer papers in the other, already signed, and smiling like a rodeo queen.

Riley, she said, had gone to begin the morning tending of the swine, and would I like to retire till morning when we could try to load up Blue Medicine, who she said was nearly impossible to load and would no doubt take us several hours to push into our trailer.

Then with her head and bangs bobbing from side to side, she grabbed me by the elbow and led me down a very narrow corridor lined with more bumper to bumper, built-in wall coolers with fluorescent lighting, each of which lit up as we passed. Like a haunted-house gag, the entire house was filled with glass fronted light-up meat coolers. Living there must've been like taking up residence in the frozen food section at the supermarket.

Escorting me into a very tiny cubicle with a very tiny springy bed, she plopped herself down onto the bed and pulled me to her side, and in a previously-unheard-by-me tone, as soft as a breeze in the reeds, she spoke in a surprising north Arkansas accent:

"I just love the way you talk about Jesus, it makes me feel, I just don't know what...!"

Taking my elbow in her elbow she said: "Please let me come with you... Take me with you this morning when you leave. I could hide in the back of your truck till we're out of the state, then I could ride up front all the way to the free and open land you described, there where you have your horses! We could have a time together, wild and free!"

Through all the wars, and close calls with would-be killers, through all the countries I'd traveled through, the political scrapes, tribal existence, or my little known life as a popstar rocker, never had any woman of any kind ever expressed an over-riding desire to be with me on account of anything I'd ever had to say about *Jesus*. Here, sitting beside me was a lady, not so unbeautiful, one of the *enemy*, wearing makeup you could've scratched your name in, pleading with me to get her out of the same hell from which I hoped both Blue and I would in a few hours begin our escape.

I was caught so off guard, exhausted, and over-Bibled, hell—all I came to do was buy a horse! I wasn't even a monotheist, much less a Christian, but the words that found their way out of my mouth only made matters more hellish. Like a stunned six-year-old, all I could think to say was: "Don't you think Riley would miss you?"

"Miss me? He'd probably give you that horse for free if you promised to get me out of his hair. Who cares what he thinks? He hasn't even so much as looked at me in five years!"

"Well, what about your little girls, you can't just go away and leave them without a mom." None of this was helping, I could tell.

"Those girls are not my children; they're not Riley's either; they are the children of his first wife by another man. He's raising them 'cause she's a drinker and gone God-knows-where. Both those kids hate me more than they hate Riley!

"Look, I loved that horse," Mona discoursed. "I nursed and took care of him. And Riley? He hated that I loved something that wasn't him, something that took money and didn't make money. So, he was mean to him; he wrecked him; he's the one that ordered him gelded. Now Blue won't even look at either of us; he's dangerous; he even charges and bites."

Holding me tight by the arm, the saga of young Blue Medicine came out of this sad woman's mouth.

Blue Medicine had been a seven-month-old colt—with a herd of ninety mares and geldings and a few foals—whose owner, after arguing with the registry, withdrew all his beautiful horses. In a rage he divided his herd and hauled them all away, out of New Mexico, giving one third to the people of the North Cheyenne Reservation in southeastern Montana, where Amarillento had originated. The other two thirds he gave to an architect, college friend who still lived on his parent's six hundred acre hog farm in Iowa, designing houses in a hip, renovated, old barn. He lived a mile east of the Dirigibles, where the Rich Kid had gone off for the night.

Hysterical and disoriented when released, several of the smallest foals, not used to cultivated land, endless muddy black soil with no rocks, and humidity, having grown up on eighty thousand acres in a half-feral existence in central New Mexico, now without their herd mare and most of their mothers either absent or dead, went running scared, undirected. Four of them fell into discarded farm implements, plows and harrows. Some were maimed beyond saving, while others recovered. Blue, with his fancy ancestry and outstanding markings, was taken by the architect's neighbor, Mona—to nurse him, for he was still suckling, and to doctor his hind left hoof, which was torn up past the hairline of the corona, a split which never fully coalesced, and something for which he would always have to be shod with horseshoes to keep it from splaying open and laming him, which in the end it never did.

Mona went through all the horse registry gobbledygook with its ridiculous high-school-bureaucracy of the day, full of official inspections and graduated acceptance appendix papers, until they actually registered the colt in her name. She planned to keep him for her own.

Some friends of the original owner, Native Dakota people from Nebraska, arranged to borrow Mr. Blue Medicine for a *Horse Dance* renewal of Black Elk's vision at Wounded Knee. The colt was two, a stallion, untrained and rowdy, but nonetheless danced with thirteen other horses without a hitch! He would always be a supernatural horse.

But then when they returned him back in Iowa, he grew glaze-eyed, sullen, and hard-headed. It was at this time the Dirigibles very unwisely let him breed a solid white mare, whose foal died from so-called *lethal white* syndrome. Instead of searching for a more suitable mare, Riley wanted him gone. A full-blown, frustrated stallion now, Blue grew more difficult and Riley was getting ready to send him to slaughter. But even though I'd already arranged to buy Blue as a stallion, the Rich Kid's family convinced Riley to castrate Blue in hopes he'd grow more amiable. So, to save Blue from slaughter as a stallion, Mona convinced her husband to have him gelded instead.

When the Father Sun began to burn off the dull, foggy yellow of a midwestern summer morning, Riley was still occupied managing his commercial pig farm when the Rich Kid showed up well-breakfasted.

"Mona, you know I can't take you home with me because we're both married. And while the one I'm married to has a lot of good points, a lot of them are very, very sharp points, if you get my drift? When she's mad, she's as movable as a loosely woven gunnysack full of horseshoe nails, and just about as cuddly, and once she caught sight of you, she'd have both us shredded into dog food. Let's just keep writing letters to each other and see what comes of it. What do you say?"

And we gave each other our secret addresses to which neither of us ever did write.

She started to give me a kiss, but then I remembered Judas, and that we were still in Iowa Hog Heaven Hell with a bunch of hard-headed white Christians with whom I'd just spent the entire night talking about Jesus. While I knew Jesus said we should love our enemies, it's good to go slow with some things, and so we kissed the rings on each other's hand instead!

Just then Riley, looking weirdly rested, well fed, and friendlier, appeared from behind the door all ready to load a horse:

"Your friend's got the trailer backed up to the corral gate, we're going to try to push that horse into your stock trailer. You want to give me a hand with this panel?"

"What panel?" I asked. When he explained, I said: "No way."

Riley positioned himself behind one end and the Rich Kid behind the opposing end of a loose eight-foot-high, eighteen-foot-wide, steel-pipe, corral-panel gate, with which, inside the enclosure, where this pig-poop-colored, hang-dog, obese horse was standing, they intended to *push* Blue Medicine toward our rig, kind of bulldozing him into the back of the Rich Kid's trailer, which was standing there with its back door wide open, the whole trailer having been wedged into the opened gate space of the corral.

This was insane of course, because that horse was a Mesteño Barb, and when cornered, just like wild bison, they can jump from a standstill over seven-foot fences, and even belly flop over eight-foot enclosures. If scared enough, or crowded into a terrified desperation, they can do much worse.

It turned out this method was considered standard procedure in Hog Heaven Hell! These people were accustomed to *gate-dozing* pigs and cattle and untame horses to get them to go where they wanted! White man horses. Blue had obviously been chased around like this before, because he started nervously moving his big self around before they'd even got it going at him. But contrary to their desires, he didn't scare away from them toward the direction they wanted him to go, but acting like he still had both his testicles, instead of moving away from the panel, he unexpectedly spun around and threw himself smack-dab at the unmanned midpart of the panel and flying straight up in the air like a big, fat, flying hog, he sailed right over those fools' heads to land back behind them, then spun around, prancing and snorting further away from the trailer than when they commenced!

I was convinced his soul was watching somewhere, running the show from a remote location. I was actually relieved, for now I knew I hadn't made a mistake by buying him. He had scruples and was just too much of a horse and too noble to be scooted around like a hog by these presumptuous turnip eaters. The best part was he'd made his point without a hysterical wreck, pulling it all off without anyone getting hurt, including himself, and there had been a lot of opportunity for disaster and injury in what they were stupidly doing.

"You see, I told you he's no good, he's an incorrigible outlaw." Riley spoke, then spat.

So like a bad government, instead of scrapping a proven bad plan, they put even more energy and hate into its execution, trying over and over to corner him. When they did, I saw Blue just faintly grin with royal contempt at these unimaginative men, letting a smile peek through the pig blah he'd been coated with. His determination to get as far away from Mr. Riley Dirigible and the Rich Kid as soon as he could was pretty much my own feeling as well, which finally brought me to my senses, slightly dulled after a long sleepless night of weird challenges.

Of course! I suddenly realized, peculiarly late in the morning, that Blue Medicine, this pig-poop colored, so-called incorrigible outlaw, for whom I'd gained the release papers with the help of Jesus, my ancestral tongue, and eight hundred bucks, now belonged legally to none other than me and God. He was *my* horse, so why was I letting these fart bags push him around like a giant gerbil?!

"Hold on fellas, put that stupid hunk of dangerous iron outside the corral. *Now*, dammit! He's my horse, not yours. We'll do it my way. Thanks." Looking up, startled by the new tone of command in my voice, they nonetheless bustled off to do just what I asked.

"Now let's have another cup of coffee, and think this out," I ordered and we did. I knew the kid had a thermos of something more drinkable in the cab.

We sat down in their designated *kitchen* and drank up the kid's coffee while they discussed how to get Blue into our Persian blue trailer.

Being the only one of us sitting with a view of the corral, I calmly had my coffee while I watched with delight at what I knew was going to happen.

I pushed with the spiritual force of the Sun in my chest to help Blue as he slowly snuck up on the trailer, stalking it like a cat. And then I watched as he very daintily reared up and quietly let his front half down over the top of the closed corral gate, and then with his hind legs dangling in the air, he wiggled his back end over the fence like a toddler into a crib, to land very neatly and quietly right into the mouth of the open trailer. After walking nonchalantly to the rear, he turned back around and stood there, big and grinning, his head facing out the back, not moving a muscle.

You could just feel him saying "come on Martín, let's get the Hell out of Hog Heaven Hell *RIGHT NOW!*"

"Hang in there young man, just a little bit longer," I told him in my heart, with my Keres language.

Suppressing a grin of admiration and a belly laugh of triumph, I got to my feet in the *kitchen* and left nonchalantly, as if going off to pee. I walked out the front of that suburban, frozen-food-mansion, and ever so slowly tiptoed up and quietly closed and latched the trailer door, petted the old boy on his smiling, wily forehead, as even and flat as an anvil, then trying not to swagger or breathe too hard, I made my way back to the *kitchen* and sat down and drank another cup of coffee.

While I was gone, Riley had developed another plan of force: "You know, guys, my neighbor has a tranquilizer gun, and I think if we shot this horse with it and knocked him down, we could halter him and get him in the trailer while he was still groggy, when he started to come around. I'll give that man…"

"That's okay Mr. Dirigible, I already got him in the trailer."

"What are you talking about? When?"

Everybody turned to look.

"Come on kid; let's get going; we got a long drive back to New Mexico."

Mona actually almost laughed, the kid did laugh and pretty hard, and Riley was stunned and not amused that force hadn't done it. But, I was still not breathing 'cause we were still in Hog Heaven Hell. So, I pushed the kid, my gear and my guitar into the truck, shook everybody's hands and got going. Blue gave the side of the trailer a big kick as we bumbled on out of Hell making it thunder as we left.

The trailer listed very noticeably to the left as we rumbled off to pick up a mare at the neighbor's, which the kid had purchased the night before, and then on toward Clarinda. Blue was way too fat, but he still had to eat and so did I, so I had the kid stop at a feed store with a diner attached. That ephemeral Dirigible Iowa chili left me feeling a little weak in the knees.

After buying and loading a couple of bales of hay, we went into the diner and eased ourselves down at a booth. When the waitress had taken our orders, a great big fellow wearing overalls, looking a little like Blue Medicine himself, with two blue eyes hammered into a red face on a head that really looked like a tiny bowling ball sitting atop a four hundred pound torso, threw himself next to me at the table, knocking me like a billiard ball to the wall, while he straightened his bulk.

Another guy doing the same bounced the kid, removed his baseball cap, and says to us: "Boys, is that Paint horse in your trailer that crazy horse from the Dirigible farm?"

I couldn't believe this, we were fifty miles away from Hog Heaven Hell and they knew our horse was coming their way!

"Yes sir," I said, "that's him alright."

"Well, I've got a Paint I could sell you that's a whole lot better horse than that mess you got stuck with there. Look, when you fellas are done with breakfast, what say we go over and see 'em? I'll give you a real good price."

"Well, sir, that's nice of you, but truth is I've already shot my wad on this one. So maybe next time, but thanks for thinking about us."

Somehow word had gotten out that we were some rich guys mysteriously running around buying up country horses, which in a sense was true, 'cause the Rich Kid's family had been buying Barbs cheap and hauling them right through here for two years. But how did all these people know who we were, where we'd been, what we bought, and where we were headed?"

"Kind sir," I continued, "maybe you can enlighten me about a mystery hereabouts! Yesterday, as we were wending our way over from Nebraska, I didn't see one doggone rock the whole danged drive. Could it be true this district is basically rockless?"

"There's a rock, a big one over by…"

"Yeah, you mean that big square piece of sandstone in Norwich?"

"Right, that's the rock, it came all the way from the Quad Cities. That's our only rock!"

"Do you guys like rocks?"

"Yeah, we all want rocks, but who can afford them?"

"Look friend, where I'm from we are all about rocks, big ones, small ones, soft ones, hard ones, every kind, from gravel to boulders!"

"I tell you what," says this big guy, handing me his card, "the next time you guys are coming this way horse buying, you just fill up that horse trailer with a big load of good looking boulders and I'll trade you even for my Paint horse!"

My luck was definitely coming up, Blue was a good luck horse. Imagine trading rocks for horses!

Finally our meals came and though I offered to buy all six of these fellas breakfast, (there were four more guys behind each of us, listening in) they all politely refused, but insisted on staring at us as the kid and I shoveled in all the food we could get as fast as we could get it in us, 'cause I for one was anxious to get out of that rockless Hog Heaven Hell as soon as we could manage to make a run for it.

Even though nothing illegal or wrong was being done, what Blue and I were doing by leaving on our own terms, heading toward our own ancient pattern of life, away from this impounded unhappy place, once a beautiful land for the original Native Otoe owners from whom it was unfairly extorted, was definitely a kind of spiritual horse raid. For just trying to get our natural souls back home to our own Native land, there was an overwhelming feeling in this place that being truly, indigenously at home was so foreign and distasteful to these immigrant descendants, that its presence set them on edge. Our implied refusal to accept this mediocrity these people lived out as some kind of superior lifeway was not only suspicious, but interpreted as ungrateful and criminal.

Outside, Blue Medicine was making an ear-splitting racket clobbering the metal sides of the trailer with his big front hooves. After all he knew even better than I, whose every natural instinct said we'd better get moving or we too might get stuck here in Hog Heaven Hell, like all these people. So, away we drove, with Blue screaming and loudly beating time, denting up the trailer all the way to the Nebraska border.

Chapter 8

Fairy Tale Cops and
the Color of Blue

Nebraska at the Iowa border was windy, real red, and fierce looking in the sunset, but I breathed a lot easier with the horses in the back and all of us heading the right direction: west!

By Hebron, rain in sheets began to crash across the highways, making darkness descend over us an hour earlier than nightfall under clear skies would have done. I was still at the wheel, the Rich Kid snoring to the swish, click, boomp, pank of the wipers bending at full blast, barely able to negotiate the torrent pounding into the windshield.

It was hard enough to keep the rig from hydro-foiling, but maneuvering the rig to keep from fishtailing and flipping over was a constant focus, for the wind came ripping in pulses of violent gusts, whose broadsides had already caused more than three semis to have jackknifed or rolled completely over and off the interstate.

As we glided into Kansas the rain was still hard, not torrential, but steady. The rich boy woke up when the flashing red and blue lights from a Kansas state police patrol car came oozing up behind us, its loudspeaker ordering us to pull off onto the shoulder as we skirted Concordia.

I eased the whole rig to a stop.

Brandishing a big, black flashlight with reflector tape stripes, the officer let his light search our cab and our hands, his mounty-type hat dripping like a shed roof, the yellow slicker he had on clattered like a tin roof in the torrent when he leaned down to examine my driver's license.

He was tall and spoke very calmly, but loud enough to hear over the downpour.

"Boys, I stopped you, because, do you fellows realize that you are driving around in the dark without a left taillight or turn signal on your livestock trailer?"

In New Mexico, most people from ranchitos, farms, and villages kept alive an old tradition of being terrified of any police authority. This derived from a time in history when all civil authorities were white and considered themselves a superior caste that held Spanish speakers and Natives automatically guilty of being potentially unruly because they were Catholics and non-English speakers. This combined with the fact that most New Mexicans aggravated the situation with New Mexico's famous, time-honored tradition that considered all ordinances, traffic signs, vehicular safety requirements, and documents only as suggested guidelines made by outsiders who didn't really understand New Mexico or her people, instead of laws requiring mandatory compliance, whose infraction was punishable by law. This reinforced both sides' opinion of the other.

This didn't mean the people thought the police were elite, or even bad for that matter. People knew cops were regular people in service to an elite that was not on their side, unless of course the cop or the judge was a relative, which conjured another New Mexico tradition altogether.

Unlike myself, who knew I was guilty of something because I was a commoner, the Rich Kid knew his people were elite, and so he poured out a plausible, elitist lie, expecting to be instantly exonerated because he said so. But this was Kansas, not New Mexico.

"Oh heck, that taillight has given us trouble off and on over the years. It's been just fine for the last few months," which was a bucket of toad farts. When we started out neither signal worked on the trailer and the left taillight was totally out, and had never worked at all since his mother bought the trailer before he'd been born!

"I can't let you guys back on the road without functioning signals, so either you fix it right now, or I'll have to tag your trailer and you guys can fix it tomorrow after you talk to the magistrate."

"Well officer, we got a couple of pretty wild horses back there, we couldn't just leave the trailer here on the road, if you know what I mean."

"Look boys, I'm sorry, but that's just the way it is." We must've looked pretty unhandy and spoiled because after a short silence, the policeman, in a very matter-of-fact, country-boy-way, spoke up.

"Well. Don't you guys have any tools?"

The rain was coming straight down, windless and relentless.

"Yeah, we do," the rich boy breathed out in a sigh of disgust, and climbing over his seat back into the trashy rear of the Suburban, he rummaged around like a racoon in the accumulated strata of disordered mechanical debris, until he produced an old dented metal toolbox.

"Could you let me see that?" the cop chimed.

I opened my door, intending to get my rain gear on and walk back to the trailer with the tool kit to see if I could fix something, but the cop lifted the tool kit out of my hands and with me following, proceeded toward the rear of our horse trailer himself.

And then, to my complete surprise, right there in the dark, in the driving rain, this man, after digging out a screwdriver, opened up the trailer lights and started methodically eliminating causes for our signal malfunction!

Inside my soul I knew that the problem lay in the fact that all the wires, for years, had been chewed to bits inside the trailer by various bands of colts and fillies, who love to chew on automobile paint and rubber wire insulation, like spaghetti, to test their sprouting adult teeth. The trailer would no doubt need a complete rewiring for the lights to function as intended.

So, standing next to the cop, I told him that I figured that the wiring had no doubt been compromised somewhere inside the trailer by the horses.

"Well, I'll just check that out," he yelled over the deafening din of the downpour on the trailer ceiling. He was going to fix it. I couldn't believe this.

When he started running his hand through the open upper rails, feeling his way along the line, I got worried one of those wild creatures might bite him or even give him a good kick before he could ascertain anything by his method, so I yelled to him over the thundering rumble of the rain on the trailer lid: "Look, officer, allow me to halter these beasts and pull them out of the trailer so's we can get in the trailer and check it out properly without you getting hurt, these horses are not exactly broken.

"Good thinking. I'll wait in the car while you do that."

Neither horse had been successfully haltered in recent history by their previous *owners*, so I had no idea where to begin, especially in this urgency, and in a storm. Blue was in front of the central partition, so I just edged my way in with a long cotton rope, and to my great surprise, with no battle or deadly shuffling, he let me put an Indian chin halter with a twist over his big, funny-old, pig-smelling head.

I unlatched the trailer rear, swung the door wide open and let him jump out into the storm, led him toward the Suburban, and tied him to the tie rungs alongside the rear of the trailer. He stood there, his eyes squinting, just as still as a mountain taking a shower in the rain as I pulled out the mare with equal ease. The officer lifted himself up into the butt end of the trailer, searched around with the stupendously bright beam of his flashlight, found six breaks and frayed wire, which he cleaned, cleared, brightened with his jackknife, shuffled back to his car, returning with a roll of electrician tape and a roll of light insulated wire. In twenty minutes he yelled to me, still watching at the rear just inside the trailer: "Tell your buddy to turn on the truck, and let's see what we got!"

And of course, when the rich boy did, the whole trailer lit up like town hall on Christmas; even the lights on the top and sides that had never functioned on this Rich Kid's Mama's trailer since she owned it were blazing and blinking away.

The cop went back to his car, returned with a warning citation for driving without a taillight, etc.

"Boys, it's about 9:30pm, you guys look beat and my day's done; I could sure use a cup of coffee. What say we go downtown and get out of the rain; this storm's bound to let up about midnight, then you fellows can get back on the road."

"Well sir, that's an enormously appealing notion, but we gotta keep trucking back to New Mexico."

"Well boys, I could ask you for your brand inspection papers and veterinary health certificates on these two broomtails, but if you come have a cup of coffee I won't ask, and the world will be just that much safer without another drowsy driver on these rainy highways."

"Yes sir, I think we should buy you at least a cup of coffee for fixing up our lights."

"No, don't do that, that's bribery," he said grinning, "just follow my car and don't try to escape."

I had utterly forgotten about transportation papers, and if caught, the horses could have been impounded and quarantined for a couple of weeks at my expense! Not to mention the fine or imprisonment. So, coffee with a cop it was!

Both horses let me lead them back into the trailer like they'd been doing it every day for a century, and when Blue plopped his overweight self into that *can on wheels*, the whole thing leaned to the left. I tied him in opposite the wiring, delighted he was so easy to handle after all the foofaraw about his savage personality.

The cop not only bought us coffee, told his life story, loved horses, but bought both the Rich Kid and me each an all-night breakfast, and told us the best places to dodge brand inspection stations for our homeward route, 'cause he used to haul racehorses back and forth right through here in his youth! He knew, in his own way, that we were on a horse raid and were trying to get out of *enemy* territory as stealthily and quickly as possible, driving at night in a storm to cover all our illegal motions. But some of the enemy were certainly friendly, and I will always be in praise of a kind police officer like him. He was not only a unique person of his own invention, but the child of a forgotten pocket of American existence almost extinct. We both took down his name and address and thanked him profusely, as the diner chef filled up our thermos's with hot coffee.

Just like he said, the storm let up and when the kid, who was back at the wheel, started laughing, making fun of the cop, I had to stop him, 'cause I knew this man had been taken over by some kind spirit sent by Blue's wild-horse-soul, somewhere out there with the Divine in Nature, to protect us and get us all back to home territory. How many people have been stopped by a cop for missing taillights and had him fix them for free, in the driving rain, in the pitch dark, then buy you breakfast?!

• • •

Having dozed off, and asleep for some hours, I was awakened by the whine of an old style cop car's siren just as we were easing our way out of Hugoton, Kansas about 3:00 in the morning.

"Guys," the African American cop with a warm-weather, dark, short sleeve shirt and big muscles, bugled into the cab.

"Do you know you're dragging about fifteen feet of lead rope out of the back door of your trailer? I just thought you'd like to know, it's probably against the law, but I just thought I'd save you some expensive rope!"

Oh no!

I couldn't believe it, another helpful cop. We must still be in Kansas!

Jumping out to fix the situation, I looked in the trailer with my feeble flashlight to check on the horses and saw, what was to my stunned half-awake self, a beautiful, bright, sorrel-red and blazing white, overweight, medicine-hat paint gelding with two bright blue eyes and wrinkly lips, like a rhino, smiling back at me, having untied his moorings, causing the rope to leak out of the trailer and drag on the road, burning off at least twenty feet!

Blue Medicine was returning, the rain of Concordia and the kind cop had cleaned off the pig-glaze, and a horse had begun to re-emerge!

"Guys, my beat's up for the night; I'm signing off. Looks to me like you guys could use a cup of coffee. Just leave the rig right here, and let's go inside. I'm treating."

The cop had pulled us over right at the Hugoton Main Street Diner, like he was trapping company, or maybe...

Anyway, we went along with him, 'cause just like the other officer, when we balked, he let us know he was going to start asking for more documentation to make sure our horses were healthy and not stolen, if we didn't come along peaceably to drink coffee!

I actually stopped drinking coffee when I returned from Central America, because it was incomparable, and for some reason, even the good stuff gave me headaches. So, I switched back to black tea. But on the road, when requesting tea in those times, what they had was even worse: heated up instant ice tea! So, on the road, bad coffee it was.

Once in the diner, this second, friendly policeman started asking us where we got our animals, 'cause he recognized them as different and non-modern, right out of the old days. Turned out this man originated from northeastern Texas, on the border with Oklahoma and Arkansas, and was from a town of all Black cattle raising families. He'd served as a pilot over Cambodia and in Vietnam during those terrible, idiotic wars, flying helicopters, pulling guys out of the field.

He hated being a cop and wondered if we knew of any more romantic jobs in New Mexico rounding up wild horses by helicopter, because he'd done it before and loved flying and wild horses.

Misty eyed himself, he practically had us crying about his life stuck here in not too exciting Hugoton, Kansas, imagining for some reason that the lives we appeared to be leading with our long hair, my buckskins, our old fashioned horses, my guitar and being on the road with no boss or check-in times, were somehow more glamorous and more worthy of the talents of a warrior like himself.

I actually did know some people who used helicopters to chase horses. I didn't agree with what they were doing, but I liked this policeman, so I told him I'd get him their contact number when I got home, a place towards which, I thought, we should probably be heading right about now.

"Look, before you guys get back on the road, I have a dentist, well he's a friend too, and he has a horse I'd think you'd like to see. I can tell you fellows are crazy for wild looking Pintos, 'cause you got a wild, old-time one there in your rig, but you should see this guy's. It's about 4:00am, I don't think he'd mind us waking him up and taking a look, wha d'ya say?"

Man, it was really hard to get out of Kansas with these two horses, because for some reason, at this moment in time, while hauling these particular animals, these particular policemen were very helpful and wouldn't let us go. It never happened again. No doubt it was a spiritual thing; some spirit was looking after us.

Well, the dentist actually was thrilled to see Zach, the cop. It was a fairytale. Since when can you just saunter on over to your dentist's house at 4:00 am, wake him up at the back door, and drink *more* coffee with him and his wife, in their pajamas, just to have a look at a beautiful, big, Quarter-horse-type Paint by the beams of flashlights and the shine of Venus, then have them serve you breakfast before the dentist goes off to work? I had to rethink my whole stigmatized working theory of America that said all police were of one mold, that all cowboys were white and mono-faceted right wingers, and dentists were all wealthy, unapproachable golfers. Education was everywhere. Blue's presence made life a bigger teacher.

After the kid and I had taken down everybody's numbers and names and they took ours, and we'd shook hands and said our farewells, it was my turn to drive into Oklahoma. With the sun to the left, just rising over the land, once we had successfully skirted all the inspection stations, thanks to the impeccable advice of our new police friends, we'd be safe again. For when we got back to that mile of detour around the tornado-ravaged bit of road at Clayton, New Mexico we'd come in on, there would be no more friendly, useful cops, no more helpful dentists, just Antelope, Elks, Flycatchers, Merlins and really big, open, rolling space till we hit the mountains of home.

My innards would rejoice again because they wouldn't have to be sacrificed to yet another cup of stale coffee in the name of the horse raid. I could go straight back to my beloved Darjeeling tea, with home-milk and honey.

I could breathe a deep, clear breath again with no chemicals, smelly feedlots or GMO corn, happy as we sailed west through the big, eastern New Mexico prairie to my mountains, gliding and rolling home, and amazed how more beautiful Blue became as mile by mile he gained his real colors the closer we got to his old home and his new life.

Chapter 9

Hatched From an Egg of Ice

Blue Medicine, as his childhood captors registered this magic horse's name, had remained invisible to his Iowa keepers. They never saw the real horse and wouldn't have seen him even if he'd chosen to be seen. He spent the first eight years of his life privately developing inside a chrysalis of difficult and alone history, camouflaged as pig glaze. There, hidden from his captor's gaze, he slowly and quietly gestated into a very substantial, majestic, never-before-seen being, who when he finally did burst into this world, he did so as an already formed adult, literally hatching out of a shell: a shell of ice, by the improbable magic of ice-encrusted Sandhill Cranes.

From that day on, an utterly new animal, a rare type of horse emerged from that startling, nerve-ripping sound of blades of ice crashing from the skies. They were the Cranes that birthed him, for they had been holding his natural soul in safe keeping all along, and the ice that brought him into this world allowed him to molt off the herdless, Midwestern hell he'd been kicked into.

I might have surmised that the migrating Cranes held

the key to finding the real Blue Medicine, for as an Abalone Horse he was the Horse of the Summer Sun, and the Cranes hereabouts were the Lords and Ladies of that change from summer to winter and winter to summer. But I didn't wake up to the fact until it happened and then it was more than a surprise and the deepest of natural magic when it did.

◆ ◆ ◆

For most Natives in what is now Northern New Mexico, the immense melodic bands of Sandhill Cranes soaring over and through their lands—in their biennial migration of forty thousand strong, south along the Rio Grande in November to the Cottonwood forests of the Big River to places like the Bosque del Apache, and then again northward in February, nine thousand miles to Siberia back along the same fly ways— are for them the inner forms of Deities who cause the land to fill with water and that rule the thunder.

These tall, wonderous birds mostly nest in cooler summers very far from us, but return, flying with half grown babies, in late October or November in successive groups of five hundred to two thousand for weeks.

Though these avian herds traveled with some migrating Snow Geese, Eagles and some varieties of Ducks, they flew faster, at greater unbelievable heights, and spent more time in the air than any other flocking, water bird migrating over land. After a group's day of hard southward flying to get to a traditional staging ground, the babies in mid-flight would often call in desperation to their parents as they started to lose strength and couldn't keep up. When the young birds, unable to flap any longer, still gliding, began to drop and lose altitude, it soared one's soul to see how phalanxes of adults would respond to the emergency by flying back and circle under them to create a great community of upward-moving cushions of air. By the force of a hundred collective adults simultaneously rising beneath the young, they were able to buoy up the juveniles, pushing up the air in such a way that caused the babies to glide easier on the air's current and hold them in a fixed trajectory, and keep them from falling just a little longer, long enough to get them safely to the next night's resting spot on the ground. Like Whales do in the sea, who using the air bubbles they blow underwater to hold their young up and give them air to breathe until they can reach the surface, the Cranes kept their young afloat mile after mile, until finally it was safe for the entire group to descend, circling. Clan by clan, family by family, flying very low, they would spread out along some well known point of night rest in their accustomed, millions-of-year-old, back and forth passageways.

These lines of flight and stopping places were traditional places, part of a story whose well-kept memory ruled the details of the annual cycles of these majestic migrations. From ancient times every group of Indigenous humans, living along these fly ways held these birds in such awe, that much of what they revere about the Cranes still forms some of the deepest foundations of many tribes' spiritual culture. Lived out ceremonially, the rituals of magic that were given to the original people by these birds is still a deeply kept secret. Any people could feel and hear the magic of this two-times-a-year specialness of the birds' comings and goings and their occasional staying, whereas certain Natives and the birds had the continued living presence of the Mythic Dream in their mutual, ritual interdependence since forever.

And that's the way it was, the same for years and years, year in, year out.

Leaves would not change, Thunder wouldn't give up blowing trees to bits, snow wouldn't dare to emerge from the Winter Goddess without the majestic flight-calls of southern migrating Cranes singing the new winter out of the old summer.

Then in spring, grass wouldn't green up, the days wouldn't cease freezing, and huge tracts of *chimajá* would never dare to summon up summer's Darkling Beetles, the little sister of summer, to call the Rain-Beings back out of the lakes and into summer action, without first having heard the life-stirring cries of the Cranes moving north again in their really hard push to get to the upper ends of Siberia's tundra and stony, lower valleys full of mud, bugs and fish.

The old-time original people here knew that the Cranes healed the land they flew over. To them it was simple physics: the collective screams of Cranes made things come alive, just as Indigenous medicine societies collectively healed the life-ravaged bodies of their people with the Crane infused medicine, over whom they sang Crane songs. That's how it always was, the same for years and years, year in, year out.

Therefore when, very occasionally, some different pattern occurred with the Cranes, it was a mystery, sometimes a miracle, and always accorded great import. It was never ignored. Even today, for modern people who treasure the sounds of migrating Cranes, and who themselves travel long distances just to hear and see them, it is always a little alarming when some different mind takes over a large group of Cranes, whose leadership mysteriously causes the big birds to leave their northern nesting grounds a little too late, to come in ahead of the crippling, high-mountain blizzards that frequent the Rocky-Mountain-vertebral-column of the country along which they migrate.

The oldest Cranes have always had the whole route and its timing encoded in their hearts and could therefore lead the flight up and over those mountain heights at just the right moment, knowing exactly where they had to be at a given time to reach specific resting places, without getting stranded and freezing to death. They knew where the aerial pressure passes rose up in the sky, down from which they could glide effortlessly like winged skiers for fifty miles, without flapping, to reach the beginnings of traditional stops down in warmer lands. They knew to scout and assess the geography of the present day lay-of-the-land, changed by modern people, to have the wisdom and adaptivity to be able to part from established tradition when necessary, to lead their bird tribes into a food-rich, shallow-water, Crane-camp-ground, off the traditional route just for the night, and steer them back onto their millenia-old, traditional migratory route in the morning!

When Cranes showed up in places they'd never been, scientists would assume they'd been "blown off course in a storm." But Cranes won't get caught in a storm unless they have lost those individuals who keep the older story of all the hows and wheres written in the corpus of the collective, mental, synaptic net formed by the birds as a whole organism in their clan, within the bigger organism of all their species.

Cranes are very organized. Like all migratory human nomads, each Crane belongs to a family, who in turn is a unit of a specific band. Out of these bands, they marry individuals of other bands, into whose new group they move into, with whom they now migrate and make babies, who in turn join their mother's band. Then there are sub-tribal groups comprised of several bands of some five hundred to a thousand Cranes. In these flying bands, there are at least three old Cranes you can always see: *out-riders* who fly apart from the rest, usually out in front. Preceding every migrating band, these out-riders scout out the suitability of what their own predetermined, internal, leadering map and story-of-the-going tells them is the next campground by flying ahead of the greater clan collective, leaving the last resting place earlier than all the rest. Being the first to arrive, they always slowly and elegantly cruise very low over various appropriate camping places within the inner map of the remembered story of traditional resting places. If everything was just so, they would describe this place in their screaming songs, rise back up and hasten to fly back to the first V's coming south and return with them. Flying in the front, they led them into the previously scouted campground these leaders had chosen for them to *camp* the night. Then these scouts would fly back to the next groups coming in and escort each of them in sequence, group by group, until five hundred to two thousand Cranes, in their respective clans, groups and families, were laid out in a strand, side-by-side, for maybe up to a mile in length, where they all rested the night.

These *leaders* knew where every one of these clans were situated and didn't spend the night with them, but kept watch off to the side somewhere, very often up on a cliff, so they could see and *talk* administratively to them all.

All night long, they would call out intermittently. The nearest group would respond first, and then the next group would call to them, the next group doing the same, all the way up the strand of camps, until everyone was confirmed present and well. This way they knew they were all there, in constant audial flow and sound location with one another, like whales in a large pod.

An hour before dawn, these three leaders would rise up in the dark. Flying quietly alone, they appeared from the south and began rousing each group in succession by cruising very slowly and low over them, plaintively calling them to action. Once all of the groups had animated themselves, signaling their readiness by yelping and calling back, these leaders would land, dropping right in the middle of the whole string. Not at the end. Not at the beginning, but right in the middle of the center group.

Like a bow string pulled back, arrow nocked, ready to release, the tension of the together-action mounted.

Then, at just the right rhythmic inhale, the collective force-field of a stretched-out mile of Cranes yelling in readiness, these three leaders (sometimes there were more) would leap up together and fly the opposite direction everyone was meant to head in the migration. When this happened, all the Cranes of that middle band would start running like ostriches, running together until they caught the air in their outstretched wings, and flapping, rise up in one majestic surge of flight. They didn't follow the leaders, but started circling in spirals of screaming birds rising up on the incoming morning thermal.

In the same sequence they had landed the day previous, they now returned back into the sky. As the old leaders flew over them, each group in succession rose up, pulled to the sky by these three yelling *old knowers*, who continued all the way to the rear of the column until every group had risen up and were together again on the light morning thermals. Once those last Cranes from the most northerly camp had risen up flapping and screaming, they joyfully jammed themselves into the dancing matrix of the entire airborne tribe, the whole now resembling a kind of swirling, aerial tiramisu of stratified, thermal-riding Cranes in a wild jazz of joyful screams.

When all were moving and the whole tribe was judged to have risen up to sufficient height, each band unwound itself out of the swirl to pull themselves into big V's, micro Vs and lines. The leaders then herded them from the north up into the skies, toward the south, driving from behind to keep an eye out for any of the young or aged who might be in trouble.

Just like human horse nomads during their various annual movements, everything during a migration in their Crane tribe depended on these leaders; for these out-riders were the living map and knowers; they had the million-year-old story of how, what, where, when, and every adjustment made since, written in their nature-educated Crane souls. They'd seen it all and had been born for their position.

They weren't like guides on a wagon train, or some outside mercenaries hired to lead tenderfeet from their homes to new homes, serving anonymous families to whom they were not related, the entire Crane herd was an organism and these leaders were the actual thinking of every Crane, consolidated in the leader's body.

If some mindless, numb human getting a new shotgun for his birthday needed to shoot something and hauled off and unthinkingly killed one or two of these leaders, as too often happens because they fly so low and slow to survey their nesting grounds, if but one survived, two or three other cranes could pick up the craft as apprentices from the remaining leader over time.

But there are often more than just one ignorant shotgun wielder strung out along the migration route. If one of these took his new goose gun and without thinking blew away all of these slow, large, easy-to-kill majestic thinkers, knowers, and storied navigators of the Cranes in succession, a lot of delay and dissonancy would ensue in the bereft leaderless group, who like bees, would find it prudent to divide up, and the resulting smaller groups would merge, crowding into other migrating bands who still had intact leader Cranes, Cranes who knew what to do and where to go.

You could always tell the *refugee* portion of Cranes in a band whose leaders had been killed, because they always camped together, off a ways and looking nervous, waited for the welcome of assimilation to be worked out in the groups.

Sometimes a band, having lost their big old leaders too far away from other bands to merge and take refuge, would be forced to develop an unknowledgeable interim leader who would divide their groups and start camping in strange uncrane-like, non-conducive locations: like the top of a dry stony mesa, or up in the high conifers on a steep mountainside, or somewhere where the scared untrained emergency leader might deem it safer than the traditional staging grounds, especially if they'd been repeatedly shot at, harassed or killed on the grounds of their regular haunts. But sometimes intact bands of Cranes are engaged in mysterious missions for which science cannot accurately account.

◆ ◆ ◆

Something like this might have been happening that night, when an unseasonal November blizzard came tearing through northern New Mexico, up into the mountains and canyons where we kept our camp. Traditional Crane migration routes lay forty to fifty miles west of us towards the Big River and no one I knew had ever seen even one Crane in our high mountains. So, in a way utterly unanticipated, late migrating cranes by the hundreds could be heard, but not seen, their cries high up in the snowy clouds, their wild, scared voices fading in and out through the bone-gnashing whistle of the terrible freezing wind.

Blue Medicine would weather the storm standing in the corral I'd made for him when he first came to us earlier that summer. Located on a rather steep Pine forested hillside, so he couldn't remain dedicated to his Midwestern-pig-farm, self-righteous depression and lethargy, I created a run, fenced with poles and barbless wire, that forced him to climb from the Scrub Oaks to the Pines, upon whose barks and tannic leaves he could scantily munch, to begin replacing the Baby Huey, pig-smelling fat his body had accumulated in the lowlands with clean high mountain smells, whose vitality I hoped would carve away his blubber of unhappiness to leave the frame of his true form upon which to enthrone his soul, if we ever found it.

To get to water he had to daily walk hard downhill over coarse rocks and back up negotiating other sandstone ledges to get to his pure mountain grass hay. Little by little he began not only to melt his fat and shrink, but made what fat remained increasingly Barb shaped. Still, I knew as an already grown horse, riding would be better than anything else to bring him fully alive, besides which, having been gelded so late, if he ever got the blubber off without having first learned how to get to work before he was fit, he'd have too much confusing, undirected juice and nowhere to put it. Without learning to ride together with me now, he no doubt would become a fierce, hard-headed dragon, a resentful, temperamental monster, a law unto himself, and beyond anyone's ability to get him to listen for the rest of his days. And who would blame him, after all he'd been a pushy, full-blown stallion until he was eight!

Though he came to us relieved to be away from Iowa, he was still a handful, and I was all for riding him. But fitting him with a saddle? That was an ongoing, comical conundrum. For when I tried putting any of my saddles on him, they looked like little fortune cookies strapped on top of a school bus, with gigantic heart-girth cinches! To melt him down to size I needed to ride him, but to ride him he needed to get down to size. I had to resign myself to training him in a kind of light Plains Indian, Gaucho-type pad saddle with big old stirrups. Though really slight and still a bit ridiculous, at least it was fast enough to buckle on, for in the beginning he naturally fought the whole idea. Even though his head and neck were so massively built, and in one careless moment he could kill you just by casually lifting up his head under yours, his mouth was so soft and delicate, uncalloused, new, firm and had a prehistoric feeling, I thought if I did things just right, his powerful head, like Amarillento, might take to my quirt *steering*. But until we got the real Blue to magically emerge from the pig tallow to show us what would actually work best, that method combined with a heavy bridle fitted with a smooth, primitive bar bit I had from an old wagon harness would have to do, and it did.

To everyone's great surprise, Blue took to being ridden fairly quickly, especially in the hills, but because of his weight he still breathed awfully heavy and was too fat to legitimately buck. I pushed him and pushed him and pushed him all summer long. Sometimes, as he began to pull into shape, we fought, especially when, for no obvious reason, he'd suddenly stonewall: planting his big hooves into the ground like the struts on a backhoe, unwilling to move in any direction, there in the middle of nowhere, both of us snarly, cross-eyed and obstinate, like a couple of horn-locked, old bull elks. The grandest, most fortunate thing about him, though, and something I always loved till the day he died as an old, old man, was whenever both of us, together, lost our tempers with one another, and we went off on each other, sometimes pretty fiercely, unlike other horses, even if I stupidly slugged him in frustration, or he tossed his massive neck and crushed me up against a cliff, both of us, after a couple of boiling and snorting minutes, would revive enough perspective to laugh about it all and he'd let me back on, and we'd always be best friends again. Just like me, he was very proud and quick to react, but equally quick to forgive. He was a hero horse, a hero, and a hero's horse.

Blue was, of all the horses I'd ever known, the horse I was closest to my whole life. From the time he came to us at almost eight years old till his eyesight got too creative to safely ride the high ridges at thirty-one years, I rode him every single day, sometimes days or weeks on end, unless I was off temporarily in another part of the world. We were always part of each other.

But in the beginning, he was just coming out of being an unemployed, herdless, pushy, hard-headed, testosterone-steered asshole of a stallion and still brooding about no longer being a stallion, but still a hard-headed asshole. But I was only in my thirties, and just as proud and opinionated, still brooding about how much I'd lost in my last life as a big leader in Native Guatemala. Though not the best ride in the world, and nowhere near as fast as Amarillento, Blue was definitely the best horse in the world. Very, very, very powerful and totally a knight's horse: honest, easily insulted, quick to forgive. He was beautiful, very male, stuck on himself, exceedingly rare and loyal. He couldn't ever be stolen, because he wouldn't let anyone else even touch him, much less ride him, if I didn't put them there, except of course a pretty woman, but then that was him stealing her. But that all came later.

In those beginning times, he was not yet so strong, plenty pushy, not as beautiful as he would get, not as loyal, just true. But after only four months of truly hard work and only grass feed, no grain, just wild horse fare, he finally sweated off the *couch*, and the three inch crease down his back thankfully disappeared. But you could still smell the pigs in his scent. His rear stopped being an apple butt, his croup reappeared, and now I could just barely get his sister Zajlani's saddle over his powerful withers, and strapped to that beautiful deep girth that housed a heart so dedicated and strong that its very sound was what comforted all our other horses at night.

As the flies disappeared and the weather grew cooler in the fall, I worked him even harder, probably too hard, and as he wasn't yet as vital and tough as he would become later on, when the cold weather in the mountains started to really drop, with a little snow and night temperatures of zero, Old Blue began dropping weight too fast and he began to cough and sicken.

Up till now, to Amarillento, Blue was nothing but another large insect; some intrusive, semi-animate object not worthy of spending his energy on. He wouldn't even waste the energy to whip him into the pecking order he had the rest of the horses laid out in. So Amarillento pretty much ignored Blue's presence. But when for two days Blue's health seriously dropped and my every attempt to doctor him seemed to fail, Amarillento one night snuck out of his flatter, more accommodating corral and *broke* Blue out of his and together they both sauntered down to the creek, where they stood together in the dark under a cliff, out of the cold wind. That was the beginning of their lifelong brotherhood.

One little, one big, one slight, one massive, one quick and mischievous, one pensive and powerful: later on, the one was never seen without the other. Nobody ever talked about Blue without mentioning Amarillento, and vice versa.

Horse people pay a lot of attention to what horses do under the saddle or how they perform, some deeper people pay attention to what unridden horses do when they frolic or speed around in the herd in their own time. But truly horse-infused people watch how horses stand together, how they graze together, for horses spend most of their lives trying to graze, slaking their thirsts with style, and standing in groups of twos or threes in such a choreographed way to make sure they are beautiful from every angle. Horses standing together are horses plotting to add to the majesty of the mind of Nature. Horses are such artists in everything they do that they even make an art form of just looking cool together. Just functionally standing, to get food and drink inside, is not enough: they have to be organized by some artistic, internal mandate to be beautiful. If there's a horse that doesn't do that… well, don't ride that one. But also, their togetherness makes them whole. When one horse is all there is, and that horse has to somehow function as a herd of one, then that horse can't pursue the necessary *together standing* that a horse's existence requires. They lose immunity. They sicken in body and soul. There are actual 14th century Mongol horse veterinary treatises that speak to this effect. I agree.

And Amarillento being the horse he was, knew this, for even as Blue was losing weight from weakness, the more he *stood* together with this little rascal, his new mischievous older brother, the more he began to revive in another way, and even stopped wheezing as much! They were only two years apart and a full hand different in height, but from then on out, they were two halves of a single organism, a kind of eight-legged, two-bodied, two-headed horse! So, I put them together in the same corral and that's how they lived.

• • •

Though they'd both been residing together now in the same flatter corral for over a month, one night in November, in a move still mysterious to me, Amarillento, using his Houdini lips no doubt, once again opened the gate somehow and let

156

Blue drift back up to his original hillside pen to stand under a Ponderosa all by himself.

When the vicious blizzard descended, the voices of flying Cranes stranded high up in the snow clouds echoed in a sort of thin jittering wail that faded in and out and back down to us in the blinding darkness of the snow-filled wind.

At first the ground was still warmer than the air, but then suddenly the temperature dramatically dropped. As the snow hit the trees and the rocks, it melted, but instantly froze again, making it so ice accumulated over everything instead of snow. In the midst of this dark, terrifying phenomena of whirling snow, a thousand misled Sandhill Cranes, old ones and adolescents and their parents tried to land. Most of them uncharacteristically hit the trees, each of their four-foot lengths wedging clumsily into branch crotches, landing stranded and sprawled in anyway they could manage. Spread out for a quarter mile up and down along the creek, you couldn't really see them, but because they called constantly to one another through the roar of the blizzard, you could tell when the whole flock had come to earth. I'd never seen a Crane in the mountains, even on the ground, but I had never seen one in a tree anywhere at all, much less a conifer. But that night, they were all lodged in big Firs and Pines, balancing as best they could, their feet not evolved for life on a branch. They must've suffered terribly in that long blizzardy night.

I had no general custom of blanketing horses that weren't sweating from work, but I blanketed Blue with a wool blanket and army blanket pins as best I could manage in the wet wind, 'cause I knew after having lost so much weight and being weak now, this type of blizzard could mean hypothermia, pneumonia, and death.

By then, all the Cranes and tree branches I could make out in the dark were glazed in ice and further coated with a two inch layer of snow that now stuck and didn't melt. The temperature continued to drop way below zero and the snow, though windless, continued to accumulate on top of the ice until the sky cleared around 1am; the stars sharp and brilliant, the temperature unbelievably cold.

As the dawn began to lighten that mountain world, I could see that Blue had torn off his blanket during the storm. It lay there frozen like an ice sculpture and snow had melted into ice on his back too. Just like the Cranes, he had turned into an ice glazed horse, some of it forming icicles two feet long in jingling strands along the long winter fur of his belly. His mane was solid rods of ice, crested with snow, and his poll looked like a frosted sea urchin. All the Pines, Spruces, Firs over and above where Blue stood unmoving were clumped up in snow-garnished ice, and filled solidly with ice-coated statues of Cranes that at first appeared dead to me, but then eerily their eyes would blink out from their snowy heads.

Several cranes *had* died, but they had fallen, having dropped like rocks from their precarious roosts. Those now lay frozen solid to the ground, buried in snow, in or along the icy creek, resembling snow covered driftwood.

To get a wider vista and a better grasp of the situation, I trudged through the snow up the cliff behind our camp to

where I daily watched the sunrise to pray. From there I could ·
see the eastern horizon a little clearer and our tents and cabins
below in the shadows of trees, Cranes and cliffs. Blue stood in
the middle of it all as still as a mountain covered in snow and
ice, his old Pleistocene nostrils puffing clouds of steam that
gathered like a blanket, up and over him, making more ice.

The sky was cloudless, windless and a solid winter blue
from horizon to horizon, and as the Sun peeked up, one had
to squint for the brightness that dazzled out on every side,
especially from the ice-covered peaks of Elk mountain and
Varelas, who each reflected the Sun so bright you couldn't
look at them at all.

After catching my breath from the climb and before
I could even proffer my offering to the rising Sun, a deep,
startling, subsonic thud and loud crackle, like an atomic blast,
rumbled out from these blazing peaks. In the instant I turned to
look, what I saw seemed like the upward thrust of scintillating
smoke of an explosion rising hundreds of feet above the tree
line, up off that peak. A mile-wide swathe of sparkling dust
accompanied the rumble that was rapidly echoing straight
towards us from twenty miles away.

Years before my birth, a tremendous summer forest fire
had burned straight up over those two peaks, whose story was
widely told. The wind-driven fire had been so hot and moved
so rapidly that though it burned through all the untouched,
ancient, living, old-growth Firs and massive Spruces that
in those times still packed the very top, only their branches
were burned completely off in the intense rolling flood of

fire, while the bark on their trunks and the long spears of the trees were left standing. For years and years the hopeful roots of these branchless spires had faithfully continued to pump sap into their inner bark trying to revive the trees and resprout more branches, but in the end they never could. Over the decades the giant spires dried standing, their inner bark totally turned to dust, leaving mammoth fifty to one hundred foot branchless tubes of thick outer bark as loose sheaths on thousands of straight, dead, tree shafts bristling on those particular mountain peaks.

That thirty seconds of continual *boom* we heard turned out to be the incredible sound of thousands of tons of ice-impregnated, one-hundred-foot bark tubes simultaneously crashing to the ground into piles of violently slivered ice and bark around the bases of the standing skeletons of their bodies. Though not knowing what I was seeing, I was watching when the heat of that morning's sun suddenly loosened the ice enough to cause the bark cannons to all slip and violently careen to the ground, raising a tremendous ground blizzard with a blinding sparkle into the clear breezeless eastern horizon. That echoing crack and rumble was so loud that as it radiated the hundred square miles out around the peaks, it gained enough force in returning echoes to continue knocking ice and snow off every tree in concentric echoing shock waves, accompanied by a rolling ground blizzard that looked like a blanket of sparkling smoke heading our way.

Because of the speed of light, I of course saw the ground blizzard closing in on us before the sound hit, but when the sound of this sun-inspired explosion of ice and snow crystals in the clear blue air of the mountain morning did reach us in the seconds after, it was so loud it shook our world and rattled all the trees with such force that it caused all the snow and ice to drop in chunks and splinters from their branches. The Cranes, who before the *boom* of the morning Sun had looked like frozen ghosts of Cranes all humped up in the trees, began to cry weirdly out from under the ice and snow that covered them. Their wild calls came from under the snow everywhere, at first muffled, then wildly echoing up and down the valley. As I stood in my blanket coat looking up and down the creek from the cliff edge, I could easily discern a quarter mile of at least a thousand Cranes, who startled by the unexpected boom of Elk Peak's rumble of falling ice, were themselves instantly trying to move up into flight, away from the frozen mountain forest.

Each Crane had her own struggle, for as if encased in glass, they simultaneously pushed out their powerful ice covered wings and trying to leap up as hard as they could, burst out of their frozen coats, continuously jumping up and screaming, their wings finally stretched out, and miraculously all of them were able to lift off. Though they'd been loaded down with ice, their feathers beneath were still dry and by flapping and rising slowly, they nonetheless all succeeded in getting themselves flying back up into the clear blue skies of our mountains. That miracle was itself accompanied by yet another startling sound, not unlike the loud tinkling crash of five thousand bowling balls hitting a million crystal wine glasses would make, for in the instant that they rose, every bird let fall from their bodies, outstretched wings, and tree branches all round, a barrage of puzzle pieces of slivered ice and powdery snow. The rays of the morning Sun pushed through these crystals as they trundled to the ground, whose fierce blinding flash of swirling spectrums and rainbows blazed off in every direction, covering everything in that wild day's white snow-covered world with exploding prismatic light!

My mind was fairly rocked and utterly stunned. In that breezeless dawn, I jumped and bumbled my way back down the cliff as quickly as the snow, ice, and hidden boulders would allow, and just as I came upon where Blue, unmoving, had stood all night, himself ice encrusted, right over him ninety ice-covered Cranes rose up to fly off with the rest of their kin. The falling of their ice slid and cracked over Blue's head and spine, their rainbows scintillating all over him. Startled by the boom, the riot of their screams, and the scare of so much falling ice and rainbows, Blue lunged violently forward, but slipped to land sitting on his haunches like a big frosted dog. His head still dazed and wobbling, he decided he too might fly with the big birds, and from that position he leapt up, shooting like a rocket stretched out straight up into the air. Just like the birds, slabs of ice and strings of icicles cracked off his body and crashed to the ground around him. As if hatched from some mythic egg of ice, Blue emerged into the air like a winged mythic horse from another time: his blue eyes matching the blue spectrums of the Crane's falling ice.

With no wings, he crashed inelegantly back to the ground, his legs all spraddled out. But returning instantly to his feet, Blue took off bucking in joy, slipping wildly all around in every direction, thoroughly adding his spinning motion in with the sparkling light until he had come totally back to life.

In the moment it took the air to clear, the screaming Cranes rose up on the morning thermal, formed V's and disappeared. The real Blue Medicine, his head erect, his coat all snow washed, his eyes bright, his attitude vibrant and alive and grand, finally returned to himself, having emerged from an egg of ice and snow. Hatched out of ice by ice-covered, tree-sitting Cranes, his soul had returned. I should have known of course, that the wild Cranes had been holding his soul safe all along, waiting for the right moment to give it back. And now they had.

Chapter 10

Blue, Put That Woman Down!

After Blue had been cracked out of a chrysalis of winter ice and scared back into life by a mountain rumble, and had his remote wandering soul shot back into his body by one thousand ice-shedding, screaming, off-course Cranes, he quickly ceased being a fat, smelly, uncooperative, depressed, former stallion from a pig farm in Iowa.

Nobody who saw him after that, who'd seen him before, would believe he was even the same animal. His physique, the way he held his body, even his colors changed, his hoof size changed, his mood and demeanor were instantly altered, nothing about him was the same. Overnight Blue pretty much became the powerful horse he was born to be, and who he'd always be till that cold December evening when he died at the age of thirty-four, twenty-six years later.

Amazed as all our visitors and neighbors were, I never tried to explain any of the details of what had happened with Blue, much less the spiritual reality. Knowing that such a reality was too much for most people who felt more secure addicted to living in a world padded with rational facts; facts that demoted Nature's magic to mechanical functions that left people with the illusion that humans, their limited motivations and scientific explanations, ran the world. But people didn't run the world, and that thought certainly made me feel safer.

But then again, I figured if anyone around us whose mind and soul could contain what I would have tried to explain about Blue, would probably already have seen what happened, or at least see the grandeur in it. So I reasoned: why bother people with such a powerful tale and risk having the power of it belittled and lost!

What inhabited Blue Medicine was a rare being that kept recurring in history as a medicine-hat horse. He kept coming around throughout the centuries to host a string of owners with his magical self.

I'd seen early photographs, from the 1850's to the late 1920's of Native women and men from over thirty differing tribes seated on all types of Barb Mesta horses, and not a few of them were seated on *Blue*. I mean these horses in these old photos and glass negatives had the same markings, the same face, look, demeanor, the same weird other-worldly eyes, the same exact sturdy capable stance, short cannon bones, the same featherless fetlocks, long forearms, the same flat, wide, anvil forehead, the same rhino wrinkled chin and lips, big-old throat latch, same wide ribcage, big heart girth, narrow chest, smooth muscles, fine thick little red ears with tufts coming out at the base, tail whiskers, everything identical. He wasn't the spitting image of these horses in these one hundred and fifty years of old photos, he *was* all those *same* horses and he was still here in my corral. He came when needed and left when needed elsewhere.

After the ice, feeding him the wild growing herbs, and grazing mountain grass, and drinking snow-melt waters, and working him the way I did, though he continued to drop weight, he stopped coughing and by spring he started putting weight back where it belonged. He grew so strong and agile, his neck became so powerful, and his hind end could push so deep that he outdid any other horse I'd ever known, ridden, or heard about.

He was no longer dull but spirited, and he scared most people with his wild two-color look and light eyes, and though he was a gelding now, he still retained that disarming demeanor of most Barb stallions that not only calmly told you he could kill you in any small move, but would just roll up and, unabashed, look straight into you, through you, and beyond you with a friendly soul-reaming arrogance that put sensible people on edge. But Blue knew he was a king and had his dignity and was never in your pocket or pet-like, keeping an excellent boundary, as all Barbs tend to do. He was not really hard to handle at all, just a lot to handle, for his mind not only took everything in, he reasoned and thought things out. Thus he refused to be *trained* by dull repetition, but could definitely learn by understanding what it was you wanted him to do, but not until both of you comprehended what the other was thinking. He only needed to see the reason for doing something and then, if he agreed, he'd learn instantly. Blue grasped the principles of reining so effortlessly that it was almost as if we could go, turn, stop, back, wait, or jump out with just my mind.

Unlike his sidekick, Amarillento, who was fast, slight, conniving, hard-mouthed, impossible to stop, and pushy, Blue was heavy duty, sure, intrepid, sensitive on the bit, stopped on a dime, and pushy.

Both horses were very courageous, but Blue was more stubborn, and tended to do things a little more by force, probably because he was so strong. Together we could jump ravines, climb cliffs like mountain sheep, walk very narrow trails over a morass, or throw ourselves at a big cow and he'd never balk. To get a bull to move, who was twice his size, we'd run up on him, and Blue would invariably bite him hard on the bottom, then anticipating the rear moving horns, jump to the side, run around the side opposite and do it again until the animal gave in and let us drive 'em where we would. Busting through brush was one of his specialties, so we could go a lot of places I could never ride before. Blue learned to let me rope anything from the saddle: logs, mares, cows, rocks. He was like a bulldozer crossed on a Sharp-shinned Hawk and a tight-rope walker.

We dragged bundles of fence posts, boulders, stumps. He'd even pull horses, cars, trucks, ATV's stuck in sink holes, quicksand or mud, straight off the horn of his sister Zajlani's saddle with a dally rope.

He had some strange mystique with wild animals of a kind most modern horses didn't seem to have. For my life as a Native doctor, Blue was a great support, for animals never suspected my motives if I was riding Blue, and often didn't flee. I never used him for hunting to keep that covenant unspoilt.

For instance, if riding Blue, we came upon a herd of wild Elk grazing in a grassy mountain park with some Mountain Sheep, they wouldn't bound away. Sometimes, if for once, I could keep my human mind uncluttered so they wouldn't be frightened by the harsh racket of my thoughts, if I was riding Blue, we could ride right into the middle of the herd! If I let him have his head, he'd often just start grazing right alongside a bunch of young Elk!

Horses are notoriously put on guard by even the slightest smell of a Mountain Lion, and while Blue would definitely stiffen up if he smelled one, he never balked in their presence, if I was on his back. And the same went for Bears, from whose very scent most horses become very flighty, and whose presence sends them bolting unless they've been conditioned to the reverse. I never did a thing to accustom him to predators, he just came out of the shell that way.

One day Blue and I, coming down the mountains, were wending our way back home about mid-morning, when right alongside our old, ridge-top, forest trail, a Lion was busy eating the insides of a Silver Fox that I presumed she'd killed. The Lion looked up and stared at me, but not at Blue, didn't flee, though she was less than ten feet away, and we passed without so much as a shiver from the horse.

Two hours later, re-climbing the same trail, at the exact same spot, the Lion was gone, but a big lady Bear was finishing up eating the same Fox.

Blue stopped and looked, the Bear stopped gnawing and looked, then Blue continued pulling up the mossy-Fir forest trail, and the Bear resumed her snuffling and crunching away behind us. On any other horse the Bear and the Lion would've disappeared long before we'd even got close, and we'd never even see them, and if they did stay for some reason, then any other horse would've been hell to keep steady, much less ride by with a Lion or Bear cracking bones behind him.

While climbing the first set of sandstone *stairs* out of our canyon up to the higher peaks behind, on a narrow bit of the path, Blue and I met a rider coming down the opposite direction. He was on top of a very anxious young red mule, trying to train him for hunting and the trail by following the rough paths we'd established on our own rides over the years.

This fellow was a Western Anglo type of guy, and very friendly. I'd heard about him because he'd bought land that contained the little draw where Juniper's singing Mouse lived, from Conrad Purdy.

The trail was too pinched for us to pass one another, so I pulled Blue to the right, up the hillside a few feet under the branches of some big old growth trees, to let this fellow and his mule get by. This man was having all he could do to keep his mule from bolting and seeing us decided to take a break. He got off and holding the reins started chatting with me about why his mule was so antsy.

I'd seen three Bears that week and the tracks of at least four others, one of them very large. So I told him I thought the mule must be sensing or smelling their presence on the mountain, and was just being a sensible young mule.

This man could talk even more than I could and commenced telling me everything about himself: his bank, his debt, his former marriage. We spoke about his almost blind little daughter and his deaf little boy he was raising alone, and how he was daily building a little timber cabin right where our singing Mouse used to sing to Juniper. I just casually happened to look to the right and saw to my startled delight that a good size, red, male Black Bear was very politely waiting there hidden quietly behind a tree, not eight feet away from where Blue and I were standing. His head cocked and sitting on his haunches like a gigantic little kid in school, listening to our entire conversation, he looked almost engrossed with our discussion, but his presence no doubt was behind this mule's unwieldy mood. Blue, on the other hand, not only kept his cool, but together with the Bear, they both very gentlemanly listened to our dull palaver without any snide commentary! Without letting on that a Bear was listening in, I went on to tell that man the story of Juniper and the Mouse. After a few chuckles, as he was riding without a saddle, he very expertly leapt back onto the bare back of his spinning, aggravated mule, and with his hands tight on the reins, he white-knuckled it all the way down the trail, sometimes sideways, or even backwards, all the way home.

Blue, I, and the Bear, on the other hand, just waited, watching to make sure he was all right, and as soon as the mule and this man were out of sight, we all pulled back up onto the trail to resume our journeys, the Bear went north and we went west!

Given the opportunity, I'm sure a Lion or a Bear would've like to have killed and eaten Blue, because he still had just a little residual pork overtone on top of a very edible sweet horse smell. I even thought of eating him myself sometimes, he smelled so delicious, especially when he was acting up. But unlike Amarillento, who would survive being mauled by inexperienced Mountain Lions several times in his life, mysteriously no predator ever bothered Blue out grazing on the wild range, probably because they could tell how very well aimed he was with his rear kicks, and not bad with his fronts. Although he never kicked at all, unless himself attacked, if he was attacked, whatever was after him would generally not survive.

In New Mexico, unfortunately, the main adversaries a rider had to watch out for, of course, were not wild animals, but dogs. Packs of dangerous feral dogs were not uncommon, but even village dogs, or fancy dogs owned by people who weren't vigilant about their dogs, who had them to guard their houses, would almost always harass and sometimes ruin a leg tendon on a horse.

We always had a couple of dogs to keep off the dogs! They knew their jobs and were very careful not to rile the horses, but I rarely took any of them with me riding, because I loved the wild and the wild wouldn't come close if dogs were present. Blue was always wary of any dog, even our dogs, but luckily they kept away from each other.

When we rode, Blue and I were handsome, and inspired admiration in some people, but jealous hatred in the more insecure sector of the population. Thus riding in populated areas had its risks, for Blue, though steady around moving vehicles, had his quirks, and his outright intolerance of loose, unruly dogs was one of them.

One time, an angry man who was raising powerful Rottweilers for tracking, noticed Blue and I crossing a street south of Santa Fe during that funny era when I had started accompanying *city people* on horseback treks out of Santa Fe, off into the hills, when it was still wide and unpopulated to the west, all the way to the Big River: riding from desert spring to desert spring.

As we were leaving the edge of town, this man who'd seen us before, just for a prank, thought he'd set his dogs on Blue to see him spin and jump and scare and to cause a conflagration of some sort. Inebriated and feeling obstreperous, this fellow began yelling obscenities and let out three big dogs who came at us snarling and gnashing and leaping up to rip Blue's throat.

But, by the time this unhappy man was done yelling, two of his misguided dogs were dead. In less than a minute, they lay quaking in the middle of the road, their skulls cracked wide open from the never-failing aim of Blue's hind legs, while the third ran home whining and barking. Blue didn't even stop walking across the street. The man called the police and ended up in jail himself. Blue was an amazing, powerful beast, friendly to all, but he didn't put up with bad dogs.

Blue never attacked any one or any animals except in righteous defense of himself or myself.

To the contrary, wild animals were always joining up with us on our rides. As we rode through the wilder areas, I remember more than once returning on the trail from the *Cross*, accompanied by wild animals trotting right along with us.

One balmy summer evening, the rays of sunlight through the forest dust thick with our hopes for July rain, as Blue and I descended a stretch of that path, which was just shy of vertical, through my half-opened eyes I registered my half-wolf, half-husky trotting on the trail in front of us, going our way. I was so drowsy that it didn't immediately dawn on me that we hadn't left the house with our dogs and when I did remember, I looked ahead again to see that who I'd casually taken to be my dog was actually a big, red-foreheaded Coyote who had now been joined by his wife, both trotting not nine feet in front of Blue. I chanced to turn and look behind us, and sure enough there was their pup, all three just amiably trotting right along with us on the trail, keeping us company, as we were, for the moment, all heading the same direction.

By the time we'd ridden to within two hundred yards of our camp, one Coyote veered left, the other went right, and the one behind us was already gone.

Once he became his real self, Blue Medicine also loved human company more than I did, and turned out to be very social, just as long as he was the center of attention. He didn't like men so much, he put up with me, and he did like kids, but was absolutely enamored of all women, especially young pretty girls.

The new Blue Medicine was so handsome and full of life, that when people came to our spot for me to work on them, the only horse they noticed was Blue. And that was as it should have been as far as he was concerned.

Invariably people would gather around his corral and Blue would slowly shuffle over next to where everybody was leaning. Parking himself always just two inches farther off than anyone's arm could reach, he would maintain his self-respect, never getting over friendly, but enjoying the admiration. But if he should swing around and poke his head over the corral rails, his big rhino-lips twitching, searching for someone to pet his face, you could be sure he'd found a young woman he wanted to pick up!

He was shameless! I never allowed people to pet horses faces because it usually led to encouraging horses to nip or bite. But it wouldn't be long before Blue had a lady rubbing his cheek and behind his ear, his thick head sliding up and down like a big faced house cat.

Inevitably he would commence snuffling all over this woman's body with his elephantine lips, his nostrils puffing, presumptuously tickling the lady everywhere. If she happened to start laughing and didn't move away, or turned to her friends exposing her back in the least, invariably Blue would search out her belt line in the back, or lacking that, he'd find the cloth of her dress, and grabbing up as much of the belt or dress into his big mouth as he could manage, he'd clamp his teeth. Then, like a building-crane, he'd lift this poor girl up into the air and start moving off with her dangling from his mouth like a mother dog bringing home a straying puppy!

Usually at this point, this woman would be screaming, and when I heard it I knew what was afoot, and would come running to the rescue from the tipis. Blue really did listen to me and no one else. But in these situations I learned not to yell, "Blue, put that woman down right now, Dammit!" Because of course, as soon as he heard the irritation in my voice, he'd open his mouth and drop his sequestered *girlfriend*, who not uncommonly would end up unceremoniously sprawled upon the ground, scared and indignant.

Strangely enough, none of this ever seemed to deter the same person from sidling up to him again on the next visit, which only galvanized the custom. I don't know if it was their perfume, their cosmetics, their pheromones, their vibe or the sound of their voice, or all of the above, but Blue was always trying to *pick up women* whenever he had the chance.

This was very troublesome during public events, exhibitions, in crowds, or when we would ride in parades, where he'd be scouting out the possibilities of picking up a girl somewhere. If I was on him, I could pretty much keep him from lifting some unsuspecting, admiring lady up into the air, but on his own in the corral, where people could visit him when I was otherwise engaged, he was always hoping for the chance. In crowds I had to keep an eye on him all the time.

While standing together in their corral, Amarillento and Blue, both heads to the other's tail, looking half-asleep like a lot of horses do, were actually communicating in their dreams, always cooking something up. Amarillento, of course, had started out mercurially inclined, but after a year of living together, the two of them developed into an incorrigible team who loved setting people up for their joint practical jokes, especially myself. Each of them on their own was mischievous enough, but Blue, over time, developed into a more complex style of prankster, whose schemes, however tangible they seemed, usually involved some ephemeral magical inexplicability.

For instance, even though he was twice as long and wide as Amarillento, like a Rhino or wild Bison, Blue could completely hide from view behind a wheat straw. He might be standing right in front of you, and if he didn't want you to see him, you couldn't find him! I swear this to be true, and others who knew him will concur, for Blue was so aware of the size, distance and nature of his shape and wild markings, that he was able to artistically contort himself by the millimeter to blend in so thoroughly with the shadows of trees and bushes as to be virtually invisible as a horse. Like a trout in a stream, he could turn himself so precisely as to make his bulk unseeable behind a fence post at a certain angle, imperceptibly moving just far enough away from your gaze, shifting as you moved, so as to be perfectly camouflaged behind some thin stalks and a shadow, as you, the halter lead dangling from your elbow, ardently searched for his lordship.

Like a horned lizard sitting on an ant pile, whose skin could assume the color of the gravel so as you couldn't see him until he moved, Blue might be standing extended in a sun-dappled shadow, right in plain view, not nine feet away but nonetheless totally blended in. Not until he was sure his prank was a success, and he could see I was stumped, would he flick his tail, twist his funny ears and grin at my own self-laughter at having yet again been bested, right up close inside his corral. Only then would he let himself be seen and haltered and taken for a ride!

Or not! Because maybe his cohort Amarillento, not to be left out, would rush up and grab my rope in his teeth and run away, for which Blue, considering this a fantastic continuation of the trick, would run away with him, playing keep away. They'd keep it up until they forced me to halter and saddle a third horse, and with my lariat go rope each of those ne'er-do-wells, one by one, wasting half my morning just 'cause they were full of the tickles.

Not one to negate the useful nature of something so amazing in such a phenomena, I learned that even with me mounted on top, no matter how outspoken we were both dressed, or how flashy a rig we were both sporting, Blue and I, as a team, could very politely walk up on pretty much anybody, or any meeting, or any cabin and not be noticed.

We could stand invisibly and unperceived until we decided to announce ourselves with a gentle "How do you do?", which usually scared the DNA out of whomsoever we'd been hiding from, while standing right out there in plain view!

I myself could not figure how we couldn't be seen: a bright sorrel red and blazing white, boldly marked medicine-hat paint with bright blue eyes, a shiny silver bridle with turquoises, and silvered saddle and bright Navajo saddle blanket, and me with my yellow calico shirt and wide hat seated on top. But it was a true thing.

Behind where we camped and lived our lives, a mile west of us, running on top of a sandstone ledge, a two-mile strip of magnificent, uncut, old-growth Fir and Pine forest stretched. One day a man from Michigan bought a piece of this rare land square in the middle of that ancient forest. Having miraculously never been timbered in the 19th century when the railroad had forced its harsh ride through the canyon, clear cutting millions of acres of old, high-mountain trees for ties and trestles, this man decided he would start cutting these old giants.

The only access for this fellow to a tiny, two-storey adobe house that already sat perched in this fellow's newly acquired property was up that same overgrown log-skid where I trained all my horses, starting with Icicles some years before. The remaining mountain side was very steep and beautifully covered in those high mountain trees, whose live presence in New Mexico was very rare and wonderful. They had become precious to me.

This man had hired chainsaw crews to clear all the ancient trees on the mesa top and all the ones lining the log-skid to make room for bulldozers to make a *real* road wide enough so he could drag an awful, double-wide, canned house and plant its ugly pollution high on top, all just so he could come three days a year to shoot wild turkeys, drink, and have a view to see out of the forest!

Though it was all vaguely legal and technically none of my affair, as I didn't own the forest he was planning on destroying, still the whole thing was obscene, unconscious, and unethical, especially in a dry climate like New Mexico, where large trees were rare treasures. I knew of no other tangible recourse than to appeal directly to this man in person and maybe get some of those mountain top trees a reduced sentence.

But the problem was I couldn't seem to get an audience with his *high and mighty self*. As to be expected, I guess this flat lander and his girlfriend didn't feel they needed to talk to unmoneyed, unconnected, local savages like us, who didn't work grunt jobs for the likes of their superior *caste*. I couldn't even seem to casually run into him, though I knew in the beginning they had to walk the two miles behind our camp to get to their *site*, because no mechanized vehicle could make the trip until they cleared the land.

Nonetheless, as the big trees started to fall by twos and threes, it broke my heart, so Blue and I intensified our search for Mr. Sanderson, both by day and by night. Both of us dressed for battle, beautiful and in our best, together we rode up to this fellow's spot, cradling a gift of aromatic ground coffee per New Mexico neighborly custom.

They'd only cleared less than a half an acre and it was the crew's day off, so when we got there, it was quiet. The man and his lover had erected a tent inside the adobe, as they didn't think it qualified as a house, though the hermit-poet they evicted to take over the place had thought very highly of his mountain hideaway.

Blue went into *hide* mode, reluctant to follow the established, torn-up mess of a trail they'd been establishing, so I took his hint and came up square across the mesa from the back, above the old Eagle nests on the cliffs and entered the *site* from the north. But it was just our luck that today, there he was, this hard-headed fellow, his fat hairy body all stretched out and naked *enjoying* the naked company of his girlfriend on a dirty mattress they'd pulled out of the old house.

We were only about ten feet away when Blue and I came upon them. Out of respect we just stood there, as still as a mountain, trying not to watch, but wondering how to make our exit without making a scene. It was a bit spooky: the lady was looking straight at us and neither one registered that a man on a horse was practically standing right on top of them. Blue, the shameless creature that he was, just stood there watching, but luckily enough didn't snort. So without even breathing, I forced him to back up as quietly as we had come and together we ambled back down the mountain, figuring this was not the time to try to talk to such a couple about the beautiful trees they were cutting down!

The next evening, toting their saws, gas, tools, and coolers, multiple tree-cutting crews trudged up the mountain behind our camp. They were going to start on widening the road the next day.

I dressed up again, saddled Old Blue again, and rode straight up behind them on the same trail in the dark of the night.

When we arrived at the site, a big bonfire was raging and everybody was dressed this time. Workmen were standing or sitting on stumps in a large, dense circle drinking beer and throwing their empties into the fire and eating Slim Jims. There were at least forty men. But I figured it was now or never, so I rode right up to their fire.

Blue courageously stood right there with me on his back, with a workman standing on either side of us. It was hard to believe. Nobody acknowledged that a horse and his rider were even present. "Maybe they think I'm part of the work force or maybe they're okay with me being here? I guess that's good?" I thought.

The Boss, the man from Michigan, Mr. Sanderson, eventually rose off his stump and started up his rallying speech, defining which group was going to cut which area the following day and to answer any questions.

Waiting for an opening to make my case, I was startled off my intended plan when someone asked *the Boss* about those crazy Indians, or whatever they were with all the horses and the tipis, who lived at the bottom of the log-skid, where this man was planning to put a road, who were rumored to be opposed to the plan.

There ensued a string of obscenities and crude hate-filled jokes defining this man's unflattering opinion of me and my people and what he would like to do to us, which was pretty horrid. At this point, when everyone started laughing and drinking up to the proposal, I realized they weren't seeing Blue or myself standing there listening, right beside them in front of the fire. We were just an invisible part of the crowd! As their drunkenness increased, with me still mounted on top, I backed Blue out of the meeting and snuck off, and we rode all the way back home through the moonlit shadows of the condemned trees.

Twice we'd not been noticed. How could you not notice a silver-encrusted powerful, blue-eyed paint horse and myself on top, right in front of your face? That horse had a powerful magic.

After their binge, the chainsaw crew was thankfully too hung-over to work the next day. Still hoping to save some trees, for yet a third time, I rode up to their *site*, and this time I finally came across this man all by himself, and this time he could see us. Wasting no time, I began talking to him about the trees.

As I expressed my love for the trees, the place, its history, and about how often I'd come to see him and had not been received, including the day of his open-air love making, and after reciting his obscene "burn out the Indians" speech verbatim in explicit detail, and about everything that had transpired, back to him, this man began to pale. Trembling in rage, or maybe fear, he renewed his threats, and adding in a few new ones he ran off looking for something to shoot at us with inside the adobe. His screamed threats grew muffled inside the walls. He was scared and not used to the magical side of horses, and was certainly not going to rethink his deforestation plans.

We'd given it a try, but I'd failed and now it was time to get away.

By the time he and his lover re-emerged with their handguns and came looking for us, we were standing *invisible* behind a tree and watched as they walked briskly past us, grumbling the whole distance back down the hill to their vehicle, without ever seeing us. When he wanted to Blue could really hide!

Whether rattled by us well-meaning Natives or overly frustrated by New Mexico's notoriously gradual and vague notion of getting things done on time, or not at all, or feeling defeat after being repeatedly warned of the improbability of finding water on that beautiful ridge, and still insisting on drilling a three thousand foot well through solid bands of sandstone and quartzite and unable to find anyone to do it, these inconsiderate, unconversational people, having already felled an acre of trees for nothing, got into their SUV parked at the bottom of the log-skid and blasted off heading east. They left down the same road Ta Shunk and I had been chased by that demonic mailbox two years past; we never did see those two unfriendly people again.

Chapter 11

Your House is My House

I don't remember precisely when Blue began seriously applying himself to his lifelong hobby of sauntering, uninvited and unseen, into and out of people's homes, especially their kitchens.

Though I was completely unaware of this new facet of that wild-eyed paint, this newly thought up habit no doubt accounted for the sudden presence in local gossip of individuals with weird claims of having found big, muddy, horse footprints all over their *carpeted* living rooms, and other people's tales of peculiar Bears or giant Racoons who, after entering their houses and leaving them untouched, had closed all the doors after dragging out half eaten fifty pound sacks of rice or cornmeal, strewing the remainders along their wooden decks or verandas!

Much later on, after we discovered the big Racoon was in reality Blue Boy, I would get to know just how far he'd go to get a sack of rice. I don't think Blue really liked the rice so much as he loved the fun of how its violent teeth-cracking-crunch rattled the thick bone of his big old brain-pan!

The first time I actually ever saw him inside a house was, interestingly enough, not out by our place or anywhere near the mountains where we all lived, but right in the city limits of Santa Fe, inside the adobe mansion of the Rich Kid's mother, the house of the Owners.

It was on the occasion of several groups of people owning Mesta Barb horses having agreed to convene at this strange in-the-city horse place in order to reload all their horses from six trailers into two trailers, in order to consolidate our transportation to the common destination of a competition where all of us together would *run* against the world in a kind of two day trial of endurance and trail riding of some eighty miles in the late summer heat, up and down canyons, long flat runs and frequent vet checks.

I loved riding Blue in long rides and Blue loved me riding him. We had all the glory of camping and staying out for days riding longer distances through the mixed, ever-changing terrain of our area, but I'd never done any long rides with other people and their horses, and never in the banded hills and hoodoos of Navajo land and the neighboring desert oil fields. I figured all people should learn as much as they could about everything, and since both Blue and Amarillento excelled at long distances, I decided we should learn what such a *competition* might be like.

I was the first to arrive with my trailer at the Rich Kid's house, and had already unloaded Blue and Amarillento into one of the unoccupied conveyor-belt pens.

Once everyone else had shown up and rearranged all their gear, the kid called us into the kitchen to drink coffee or tea and discuss the plan of action.

Excitement was running high and we were all chattering away as we walked through the courtyard, through the single central doorway, into the foyer and on into the tiled kitchen. Stallion style, I was pulling up the rear as usual, and noticed what a hush had come over the crowd all of the sudden. When I walked through the doorway, there stood Blue, right in the kitchen, leaning up against the beautiful Mexican tiled sink counter, just as cool and calm as only Blue could be. Like a hip yuppie at a wine bar, he was casually waiting to join us in our council of war, and probably a cup of tea as well. (All my horses learned to like tea, but Blue loved tea). When you saw him standing outside, Blue was a small powerful horse, but in a kitchen he was huge!

Luckily, these people, being horse people, were wise enough not to start screeching and stayed quiet, afraid any commotion might set the horse into a frenzy. I always wore a big neckerchief and a leather belt with a very long excess tab that hung out of the silver buckle. Tying my silk kerchief with a sheet bend to the buckle, and wrapping the silk around his neck, we exited the premises together in a very dignified strut, after which I put Blue back into a commercial halter and tied him and Mari back into my trailer. It was a mystery, for nobody had seen him go by and he had to have gone past us, for there was only the one door and we'd all been between the pens and the house! But he'd got there before we had, opened the door, entered, waited and didn't freak out, break anything or poop. He was truly a gentleman. A magical one!

After that, Blue was often found in people's houses, but only very rarely did anyone ever see him enter, and those that did watched how he used both his teeth and his old tapir/rhino lips to slip the door latch.

Invariably, if nobody was around, after searching the house until he located the kitchen, he'd just stand there patiently waiting until someone showed up to show him where they kept their rice.

The funniest thing was how distracted people sometimes are, so locked in their thoughts and on automatic pilot, and not really expecting to see a big blue-eyed, spotted Indian Pony waiting in their kitchen, Blue could be standing there as still as a mountain for quite a spell, while people bustled about their business, and it wasn't until they needed to fetch something from their refrigerator or a cupboard that his Lordship's handsome, furry bulk was blocking, did they actually notice him! If they were awake enough to not start stupidly screaming or rushing about like demented rodents, then Blue wouldn't leave, but he'd scoot over just enough so you could get the milk out of the fridge! He really wasn't a bother, he just took up a lot of room!

Blue just knew he belonged wherever he wanted to be. He never once pooped in a house or left one of his notorious and prodigious firehose pisses on the floor. He did on unpredictable occasions rummage about till he found a bag of rice or oatmeal, which he would tranquilly crunch as he waited for the occupant to return!

It was in that era, as he turned nine, that all his budding peculiarities matured into fully developed quirks. Several of them surfaced during the badland-oil-field-competition ride itself, but thankfully we'd already worked through the *syndrome of the yellow line*, not that it disappeared, but at least we knew how to get past a yellow line.

People were fond of stating, "it's so funny to see how Blue is afraid of yellow lines."

By which they meant the three inch yellow lines painted on asphalt and highways. Blue, once he'd seen it, would under no conditions: blindfolded, pushed, pulled, spurred, or whacked with a quirt, cross over a painted yellow line on a highway! Blue was a thinking horse, and he definitely had his reasons, but what those reasons were, in this case we didn't know. But I noticed he didn't spook when he came up to a yellow highway line, he wasn't actually afraid of them, he just wouldn't cross them. Trying to cross a highway, no matter how small, or unfrequented, if there was a yellow line running down it signifying no passing, Blue was willing to walk or run right up to it, but would come to jolting halt at the line.

He didn't shy or balk, he just wouldn't cross it. To *ford* such a road, we could ride right alongside, parallel with the yellow streak for a mile with no problems or snorts until there was a *break* in the painted streak, and through that we could cautiously pass, just as if it were a gate in a fence. This could play havoc in a city, or in competition where any roads were to be crossed. He'd cross a white line with great suspicion, but eventually he would do it. But a yellow line? Never.

Blue could jump mountain ravines, climb under waterfalls, ride in lightning, alongside moving trains; what were these yellow lines for his big blue eyes that he wouldn't crossover?

Sometimes on long rides out and away, we came upon a long section of fence without a gate that we had to cross, but which I didn't feel like cutting and repairing. To negotiate these, I'd learned young to always have a blanket tied to the saddle.

After climbing through the fence on foot, I draped the blanket over the top of the barbed wire (cowboys use a slicker). Then pulling the top wire down as low as it could be pushed, I urged my horse to jump over where the blanket was stretched in hopes the slicker or blanket would protect the horse's belly and feet from getting razored up or tangled in the barbed wire.

On Blue, I could ride right up to the fence, lay the blanket over the top wire and then together, mounted, leap right over the wire wall, pick off my blanket, tie it up and keep going, without ever dismounting.

It occurred to me one night, driving a long distance, late and tired, after having noticed how the sparkling phosphorescent particles in the paint of the highway lines would seem to lift off in the dark and start to float up into my lines of vision, taking on a kind wall-like depth. "Maybe," I surmised, "what happens with Blue is that his eyes aren't just seeing a line of yellow, but some kind of three dimensional wall of reflected light! In his extraordinary, crazy blue eyes that wall was probably as tall as his sight, which was why he wasn't afraid exactly, but felt that it was not possible to just pass, because what he was seeing was a solid yellow wall running for miles!"

To test this as a possibility, at the next opportunity, I strapped a rolled-up basic canvas tent cover onto my saddle and took Blue to the yellow line that ran straight along the highway in front of the entrance to our camp. As usual, he stopped right in front of the line and refused to proceed.

I dismounted, extended the tarp over the yellow line and asked Blue to walk over it and while he wanted to, he didn't. So I climbed on top, took us back a bit and rode straight at the tarp covering the yellow line, and up he sailed right over the tarp, just as if he were flying over a five foot fence up in the hills! The tarp was not simply obscuring the yellow line, causing it to have a break, it was showing Blue where the top of the *wall* was so he could jump it, just like he jumped the fences with a blanket draped over it!

It was obvious then that Blue could distinguish three-dimensionally represented images on a two dimensional surface, something science said was not the case with horses.

Science also said that horses weren't capable of abstract thinking. But when Blue jumped the yellow line with a tarp placed on top for safety, what he saw was a wall. Blue was seeing a barrier drawn there, which of course is exactly what the highway department meant it to represent for the motorists: a barrier against passing!

Trying to think as much as I could like a horse, I reasoned that if Blue saw a very convincing barrier *written* on the road that stopped him as much as a *solid wall*, then maybe he could also see a tarpaulin of safety abstractly *written* across the wall that would protect him as much as a literal tarp!

So the next day, I took a big piece of charcoal from our woodstove ash pile, rode with Blue up to the same place where he'd jumped the *yellow line-wall*, dismounted, laid out the tarp. Then with the charcoal I drew a line across the tarp and had Blue jump the *wall* again, which he admirably accomplished. Then I removed the tarp and drew a thick black charcoal line perpendicularly across the yellow line directly on the pavement where the tarp had lain. Remounting, I asked him to return back the opposite direction across the yellow line following the thin black streak to get across.

Blue turned his head sideways, then put his eye down to scrutinize the black line as if it were some strange creature, and then very daintily walked right over the yellow line, back to the other side!

I was so amazed I gave him a kiss (about which he didn't give a damn: he only liked girl's kisses!). In his big-old beautiful head and behind his white eyelashes, Blue was a thinker. The yellow line was an abstractly represented barrier, for which the tarp was able to show the top and give his belly the same safety it gave him when crossing barbed wire fences. The charcoal then was the abstractly represented safety of the tarp, which when written over the top of the abstractly represented barrier, he could now in good conscience tangibly cross over the whole in safety. Wow! How amazing. Everything about this crazy horse was like this!

Scientists who *test* animal *intelligence* are often preoccupied with testing for an animal's problem-solving ability, i.e. tool using, escaping mazes, etc. They never talk about the negative intelligence *quotient* of a creature's ability to *create problems*. I'm sure so-called human intelligence excels all other species in problem *making*! Especially problems that other species have to negotiate!

By the time we got to that desert-oilfield-endurance-trail-ride-competition, I always kept a nice, little cotton sack of charcoal nuggets snug in my saddle bags in case we ran into any unforeseen yellow line barriers. You can never tell where one might materialize. Paved roads were everywhere, yellow lines painted on them.

At the designated campground for the race, both Blue and Amarillento stood in a portable-panel mini-corral wired to the side of my little trailer, next to our camp by a couple of big Alder trees, under which we were roasting our corn and heating up our meat, when the vets made the evening rounds.

Though his pulse was beautifully slow as usual and his vitals all grand, one of the vets was a lady, and of course Blue had to lift her up in the air by her belt when she bent over to lift his hoof, which gave us an immediate *demerit* in our scoresheet for a badly mannered horse! Oh well. Some people just have no sense of humor.

Then the next morning all the contestants cued up, holding their saddles, to weigh in. Once I got up to the check-in guy, he didn't much like the look of me and said my saddle and my headstall weren't standard equipment, and the silver was excessive and weighed way too much, all of which became the source of yet more demerits on our scorecard.

When everyone was tacked up, the judges and some vets came by to check each rider and horse and noticing my unique saddle bags, one judge asked to see the contents. I had a medium sized enamel cup, a bag of loose tea, a spoon, some dry milk, fire tinder and a flint and steel, a pliers, a knife, a sharpener, a small sack of dried meat, another of dried chokecherries, and a little cotton bag of charcoal chunks.

"What are these?"

"Those, Sir, are pieces of charcoal."

"I can see that, why are they in your bags?"

"Haven't you read the old Russian, Hungarian, Mongolian horse tales? All the magic horses are fueled by hot coals!"

" Sir, we don't allow any steroids, or artificial substances to boost your horse's performance, you'll have to step out of the competition if you insist on bringing these."

Then, of course, I told him about Blue's tremendous cognitive mind, and the traffic paint, and how his willingness to cross the line necessitated the charcoal. He almost gave me that look of fear and indignation unimaginative-imperial-servants adopt when feeling defeated, but finally smiled, "I liked your first story better, its more believable. I get it, the charcoal's some weird kind of good luck charm. Alright, you can keep it." And he gave me a number.

With all the horses inspected, their vitals taken, and over one hundred riders had been read the rules, given a map, their gear checked-in, themselves weighed and searched, now at 7:30 am in the much appreciated, very slight cool of a single cloud covering the Sun Father, the race was ready to commence. The late summer heat here in the low badlands would soon begin to mount, saturating the cracked pebble clay in a couple of hours to a 100°F so it was good to get going early. With all their riders up these horses stretched out standing in a long single file cue, from which they were sent peeling off two at a time, onto the ribbon marked trail, to be clocked, calibrated, and logged by two judges.

In all the excitement and horses finally in motion, Blue was pretty wound up and ready to conquer something, so we took off a little too fast, which was outside the tradition and ordinances of this association, whose well-meant rules for management of a horse's health on long rides meant pacing yourself and not burning your horse up early on, but also to ascertain how well people could manage their horses. But some horses get more stressed, burned out, and use up more precious energy having to hold back, basically running in place, than they would by starting out with a mild, rocking horse canter until they could get all their *levels* in place, then settling back into the alternating walk-trot-canter pulse of which such long rides are usually made. Our blast off beginning earned us a couple more demerits!

But away we rolled, passing some thirty others dutifully *holding-back* their Arabians. The air was deliciously rank with Saltbush, and Wild Buckwheat flowers, and yellow Chamisa blossoms; this early part of the trail having been placed so as to cause people to tiptoe their ponies through the big stands of Navajo tea, but through which we broad jumped and cantered happy and breathing easy as if we were in our home, which we were.

A few miles along, there was a nice little valley, strong with the smell of Dwarf Pennyroyal, richly grown up from the rains, up which the first riders, with their baseball caps, were trotting. Unfortunately, a narrow paved road ran across the designated entrance to the valley trail with three yellow lines *written* on either side and down the center, across which we had to travel to stay on the trail as it was marked. We slowed down, but keeping Blue in motion I leapt down, dragging the tip of our oversized braided rawhide reins and dropped them on the road, and already prepared with a chunk of campfire charcoal, I ran up and taking no chances, hurriedly scrawled a thin line completely across the asphalt, crossing all three lines just as Blue came up, jumping back into the saddle as he moved across the road like the warrior that he was. We deliciously coursed up the treeless, shrub-lined valley between a canter and a run for some three miles until we came across that same damned road, it having unexpectedly curved around and blocked our trail once again!

Like a well-rehearsed army procedure, I leapt from the saddle while still moving at a walk, then running out front, I charcoaled the lines like before, and then jumped back onto Blue as he moved across the asphalt. Two riders coming up from behind, who had witnessed our road ritual, had to control their horses, who unlike Blue, liked the yellow lines alright, but were utterly suspicious of our black charcoal lines! They balked and reared and backed up, eventually forcing their riders to dismount and pull their spooked horses across the road, snorting all the way at these scary charcoal lines! This got reported at the first vet stop and I was given more demerits on my score card for *defacing* the local property, and purposefully laying out distractions to frighten competitor's horses so I could more easily win!

The valley was open and unpopulated, the gorgeous wild land just kept rising up and up. After a mile, the marked trail veered up a big sandy arroyo, whose workout on horses' legs was the standard terrain of most of the rides of my childhood.

Blue trotted up that winding serpentine wash like a steamboat on the Mississippi, his big old hooves paddling up rooster tails of sand and propelling him so proficiently past the others plodding away, that when we got to solid ground again, where the trail took off to the edge of a shelf that rose some two hundred feet above a ravine solidly choked with mountain mahogany bushes, we were in record time. He was a marvel in sand.

There, riding along that shelf, we came upon a lone woman rider who seemed somewhat nervous. Perched on top of a pretty and very perky three or four-year-old dappled-grey Arabian gelding who marched along looking like he really wanted to get moving, she had his snaffle locked back hard.

The only part of this person one could actually see was her lips, which were covered in a chalky sunscreen. She was wearing very big shiny sunglasses, her head was totally bound in and covered by the hood of a down-filled winter parka, which she had zipped closed! She had on cotton gloves and knee boots. The parka was at least three or four inches thick and bright pink and I don't think I've ever seen anyone who looked as warm, considering the temperature was getting past 97° with no breeze to give some alleviation. In a stepped ravine that lay at the base of a mesa that rose some three hundred feet straight up from the narrow desert shelf upon which we rode, the convection heat of the sun that rippled off the solid pebble scatter was like a forge. I couldn't imagine why this person was so bundled up.

Because her horse was so hopped up and ready to bolt, and his rider was so weirdly armored in the heat and looked very unsteady in the saddle, Blue and I drew down into a slow walk as we approached, to be careful not to spook them as we pulled alongside.

When she finally noticed us riding there beside her she instantly began her supplications.

"Oh, it's so good you came along now, could you ride with me and help me because I'm new to riding, and help me get at least to the next rest stop?"

"Well I guess we could do that, the next vet check and water stop is right on the flat top of that mesa in front of us, up which we'll really have to gun-it hard to get to the top, 'cause there's no way to walk up that, you couldn't even lead a horse up that narrow strip to get to the summit."

She was from Utah and her husband bought her this horse, but Joyce had not ridden outside of an arena, and then only a couple times, and never on this new horse, which to be honest would be a handful for anybody, but definitely perfect for this ride, if you knew how to manage such a sparky little beast. The husband made her promise she'd don her parka and never take it off while riding, because he figured its extra thickness would protect her in the event of a mishap! This woman was dutifully wearing this parka in weather that would have keeled anybody else over from heat stroke.

By rumor, this ride was going to get increasingly more difficult as the day wore on, so I said everything I could to give advice on how to ride her horse, how to lean, and when, how not to steady oneself with the reins, how not to pull back when making a big push, but to always lean into the direction of the motion and a hundred other little things, when the trail heading up the big mesa was only three hundred yards away and looking mighty steep, she said to me, "How am I going to get up on top there? Can you tow us? I don't think I can do it, can you help me?"

"If I were in your boots, I'd think the best thing to do would be to pull out of the competition this year. It's only going to get harder and harder, that's how they make them!

If I get to the top there, I'll inform them and someone will come fetch you and your horse and get you to shade and water and back to your camp! When you get back to your home in Utah, give yourself a year and get some experience riding this good-looking horse and then try again next year, you'll both be ready for all of it."

"No, I won't do that, that's what everybody else said who came past. I want to keep going, can't you just pull me up that mountain?"

Now the truth was that Blue probably could have towed her horse up that hill without her on top, and then come back down, and after getting her to wrap her hands firmly into his tail, we might have succeeded in dragging her up that incline to the top as well. This was standard emergency riding. But I worried she might get hurt even on foot; it was awful steep.

"Look, the only way I can figure, if you really want to ride it out, is to do exactly what I say and no different. If you can promise me, then I'll help you, otherwise we can't risk you or your horse getting hurt."

Blue very slightly turned his big painted head and gave me one of his looks of disgust; he knew I was being an idiot. He was right. After all, we were on a ridge above a one-hundred-foot, sloping drop, and from that shelf the mesa rose another four hundred feet. The grade of the indicated route was extremely steep, but what made it harsh was that the *trail* one was required to take ran on top of a razor edge buttress that was less than a foot in width and any misstep could bring horse and rider tumbling four hundred feet into the ravine on either side of the shelf.

Blue excelled at climbing, but even we would have to come at it running and leaning and pushing to get all the way up and over the hump at the rim to land on top.

"All right. This is what we do. Do you promise to do exactly as I say?"

"Yes I do."

"Good then, the main thing to remember is once you get running, DO NOT pull back on the reins or you'll go rolling down the hill. Do you understand?"

"Yeah, yeah, got it," she mumbled, sounding kind of resentful.

"Let's take a breath. Your little horse here can very easily make it up the side of that hill, if you balance yourself according to his angle. Pretend like you're the trunk of a tree growing straight out of the side of that hill, keep your back at that angle in the saddle no matter how vertical your horse gets, this means toward the top of the mesa where it gets steeper, you're going to have to keep your butt sticking out, straight down, your legs out front in the stirrups, and the rest of you leaning into and hugging his neck. Under no circumstances pull the reins back once you get going up, but for God's sake don't drop the reins either. Give him his head, 'cause he's got to be able to stretch way forward to get up there.

"Your horse is pretty wound up and looks like he's ready to run, so I'm fairly certain he'll just follow Blue here perfectly, right up that hill, just as if we were pulling him. So to begin with, hold your horse back, and let me get going first, then as soon as you see me start going up that hill, start counting from one to ten. When you get to ten, let the reins relax, give him a kick, lean forward and keep urging him on and hold on tight. He'll run right up behind us to the top. Your job is to just stay on, he'll do all the rest.

"Do you understand what you gotta do?"

"Yes."

"Okay, good. Are you ready?"

"Ready."

Blue and I returned back on the trail a bit, turned around and started walking, then came trotting, then cantering and then hit the hill running hard. Up and up we climbed like a hummingbird on a zephyr. When I looked back the lady had let her horse loose, but once he started to really go, which he could really do, she did exactly what she promised not to do and pulled back hard on the reins, causing the fast little Arabian to flip over, sending the two of them tumbling separately head over heels, over and over and over, all the way to the bottom of the ravine, until the big, pink Parka Lady hung unmoving, laid out on her back across the umbrella of a stand of mountain mahogany, while the horse disappeared into the dust, sliding and rolling out of sight down into the ravine.

Horrified and in an even bigger hurry, I pushed Blue to pull up and over the rim of the mesa to land on a very flat-desert-pebbled strata where twenty or so horses were being held back for bad vitals or signs of dehydration.

I galloped up to the paramedics and yelled, "horse and rider down! There's a rider and horse down, just rolled down the side of this hill right there to the north."

Two official looking people ran to the edge, took a look, and jumped into some jeep and zoomed down a road that ran off the opposite side of the hill. One of the vets asked me to dismount and began her inspection of Blue. Right then that Parka Lady's funny little Arabian came running up the opposite side of the mountain onto the top and screaming, ran right up to Blue, where with only a couple of normal scrapes and the saddle twisted to his girth, he stood there snorting and grinning like a rookie, bird-dog sent to retrieve a pheasant and returning with an old boot.

"Was it that lady in the parka rolled down the hill?" the vet asked.

"Yes, it was actually, do you know her?"

"No, thank God, but I have a feeling I will," staring at the little Arabian. I told her what had transpired.

"You're good to go," said the vet. "Your horse here came in at 240, and in three minutes was down to 30. No sign of dehydration. If you want him to have water, there's a tank over there. That's a good horse you got there – tough!"

"No, he'll drink sometime tonight when he's totally cool."

I didn't go, but hung around worried that the Parka Lady must be dead or badly hurt. And just then the jeep returned up top and out popped the Parka Lady, plenty ambulatory, and like her horse, she arrived screeching: "That's them right there," pointing at Blue and me. "He pushed me over the edge. He tripped my horse by barging past us and shoved us over the edge on purpose. I want him removed from this competition right this minute!"

I couldn't believe it. Blue looked at me grinning and with the one blue eye I could see he said, "What else did you expect, you moron?"

An old vet came up and swatting Blue's butt mumbled, "You're good to go guy. I heard your side of it. Best just to get out of range and keep moving."

And away we went.

To let the wind lick the humiliation off my betrayed heart, once down the other side, I started Blue into a vicious wild run up and down the sides of ravines, over eroded cracks at a breakneck pace, which we kept up until we were past *all* the entire bevy of contestants and onto the next vet check ten miles down.

Here, all were required to dismount, rest and wait, eat lunch and water their cooled horses, after which everyone was to start out again in the same order they came in. But I knew, because Blue had been working, he was too smart to risk drinking.

So, I took a short nap, then built a little fire, cooked my lunch and was boiling up some tea in Blue's three o'clock afternoon shade. Every contestant was in now, including, to my great surprise, the Parka Lady, who set her sweaty horse to drinking right away. Very bad, that could've killed him. A few horses whinnied and all was peaceful.

Then, just as the water boiled, Blue's head lifted. His ears moved way forward and he pulled away from me, leaving me in the sun to make the tea alone, and uncharacteristically headed towards the troughs.

Acting as if he were going to go drink, Blue entered the large circle of horse bottoms sticking out from at least sixty tired horses, simultaneously sucking in gallons of water from a circle of water tanks.

But instead of bullying his way between two horses to get to the water, Blue just walked along very slowly from butt to butt, sniffing and inspecting each horse's rear very carefully, moving along in sequence, until he'd found the one he was looking for and stopped.

Very relaxedly Blue sniffed again, just to make sure it was the right horse bottom. Then pulling out of his slit-eyed, midday, balmy trance, he arched his neck, flared his nostrils, bugged out his eyes and danced on his front legs a couple of times, then lifting up into a levade, he squealed and dropped down whomping that particular horse high and hard on both his gaskins, knocking his rear to the ground, then reversing himself in an instant, Blue sealed the incident by squealing and mule kicking that same horse in the rear with a thud. This excitement set off the entire grumpy mob of drinking horses into a riot, who backing out of their slots commenced to rear and kick, bite and buck, all of them swirling in such an incrementing free-for-all, raising so much choking New Mexico dust, that their owners running up from the caterers couldn't make out the form of any single beast, much less their own. There was a head there and a bottom here, every creature screaming, kicking, striking and swishing, and flashing legs and gnashing teeth, and from whose thick haze of commotion and dust, like a mouse crawling out from under a bar fight,

Blue emerged unwounded and uninvolved to casually wander back to where I stood off aways from which vista we watched all the ruckus, while drinking a cup of tea, which Blue helped me finish.

With less than thirty seconds of sniffing and five seconds of kicking, Blue had set off thirty minutes of general chaos.

All the riders had been down at the caterer's tent eating or sprawled out in the shade, and knowing that horses jammed so close would always squeal at each other, no one paid any attention to Blue's initial part in it all, for nobody else even saw it. But when the dust settled, the Parka Lady finally arrived on the scene brandishing a bag of chips and saw her horse limping. She started screaming about the evil nature of me and my horse again.

"That man's horse is just like him, he's unruly and dangerous, I order you to remove them from this competition. If you don't that horse is going to hurt someone, you watch, he maimed my little Pearson."

By this time the mayhem was so general, and everybody's animals had sustained some minor contusion somewhere from some undetermined horse in the brawl; nobody was really listening to her. But because they had to find something to charge us with, another complaint was entered against Blue and I for making an open fire! The Parka Lady's horse had to be scratched from the race at the insistence of the vets, and this probably saved her life, in the end. But the little Arabian was not seriously hurt, a couple of days rest and his bruises would let him be ridden.

That's when I realized, for the first time, that Blue: who could pick up women, walk uninvited into people's houses, see two-dimensional images, and make himself invisible, could not only reason out a long-range plan, but that he had a very strong tribal sense of punitive justice that operated in grand subtlety. Having seen everything that happened, he actually waited till just the right moment, and never forgetting who had dissed us, he very precisely whomped the very horse of the lady who'd falsely accused us of attacking her, then covered it up with a diversionary horse riot from which he emerged unscathed. He could really keep his cool!

Chapter 12

Just How Far
Will This Dead Horse Go?

The next evening, when all was said and done, it was a depressing jolt to the people with their fancy trailers, RVs, stretch pants and helmets and thirty-thousand dollar horses, and a big surprise to me, that by points, horse fitness and time, Blue and I came in number one in the results of that crazy, two-day ride.

Most of those riders didn't come to compete for the local prizes, having ridden only to rack up mileage and good marks on their score sheets, as applied to accumulative rating for a nationwide, annual prize in an association to which I didn't even belong.

All that being the case, in the meeting at the end, the judges said they couldn't award first place to Blue and I, though by speed, fitness, and *performance*, we'd taken the field. But on account of so many technical demerits for our saddle, bridle, my chalking up the highways, making open fires, and contestant complaints registered against us for running where we should've been walking, and for being the suspected source of general mayhem, etc., we didn't have enough *points* left to win.

What clinched it all were those damned gas wells.

Though both days the ride occasionally led straight through oilfields where oil pumps of every color and size bobbed up and down in their drone existence, Blue was totally non-plussed. But only a mile from the camp and the finish line on the last afternoon, after fifty miles of sweat, and after we had already aced the entire race both days, the trail led past the first natural gas well we'd seen during the whole race. This turned out to be as bad as a yellow line!

We were at least an hour in front of every single contestant, and Blue wasn't even the least bit worn out, but he wasn't prepared to go past this one idiotic gas well.

I couldn't drag him, lead him or even push him blindfolded. I tried everything, but nothing would do it. "Maybe," I thought, "if another rider comes up and his/her horse goes past, old Blue's hard head will follow the other horse." For in this case, unlike the yellow line, Blue actually was spooked by the suspicious gas well, which unlike the rhythmic clank and sucking racket of the up-and-down of the oil wells, the gas wells were almost silent, not moving, obviously plotting something violent, just like those mailboxes with Ta Shunk years back.

I waited. Nobody came. Totally pissed off, because we were so far ahead and in such good shape, now I had to wait till the rest appeared in hopes he'd cross with a group of horses, and come in with their same times.

Overly restless to just sit there, I rode back twenty minutes to the first knot of riders and their tired horses and when we got to the gas well, Blue balked so convincingly, nobody else's horse would pass the well either! It was not until the next group of slow pokes showed up that all forty of us finally waddled nervously past this funny old well, at which point I pushed Blue into a blazing gallop to get to the end zone first, which we did. But...everybody started yelling as we passed, "We don't do that sort of thing here buddy!" etc. and so on.

So we got over forty more complaints, which added on to all the other demerits accounted for our second place trophy: a little sand painting stating the same. All I could do was smile, the judges were really nice about it and the vets even better, but we hadn't actually come having to win, but to educate ourselves in the nature of these sorts of events, and of course just to ride 'cause we loved it.

We secured permission to stay over camping one more night, everyone else having already departed, including our Barb contingency, fuming about our *win*, though I don't know why, as they all did very well. The vets came around in the dark and accepted food at our camp, though they wouldn't sit down. The one lady veterinarian said if things ever got so I needed to sell Old Blue that she'd buy him in a second and gave me her card.

I had brought Amarillento along with us, partly to keep Blue company and also because we were on the Navajo

Reservation and my old friend Becenti thought he'd bring his family up to see us and Amarillento, who he'd been the first to recognize as fast years past. Becenti came up with his people in two Blazers and everyone started cooking under the trees and shooting the breeze.

The following morning Becenti, having brought his own black Quarter horse, saddled up while I saddled Amarillento, leaving Blue to rest in the little corral there with the people.

Becenti saw he was vindicated in his assessment of Amarillento as we zoomed over some of these desert trails. On our way back, laughing and talking about all the crazy things that happened on that ride, we were close to camp when we met two of the vets who had packed up and were heading out.

Looking awfully contrite and down in the face, the older man of the two yelled from his truck window, "I'm so sorry about your horse, it really is a shame."

"About what horse? What are you talking about?"

"Oh poor man, you haven't heard? Your beautiful paint horse is laying there dead in his corral. The race must've been too tough on him."

"Really? No way!"

Becenti and I ran our horses all the half a mile to our camp where our families and other people were gathered around the corral, heads hanging sad and talking.

Dismounting and pulling Amarillento behind, I pushed my way through the crowd, and there on his side, not moving, all four legs straight out, mouth half open, tongue dragging in the sand gathering ants, eyeball rolled back in his head, lay beautiful Blue Medicine, looking deader than all the dead horses I'd ever seen.

The vets came rumbling up, and rolled out of their truck. I handed my reins to Becenti and climbed into the corral, dropped to my knees and put my ear to his body behind his shoulder blade.

Though truthfully I was already misty-eyed, I stood up and kicked him hard where the "calf sucks," as they say, and yelled, "God dammit Blue, stop scaring everybody to death, get up you old bluffer!" And I kicked him again.

His red ears twitched and motioned back and front, his tail flipped up and slapped the dusty ground and then, to the great delight and chagrin of the cheering crowd, he got up, shook himself off and turned around and mooned me!

Blue could really act.

That horse had a pride as big as his ego, and an ego as big as the moon. He was *my* horse and I was *his* rider and if I so much as rode any other horse before I rode him, or instead of him, he'd always moon me and make himself hell to catch and then stubborn to ride.

But if his big pride was wounded by not only being *first* in everything I did, and he deemed my crimes to his heart were too severe and I'd gone too far, he'd always go ahead and *die*.

He played dead in so many ways and would end up fooling so many of us, so often, all the way into his thirties. He got better and better at it and more than once totally fooled me. He learned to control his breathing, and to not jump to life with a simple kick or a yell; sometimes you'd swear he'd really finally departed this world, but once everyone began weeping and he was convinced you really did miss him, then he'd twitch his ears, flip his tail and jump back to life, all just to punish you for having ridden some other horse besides his lordship!

The vets couldn't get over it. "Man he looked as dead as any dead horse I've ever seen, but you could pick up his heartbeat?"

"Yeah, he's got a big old heart, there's no mistaking that, but he always fools you as long as he can!"

Blue's pranks were so sophisticated and reasoned out, that once over, they always put things back in proper perspective. Everybody was laughing. Becenti almost laughed himself skinny. We unsaddled and let Amarillento back into the corral, who for his audacity to allow himself to be ridden first, took a good licking from his companion, but like the rest of us, they soon settled down to eat side by side. It was a good day winning both second and first, Blue back on his feet, and everybody seeing one another again.

Chapter 13

Admiration: The Saga of Ojo Sarco

In the spring, when the Sun's welcome gaze returns to warm the world after weeks of winter's cold air and frozen ground, like eggs frying in deep oil, a lot of horses will lay down on their side to soak up the warmth from both the solar heated Earth on one side and the Sun on the other, often stretched out for quite a while looking like they're pretty dead, but usually you can see their rib cages rise with the in-breath, and their nostrils raising little puffs of dust off the ground on the exhale, and the occasional ear twitch or a swish of the tail.

For Blue such things were just part of being a horse and he did all that too. But he took his theatre career very seriously, and since playing dead was his most famous acting role, he kept adding to his repertoire until it took on battle proportions. If he felt really insulted he would even mimic a horse already dead a while, stiff in rigor mortis, bloated up with all four legs sticking straight out, two of them hanging unbending in the air, head thrown back on a contorted neck, with breath so shallow and controlled you couldn't see him breathe. It was really disconcerting to come upon and he'd play it for all it was worth. Anyone raising a lot of horses for a long time has usually had the unhappy experience of coming out to check on her animals and finding one killed by lightning, poisoned, shot dead by a careless hunter, or dead from colic, or one unfortunate cause or the next, so this always made me take Blue's ruse seriously and he knew it.

Of course all his quirks were a sign of his enormous thinking intelligence, but Blue's entire family bloodline of Spanish-Mesta-Barb-Pueblo-Indian-Horses seemed to be endowed with some capacity for concocting precisely acted out, long-range hoaxes to get their way! Blue's brilliant sister, Zajlani with her three hour saddle limit could also play dead almost as well as her big brother.

But they both had a cousin who was definitely at the top of his class when it came to thinking himself out of an unwanted situation. He turned out to be not only a consummate actor, but a veritable playwright. He wasn't just a mischievous, clever horse looking to get more food, or garner more attention, and he was definitely not into making trouble because he could, he had a real purpose and a good one: he was looking for real praise for the nobility of his real being, looking for true admiration where none was forthcoming. He was looking to escape the innocuous spiritual landscape of the shallow people he was stuck with who were incapable of anything but pity or cutesy-pop-talk.

This horse was appealing and handsome all the way around. I'd been trying to buy him for two years, but to no avail. A solid *alazán tostado* or toasted sorrel, he had a blaze that covered his entire forehead, then ran down and over his nose right into his rhino-wrinkled-lips, as if he were drinking it. His right eye was wild, blue and piercing and his left eye black and deep brown like the eye of a Mule Deer baby: a pool of deep, intelligent *looking*. His mane and tail were red with a darker deep red stripe down his back connecting the two. With just one white fetlock on the right hind, he was otherwise a solid red horse.

His build was not full of bulgy muscles like modern horses, but smoother, more powerful and lithe. Lacking the Draft-horse-derived wide chest of the modern Quarter horse, Sarco's chest was narrow but deep and powerful. Sarco's beautiful head didn't sit on one of those spindly necks of modern horses. He was a perfect old-time cowboy horse, Indian warhorse, a Spanish horse. With the color and hardness of black bull horns, wonderful hooves had he, whose hoof wall measured three quarters of an inch thick all around!

In one small look you could tell right out that he'd be the best ride in the world. Blue was the best horse, Amarillento was the fastest, Ojo Sarco was the best ride, for I'd ridden him and would have loved to have been able to call him my own. Once a person got a hold of a horse like him, the love affair between the two made a heroic deliciousness jump back alive into both, pulled right out of the land from a time no longer seen. He was that kind of horse.

One evening the wealthy young wife of one of the Rich Kid's brothers called me on the phone to see if I could take a look at her gelding. This horse was none other than this very same Barb gelding, Blue's first cousin, Ojo Sarco, who had reportedly gone mysteriously lame on his right front. But their *specialists* in Texas, after x-raying and testing all the parts of that horse they felt might be causing his lameness, came up with only a vague and non-committal diagnosis involving something with the flexor tendon. The coffin bone was where it belonged, the navicular was good, he was too young for ringbone, he wasn't stone bruised, and there were no detectable fractures. Their suggested treatment was some series of *residential therapies* that would involve six weeks with them at a cost five times beyond the price of the horse.

In those days I was doing a lot of doctoring, mostly humans, a few dogs, some horses, and a lot of broken hearts.

Although surprised when this lady, whose entire family didn't much care for me, petitioned my help, I responded instantly because I admired her horse, and he was worth the blizzard of classist oppression and passive aggression I knew I'd have to bear to do so.

After driving my old red Ford pickup to where they lived, down on the flat land out of the mountains at the edge of the city, I watched as they walked him about in a round pen to show me how he limped around and bobbed his big handsome head. They let me feel around his withers into his shoulders and all around his body, slowly searching for any sign of the trouble for an entire hour. But all I found was a very good horse with a good smell and a good whinny. There was nothing that I could find or feel that would account for his lameness.

Thinking it out, maybe if I could live around him and watch him at my own rhythm, he might eventually reveal what caused his terrible limp. I suggested they bring him over to our camp up in the mountains and leave him with me for a few days.

The following morning, beautiful Ojo Sarco arrived up in our mountain's canyon. I led all fourteen hands of him into Blue's former mountainside, vertical pen to see how he would negotiate the terrain. At first his head hung very low and he *scootched* about looking awfully stiff and misplaced, but it was all theatre, for as soon as the trailer he'd come in had driven off, his eyes brightened, his head lifted and quickly grabbing a mouthful of his breakfast of mountain grass, he squealed like a banshee and with tail up he whinnied and complained, marching the perimeter of the corral, searching for a hole to escape through, leaping from rock shelf to rock shelf like a goat with absolutely no sign of *lameness* on any foot whatsoever!

Maybe he wasn't lame? Maybe the higher altitude or the mountain air had cured him?!

I was definitely smiling and bemused, but in my horse greed and really in love with this real old-time, red beauty, I wanted to do right by him. So to truly test him, I saddled him with one of my own homemade saddles (I'd made a couple) and bridled him with a heavily-silvered, old headstall with a medium curb bit installed, and with some light reins, got myself up into the saddle and rode him gently along the soft river mud to test his lameness. There was none. Then I rode him upstream into the river along its rush of water over the slippery cobbles of its bed. Still no sign of lameness! "Well,"

I thought, "maybe it manifests as his joints warm up." But as we rode, he only became more and more limber and more antsy to get moving. He was a wonderful going-horse.

All the time digging the powerful, lithe, athletic lusciousness of his motion, I very carefully rode him up the mountain, at first walking the log-skid, but then at a trot straight up the mountain incline. But no lameness appeared that I could detect. So I let him canter, to the left, then to the right, then even downhill at a trot over the rocky trail. If he was lame that would have shown it, but he was fabulous at everything and a happy goer at every gait!

Well, I figured, maybe the lameness would show up in a couple of hours, when he'd cooled off and stiffened a bit. So I unsaddled him, let him back into the hillside corral, fed him and returned every ten minutes to watch him. Strangely enough never once did any lameness appear! Sarco had only been at our house for less than twenty hours, and had never exhibited lameness.

The day before, I'd seen him lame in the city. And everybody who knew this horse said he was lame. The vets said he was lame. But at my house he was utterly sound! So of course I did the only thing I could think of: I rode him harder! That proved to be an utter joy. Almost forgetting that he wasn't mine and that he'd been *remanded* into my care to cure a case of mysterious lameness, I rode him more and more every day for six days, semi-rationalizing it all as part of some *special cure* I'd developed!

While I was *busy healing* Ojo Sarco by riding the hell out of him, Blue was beyond all jealousy and played dead every morning and every evening for four days, looking deader and deader every day. You couldn't blame him really, for his cousin was a wondrous horse.

I knew we were having too much fun, so I finally succumbed to those incessant nagging waves of protestant-bad-conscience and phoned up Sarco's owner and soberly told her that, "I think I finally got his lameness licked," and that she could come pick him up. But they sent Gilly, their horse slave, with one of their family trailers and Sarco went sadly back to the city.

Two days later, in the morning, his owner, the young Texas lady, called me up again. "He was fine for two days but now he's gone lame again, this time on the hind left, what did you do to my little horse to cause this? Do you think maybe he hit himself when Gilly was trailering him?"

How mysterious! Sarco was fine when I sent him back! With both my truck and trailer I drove back down into the city.

And when I got to their place, to my great wonderment I was shown a very gimpy, head-bobbing, red horse with a pronounced limp who acted like he had a bruised stifle, unable to put his foot down properly in the back!

They let me take him again, and back to our mountains we went, this time in my own trailer, out of which I unloaded him into Blue's old corral again, intending to watch him. After about six minutes this horse lifted his head, put all four feet squarely down, lifted his tail, screamed like a banshee and leapt from shelf to shelf like a goat, with no signs of lameness anywhere! "H'ah!"

After that, to continue with his *cure*, Sarco and I rode for six hours a day over harsh terrain and steep hills for a week, and never once did he ever stumble or show any sign of lameness whatsoever. He was even starting to get into pretty good shape for all the work I put him through.

My annual autumn trek to gather the wild-growing plant medicines I would need for healing all the people, animals, and family during the coming winter months was coming up. I thought to take Sarco, to lead as a pack horse into the high country, with me riding Blue—camp, pick my plants—then switch them around and use Blue to pack and Sarco to ride back home.

We rode up La Cueva Canyon into the deep narrow ravine of banded stone, right behind the little waterfall, and up onto the steep shelves of aspen glades, then over to the vehicle road that would take us up ten thousand feet to the Glorieta Peak Smoke Tower.

Already halfway up and smiling, our chests full with the fall mountain air on the crunchy gravel road, Blue happy, Sarco a trooper, powerful under my tent and food, the grinding sound of a small car swimming in the newly-laid gravel labored up the hill behind us. We pulled to one side to let whatever it was go past, when a little gray-blue sedan, looking very squat with tiny wheels, and too close to the ground, pulled right alongside us, out of whose windows two voices hailed me by name.

"Hey Martín, its Randy and Beth, remember us? The people down at your place told us we might find you riding up here on the high road." Then pushing a hand out the window, clutching an envelope thick with American currency, Beth blurted, "Look, we just came to return the money you loaned us. We can't thank you enough, it got us through a hard stretch, now we're good again and we wanted to give it back to you in person."

This was not totally true, for I never loaned out money to anyone. In certain eras we'd been too often less-than-poor in cash and I knew all too intimately the vicissitudes of taking out loans, to repay other loans, to repay more loans that were all the time increasing in interest, to people who seeing our poverty only saw an opportunity to make more money. Instead of alleviation, these *lenders* only further dug the poor into a hole of increased dependency, stuck in the bottom of the social bucket. For that reason I had a policy of never loaning out money. But I did *give* money to those who truly needed it. When I had it to give, beyond what we needed to sustain ourselves and our animals, I often made gifts of money to people who I knew would make good use of it, but I never issued money as a loan. Never demanding it to be repaid in any form, I figured if they needed it, and I had it, I would give it, and when I needed it, those who had it would give it to me with the same conditions. That way I didn't have to chase people around to get my money back, and we could always stay friends. So I gave only gifts. If I couldn't afford to give an amount without *needing* it back, I would never loan it. Life was better that way.

Almost invariably people would pay us back and that was fine, but not because we demanded it of them, and never with interest. We never lost our allies or ever bought things we couldn't pay for on the spot.

"Well guys, that's awfully nice of you both, but if it's alright with you, could you be so kind as to leave that package with my family back down at our camp, 'cause I don't like riding around having to worry about losing it up in the hills? Plus this horse is going to try to stick his head inside your cab if you don't roll up your window."

I knew if I rode any closer toward their car to fetch the money packet in that lady's outstretched hand that Blue would unabashedly force his hand and push his big-old head right into the cab, just to get a look at his own eyeball in the rear-view mirror, like he always did. The driver would invariably have to scramble out of his seat into the passenger seat to make room for that head. It was true! Blue loved mirrors and once he saw one he'd do anything to go get a good, long look at himself.

But his favorite thing of all was to get his head right up on the central rear-view mirror on the windshield inside the cab of a truck or car and study his own eyeball looking back at him!

And let me tell you, ladies and gentlemen, it was like trying to put out a forest fire with a squirt gun to pull that crazy horse away from the strange reverie his eyeball-gazing caused in his brain. He was glued to it, and the trance it caused him made him oblivious to everything going on around him. Nothing could pull him away!

The only way was to sneak your hand past his big-old head plugged into the cab and somehow manage to drape a scarf over the mirror to block off the image he was seeing and break the trance, which was harder than it sounds, because his eye was not an inch away from the mirror!

More often than not he'd end up knocking the mirror off its mooring and then you could drag his lordship's big, determined self back onto the road!

Which of course is exactly what happened to these well-intentioned hippies, who, terrified when Blue's head evicted Beth onto Randy's lap, both evacuated the car by scrambling out of the passenger door as Blue, his neck craned, stood glued, gazing at his own funny, wild, blue eyeball, until I could get my scarf across the mirror and pull him off!

I'd warned them, but they thought I was joking.

Supposedly, by science's decree, very few animals recognize three dimensional images reflected or projected on two dimensional surfaces, especially not horses.

While that may well be true for some horses, in my little herd there were three horses who definitely could see and recognize three dimensional images on two dimensional surfaces, including photos, picture windows or mirrors of any sort, the only provision being that the images were life-size.

All horse people have seen horses jump back at seeing clouds reflected in puddles and ponds. What was unique about Blue was not only could he see a life-size painting of a bird and see a bird there, but unlike his other relatives, who when they looked in a window and saw a horse, they always thought that image was some other horse, Blue recognized himself as the animal staring back at him beyond any doubt!

For now began the era where when Blue snuck into a house, instead of searching for kitchens and rice, he'd learned to scout around until he found a full length mirror, where he'd stand for hours staring at himself, turning around to see how well his tail was hanging and how great his butt was looking. Like a lady fluffing her skirt getting ready to go out on the town, Blue would check out his right side, then his left side, as if looking at himself was some kind of delightful meal, and then for desert, without fail, he'd walk up, turn sideways and forever gaze into the reflection of one of his crazy, blue eyes—on one side, then turn around to the other side!

Even in a camera, he'd learned that he could see his eyeball in the lens. Sometimes out on the range running in a herd of more than forty horses, when our herd had grown to such proportions later on, in order to separate and catch Blue, the easiest way was, embarrassingly, to produce a *professional* camera with a big telephoto lens, and he'd walk right out of the swirling, recalcitrant group to stick his eye on the lens to see his *eye* in the reflection, while you put a halter on his funny old hypnotized head.

Sarco, on the other hand, had no interest in mirrors. All loaded up and standing patiently off a ways, he watched in good humor while I dismounted, and struggled to withdraw Blue's big head from the cab of that dinky car, calm down its owners and get us back onto the trail.

Blue's head, though substantial, was the well-proportioned head of a handsome horse, but when his head and neck pushed themselves into your car's cab, they were as big as a person, huge and scary, over two hundred pounds of it. To unplug him from a mirror in a cab was maddening, ridiculous, took forever, and was pretty dangerous, because if you covered the mirror and broke the trance, and he realized his head was stuck inside a car, he usually panicked, lifting his head and pulling until he was sure he'd gotten clear, leaving the car or truck rocking like a toy sailboat in a storm. You had to get out of his way before he got moving or you'd be hurt.

Once I got his big, hard head out of their frail, little car, the people, still shaking and wide-eyed, very quietly reclaimed their vehicle, got in, turned around, and puttered back away from the mountains.

The three of us, with the money package tucked into my saddle bags, continued pushing our way up to the ridgetop from where the vast view below and the smell of that gorgeous mountain universe held me in a kind of mirror-trance of ecstatic hope and nostalgia of its wild, delicious heart.

"Those are some beautiful little horses you got there Sir, where'd you steal them from?" A kind, old, croaky voice, a little mossy and frog-like, startled me from the spell of fall in the Sangres at ten thousand feet, and the incredible vista that stretched out for a hundred miles below.

We said our hellos and shook hands, and though I'd never met him, he confirmed what anyone would suppose, for standing as we were next to the Smoke Tower, this man, a person very few had ever really met, but about whom the entire world seemed to have a story, was none other than the old cowboy-professor and poet Bill MacAllister, who had manned the Smoke Tower lookout up here on top of Glorieta Peak for over four decades.

Every day, for almost fifty summers, he'd ridden his horse up the roadless west face of this mountain from his home on the upper dribbles of the Apache Springs to voluntarily watch for forest fires along the high ridges of the Sangres.

"Where exactly are you three headed off to? Up to the high-line trail perhaps?"

"No, still too many hikers for me this time of year."

Almost eighty now, MacAllister, thirty years a college professor, smiled.

When I explained about Sarco's weird, location-specific bouts of selective lameness, and his miraculous, instantaneous cures upon his arrival to our place, and how I'd been trying to buy him for years, and how they wouldn't sell him, he laughed and added, "He's pretty brilliant then; doesn't like his home, he wants out; he likes your life better, so he's just bluffing."

"Yeah, maybe so. It's a bit mysterious."

"Well, I tell you what, just sell him to me, and tell those people he ran away, that'll fix the whole situation!

"My last horse, Mingo, took me up here and back home for over two decades, pretty much every day in the summer and twice a week the rest of the year. But he finally got too old and I had to put him down last spring. I've got a three-year-old filly at the house who's not ready and probably wouldn't grow to be strong enough to take this trail anyway. So, I'm on foot these days."

By the road we came up on, one could reach the tower by truck. But by that very circuitous route, Bill's house was over thirty miles away. On the west side trail it was a steep seven mile walk. There was no vehicle at the Smoke Tower. How did he get back and forth now that his strong old horse friend was gone? The fact that he rode his horse back and forth was very common knowledge and full of great embellishment, for his horse had been a gray of the *old style* as well.

"So now, I just walk to work and back home! The only reason I kept manning this tower was for the joy of riding to it and back every day throughout the seasons! So until I find a horse that enjoys it as much as I do, I'd rather walk than drive!

"Now, if you'd just soften up and sell me this beautiful sorrel you're wasting under a pack, then I'd have found my ride, because you can tell he loves it up here and is plenty strong and gonna last."

He was totally correct, and I myself would've loved his job, and riding to work and back!

It was already about 4:30 in the afternoon, and I had intended on finding my way down the very trail this old, erudite cowboy had created and camp on one of the springs where it bottomed out, and in the morning gather certain plant medicines I knew would be thriving in great profusion there. Plants full of the power of the Wild.

"Why don't we just go to my house?" Bill said. "I live on one of those springs; pick all the plants you want."

So we did.

Having always survived by considering fluidity as the best policy in most life situations, since I was no longer going to camp, I didn't need a pack or a pack horse. So I cleared Sarco of his pack, which because we were running light, I'd simply employed a homemade, double-bag morral that had openings which slipped over the cantle and horn of a riding saddle. After stowing our un-needed gear in the Smoke Tower, I asked Bill if he'd like to ride Sarco instead of walking, that way he could show us the way down, which turned out to be a really good idea, because about half ways down there were a couple of tricky switch backs that actually kind of bumbled back up and around before they went down again, which on my own I might have easily missed. That is how I came to be familiar with that beautiful area of Northern New Mexico.

"Bundy!"

"Veníte, mira a mi caballito nuevo…"

Bill yelled in beautiful Spanish when we got to the deliciously hidden forest house right next to the famous upper head waters of the Apache Springs. It was like an old fairytale.

His wife, Abundancia, a good looking, old-style, mature New Mexico lady walked into view from behind the house in the almost dark of the deep forest shadows of the evening.

"Wow, Billy, mira que lindo. Where did you get such a beautiful horse?"

Too bad that Sarco wasn't mine. I would've given him to these beautiful old-time people, living in love with each other and their life up in a canyon where this horse, who had not so much as even hinted at stumbling as we all pulled up along the tortuous grade to our goal, would truly be at home.

We put up the horses in his corral and fed them, and were in turn taken and fed by Bundy, who had a little guitar, and so after that very good dinner, I played and we all sang till we couldn't stay awake. But some horses, with minds like rivers, run their own wandering force in cahoots with another mind of Nature bigger than the square cookie-cutter of most human imagination, and while we all slept, I guess that was when Sarco galvanized the plan that eventually became a reality.

The next morning Bundy had everyone loaded with lunch and Sarco saddled and after sending Bill riding back to the Smoke Tower, I spent the day with Blue picking plants in the canyon. When I'd finished I rode Blue back up to the peak, put the pack on Blue and after taking down Mr. MacAllister's phone number at the Smoke Tower, 'cause he didn't have a phone where they lived, I pulled myself on top of Sarco, and with Blue packing our gear and medicines, we made the downward journey, all the way home to our camp.

Sarco had been in *treatment* with me ten days now, and the messages on the answering machine from his owner were thick and increasingly cross, so since he seemed to be pretty *cured*, I reluctantly drove him back to his legal owners, putting an end to almost two months of wonderful summer and early fall riding during which I did absolutely nothing to cure him but ride!

Sarco was sound. When his lady owner saw what good shape he was in she was ecstatic. Running him over her little cavaletti, and around her silicone slalom poles, she *dressaged* him around with an arched neck in the arena with an instructor yelling through the electric megaphone: "more heel ma'am…lean forward…now by the left lead…now the right lead," and so on.

His soundness held for a week and then I got a call, "He's lame on the right front again Martín, what can I do? You had him all just fine and now he's lame all over again!"

This time when I came to where Ojo Sarco lived in these flat-lander's fancy square palace, I'd pretty much come to the conclusion that his owner, the rider, must've been using some small method, or some tack, or some maneuver that was causing this handsome, wild-eyed gelding to *act* like he was lame whenever he got in action with her. Otherwise why was he lame here at his owner's place and not over there with us?

In frustration, I figured I'd have her go through and do absolutely everything she always did in her normal riding routine, while I watched every detail to see if there was just some simple thing we were all overlooking.

After waiting dutifully for this young woman to put on her polo shirt, her stretch riding pants, pull on her leather wellingtons, and emerge from the house strapping on her helmet, I even watched her unlock her tack room, watched as she grabbed a leather racing halter and a lead, and watched as she went to the corral to fetch Ojo Sarco, whose head was already bobbing, and who was limping very notably on the right front, eluding capture.

When she finally got Sarco to stand still and she haltered him, and led him out of the corral towards the hitching bar at the tack room where she tied him up, with me still watching her every move, utterly unsure as to what it was I might be looking for, this young woman was about to put the saddle pad and her English saddle on all at one go, when Sarco, with no apparent lameness started dancing back and forth, unwilling to stand, something he hadn't done with me. Ah ha, I said to myself, he probably doesn't like this particular saddle.

Then his owner started talking to him, which we all do of course.

"Now Bubblehead, you stop that, you always make me look bad when everybody's watching." But the horse was still doing a pretty good mambo.

"Bubblehead, stand still, dang it." For which command he did not stand still.

"Bubblehead, you're nothing but trouble, what's wrong with your brain anyway?"

There it was. The whole situation.

"Ma'am," I called out to her to get her attention. But she wasn't listening, too intent on getting saddled, which she finally achieved. Then after bridling, she had trouble getting Ojo Sarco to stand for mounting, for which she yelled smartly like a master to her slave:

"Bubblehead, stand." And tapped him on the neck with her crop, for which command he finally stood.

She mounted. And he was lame.

After she rode him at a lame walk both directions around her arena and had put him up, in a kind of impatient snotty tone she asked me: "Well? Figure anything out? Am I doing anything wrong?"

I waited a while to respond, thinking about all the beautiful riding we'd had with Sarco and Blue all over the mountains, and how even unshod and in the most compromising terrain with the most basic feed, this horse had gone sailing gaily along: happy, fierce, indomitable. A very good ride; a very good horse.

"Aren't you going to talk, did you figure anything out? Or not!"

Not sure where to begin, or if I should have even tried, but I was born a Prechtel and no matter what, we always have something to say, and we usually start at the end and go backwards to the point, but this time when I spoke I went right to the middle.

"You are afraid of this horse, that's the problem."

"What do you mean, I'm not afraid of him. What's that got to do with his lameness anyway."

"If you are not afraid of him, why do you call him Bubblehead?"

"It's just a little nickname I have for him, that's all, it's nothing."

"No, with all due respect Ma'am, I disagree. You are afraid of the possibility of this horse's natural power. You would like to possess his beauty and want his power for your own, but in your fear you try to make him less formidable by calling him Bubblehead. You diminish him by your talk to make him seem less powerful so you can deal with him. The funny thing is he must love you so much that he does just exactly what you ask of him, which is to get lame, sick, and demented enough for you to get on him without being afraid of him!

"Horses are spirits. But some horses, like this one, are truly grand; they have big powerful souls. It probably wouldn't even matter if you went upside his head or rode lopsided, that would not even be a problem, you guys would work it out in the end. But a horse like this is proud and can't withstand being made less of, and still be expected to stay healthy. Every part of your body, the way you move, the way you sound and the pheromones that go with the way you feel, all direct him to be lame. The way it stands right now, 'Bubblehead' is written in every single scared motion you make, and so you make noble, powerful Ojo Sarco into limping, stupid Bubblehead. He doesn't do it because he's put together wrong or sickly, but because he's brilliant, and you ask him not to be.

"Your gear is fine, your riding is alright. But you fear him and therefore your need to dominate him out of fear makes him lame up. His body isn't lame, his soul is wounded and limping.

"He's already got a fine name, a hero name. Use that name, or some other name that praises him, not some bullshitty, cutesy handle. Admire your horse, give him power, then he'll do anything for you. Horses like Sarco need Admiration, not condescension. True Admiration. But if you give him Admiration, he'll get more noble and more powerful, and unless you find even more courage in your love for him, you'll get even more afraid of his increased grace and presence."

She looked at me like I was some incomprehensible drunk off the street, or a coolie talking out of his station, but she was a little misty-eyed when she stomped off, muttering.

They never did pay me, as they'd promised, for my time, expertise or work, or ever let me touch that horse again, because of course they were *superior* in all things and couldn't be criticized. And since they were still making their horse lame, they decided to spend money with their upper crust vets to prove that the lameness was purely mechanical!

I knew they wouldn't thank me, much less compensate my time, and I tried not to care. I'd had such delight in the *work*, it didn't matter. But I do wish they would've sold him to me. Plus, in the end, I hadn't done anything I could bill them for anyway. You can't charge somebody for liking their horse. If I'd been a real shyster, I could have worked it so I could have bought Sarco as a lame horse. But that beautiful Indian horse's pride needed admiration, and when I gave it, he would always be sound; if I made him lame to buy him cheap, he'd stay lame and cheap. So it would never really work. I would never be a good businessman. But all that being said, Ojo Sarco wasn't finished, he had an even bigger plan beyond us all.

That winter following, people kept telling us stories about the sound of wild New Mexico Wolves wailing up on the Apache Creek, in the snow at night. Though reputedly the last native New Mexico Wolf was shot outside Santa Fe the year that I was born, new agers started claiming Wolf sightings in every far away niche of the state. Maybe it was true. Having heard Wolves singing in Canada, I knew how they sounded, how powerfully they filled the nights.

Then, one clear late winter night, in the moonlight, riding Blue through a foot of snow under the Pleiades, I myself heard a mournful Wolf-like yowl roll right over us. We stopped and listened. Blue's ears, one forward, the other going around like a propeller, tried to get a heading on where these wild sounds were coming from, when Coyotes on every side interrupted with their yips and non-stop skitter, taking over the soundscape. Then silence. Then again the yowls of Wolves, but this time they morphed into something rather different, sometimes even sounding like a Bach counterpoint partita echoing through the canyons. Then Coyotes. Then Wolf yowling, then silence.

I followed Blue's ears to the sound and after a mile we found it!

There in the middle of a small snow-filled arroyo, on a blanket in the moonlight on a cleared off boulder sat a man all bundled up, with a battery-driven amplifier sawing away on an electric viola, playing his heart out to the sky! We knew each other, and he'd seen me coming and just kept bowing away.

The snow slid his sound into that still night, running in echoes out for miles, echoes that mutated the music into layers that were digested and sifted through the branches of

Pines and Spruces, canyons and swales, repopulating again, at least the air, with the wild songs of bodyless Wolves from the past, whose echoing on top of their own echoes made overtones that sounded just like their pups wailing on top. It was amazing, the night really was filled up with Wolf singing coming from this wild man's bow.

A kind of uppercrust Native American, a Penobscot man from Maine, old now, but always in good shape, a one-time poacher, arrested and converted into a mountain Park Ranger, he was well acquainted with Wolves of every stage.

"I didn't know you played viola, Earnest."

"Every winter I come play my sounds out in the snow-covered hills to the souls of long killed beings whose souls still wait inside the land, songs of past Wolves, and my Bach life, long past. You know what I mean Martín: if we have a gift, we must make a gift to what gave us the gift, a gift to what was and what still lives under it all. I trained as a classical cellist in my youth, but all my music always came from the Wolves in my Indian soul. So every winter I play them my Wolf and Bach music, that way all their souls can sing again."

We talked and laughed and drank hot tea from his thermos and rummaged about for gossip and news, enjoying the Coyotes returning their own crazy, artful singing that spelled more snow, but the end of a good wet winter.

From where he lived outside Santa Fe, just some seven miles from Bill and Bundy, he owned a tiny rat-tailed Appaloosa mare that had gone missing, whose whereabouts he finally discovered, but could not seem to catch and reclaim.

Horses around Apache Canyon had been disappearing—tame riding mares from yuppie houses and little ranchitos.

Theories of modern horse thieves began to circulate along with rumors of wild horse-eating Wolves.

But my viola playing friend knew. He'd found them all roaming around free in a little band of nine: eight mares and what he took to be an old-time looking red stallion with one blue eye and one brown eye!

It was Ojo Sarco, of course.

Though none of that branch of the Owners would have much to do with me after our *talk*, I'd already learned through flyers posted on every lamp post and feed store corkboard that Ojo Sarco had gone missing. Like people trying to find the whereabouts of their lost poodle, they'd posted a reward for his return, or information that led to the same. The Owners even sent someone to check around our camp, no doubt thinking Sarco might be there. Instead of being insulted, I tried to put myself in their shoes, and I guess I'd have thought the same thing.

Wondering if these horses were still up there in the mountains like Earnest said, during the next spring run-off I took Blue that way to scout out the herbs sprouting in those meadows and hear the frogs of the ponds up in those springs.

Horse tracks were everywhere in the spring-mud around the main pond, along with tracks of every other animal, all come to get snow-melt drinking water. I followed the horse tracks to behind the Barbería, almost to the door of Abundancia and Bill MacAllister.

Tying Blue to a stout Ponderosa with a long mecate, I moved off behind some trees to have my lunch and drink a tea. Blue's smell in the neighborhood would bring a stallion to drive him off, if he wasn't Sarco, or if he was, the two geldings would parley and scream and stamp until they found a way to be together in the same space. But for sure, if those horses were there like Earnest said, they'd show up to find out what the hell Blue, who because he was gelded late and still smelled like a stud, thought he was doing by invading their *district*.

And it worked.

Almost too well.

Maybe excited by the life of Riley these city horses were leading, acting out their roles as mustangs in Sarco's stage play of freedom up in the wild canyons, Blue tried to join the swirling mob who descended on him, led of course by none other than a much transformed, burr-encrusted, dread-maned, wild, fierce and definitely not lame Ojo Sarco.

After jumping out of his container with the rich folk, and fleeing his *Bubblehead* designation, Ojo Sarco somehow managed to tiptoe straight through the city unseen, negotiating lawns, walls, on-ramps and off-ramps, and highway traffic, to miraculously land himself square back up in the mountain canyon he remembered, where we'd ridden with horseless Bill MacAllister. From his new forest hideaway, with great spring grass, plenty of water, and no boss, Sarco began his new life by raiding ranches and homes, running off their mares. Though long since relieved of his gonads, he had a precise plan of living his new life *acting* as a herd stallion, a plan, which, with his eight stolen mares, he pulled off an admirable facsimile. Though he couldn't actually breed any mares, being a tremendous actor, he knew perfectly well how to act out the part!

His owners never did find him, and with no leads, finally gave up looking. A lot of theories abounded, not the least of which was that I'd stolen him and had him hidden off somewhere. But I knew Sarco had been planning something all along. By feigning his various lamenesses, he managed to get himself sent around to see the surrounding world, scouting places where he might make a run for it, then when he finally found one that suited his fancy, he busted out, jumping his pen, and took up a life of freebooting, open grazing and a harem of multi-cultural girls, consisting of three Arabian-Banker pony crosses, Ernest's old-time Appaloosa, a lady donkey, a Pasofino, a Quarter horse filly, and an old red mare. He had it made; he'd done it!

But now winter was coming again. He'd have to move to better winter grazing 'cause the mountains would fill with deep snow. The only direction for them to head led through overly-populated areas before he could have found his way to the great grass, south and east towards the plains.

Well, he never did move his herd, and like run-away teenagers, his mares all got tired of the decreasing food and another cold winter, and after a year of having "run away with the circus," one by one and three by two, they all meandered back home to the delight of their original people.

All except Sarco that is. The ownerless, old red mare was the only one who stayed by him and she died under the snow that following winter.

One morning that January, Bundy woke Bill to see Sarco standing skinny and knee deep in the snow, nose to nose with their mare. Bill let him into the corral, fed him, drove out and called me. I told him that the horse had been long since given up for lost or dead, and since Bill had liked him so much and felt so lost without a good horse that he should consider himself found and chosen by Sarco himself to be his person.

Over the years someone told one of the Owners he could have sworn he'd seen a man in his mid-eighties climbing up Glorieta Baldy in the summer on top of Ojo Sarco. Bill and Sarco were so gloriously beautiful and happy and just right together and so much time had passed, and since the original lady Owner had divorced her Owner husband and gathered up her own *herd* and gone back to Texas, nobody ever said a word.

Ojo Sarco was a really big thinker. He'd had a plan. These old Barbs could reason and navigate, and that horse could really act, he never was lame and never got lame. Bill loved him and rode him till the day he died. By then everybody knew what had happened, but they were so perfect together and so impossible not to admire, nobody could say a word against it.

Chapter 14

Parade Permits, Street Sweepers, Parasitic Traders, and Yes, Ladies and Gentlemen, that Horse Poop is Historically Correct

In the natural world, every tree, every plant, every mammal, fish, and reptile has its traditional internal and external parasite.

When Blue Medicine, Amarillento, Zajlani, Cicatriz, Moehna, Zanic, Ostone, and over fifteen other old-time Barb Mesta horses began filling up our corrals, our land, and our lives, some clever, shystery people began to frequent our camp as well, just like parasites.

Like most parasitic species, they were pretty innocuous at the onset, and even interesting, their presence just snuck up on you. It would take me a while to catch on to what they were really up to. Blue on the other hand recognized right away what was staring at him from the top rung of his corral: entrepreneurial traders of historical artifacts. That horse wouldn't go near any of them.

Often disguised as *historians*, many of these operators supplied multi-million dollar operations and *art galleries* with collections of *artifacts*, which in turn were sold to wealthy collectors; artifacts whose authentication was often established in *authoritative* books written by these very traders themselves. Books which specialized in making relics of ancient Pueblo Natives: pottery, sacred fetishes, offerings, masks, or even more recent *material culture*, like 19th century cowboy gear, or Plains Indians beaded ration card holders, collections of old Indian or settler tools they peddled, into expensive *collectible art*. By detailing the origins of all these *collector* items, and rating the same artifacts, they sold according to their scarcity, they manufactured a market of investment for these *rarities* among their wealthy clients. Some of these *traders* were able to create a great lucrative trade in high-end New York, London, Paris, and Santa Fe *art* auctions where *one of a kind*, recently surfaced artifacts sold at very high prices to wealthy collectors, but which were very often just adroit forgeries of *old looking stuff*, orchestrated unseen in personal sweatshops by these traders themselves, authenticated in the books the peddlers wrote. Even the dealers and galleries that didn't knowingly deal in such counterfeits, pretty much left the same bad chemical taste in your mouth every time you had to deal with one. No matter how you cut it, they all sold dead people's stuff to barely alive rich people for a huge profit.

These dealers could appear in many guises and in all echelons, but all of them made a living selling to people who probably deep down really needed the beauty, fascination, wildness, and reality of a romanticized past they could have never survived in order to feel alive. By having these *collectibles* dried and stuffed on their walls and inside glass exhibitor's cases, the collector could rationalize this desire for the past as an *investment* whose resale value would later increase, as guaranteed by the dealers, when they got bored or changed décor, meanwhile basking in the cultural integrity of peoples made extinct by their own lack of the same.

To people like me, who still used half the things these collectors framed and auctioned, it seemed that these collectors resembled lap dogs from the city, who when let loose during their owner's vacation in the West, coming upon a dead Elk carcass out on the range, would frenetically roll around in the putrid stench to get the *real wild smell* all over them to compensate for their big-city little-dog emptiness. These collectors, in just the same way, wanted to roll around in all the beautiful cultural stuff of people long dead, just like their dogs. Making sure the "real Indians", and the "way things were" were for sure "extinct;" maybe they felt powerful for having a *piece* of that old life close, but at arms distance, without having to actually deal with a live Indian, or a real rancher, or a live Elk. Kind of like taking a scalp and hanging it on the wall: a trophy they imagined the monied power of their privileged situation had somehow taken. I always wondered if the everyday lives these collectors actually led in their boring clothes, computers, iPhones, and money markets would someday be collectable and hang on the walls of other empty people in the future? Oh well. None of this should have affected us, and didn't until some of them decided we should be for sale!

For the dealers that started coming around us, the life I lived and the old-time way I lived it was assumed to be a theatrical act. I was just an actor modelling sellable artifacts from a bygone age in the form of my silver jewelry, clothing, and tools. Blue Medicine himself was just a living artifact from the past! Our whole lifestyle was just an artifact to them. It only remained for them to find a way to market us.

Unable to comprehend, that to us, our lives were our lives, they were real, not some reenactment, or rehearsal of history. To them we were a trunk-show choreographed to sell the Old West, after which we'd go home to our drywall condo. The stuff we made, the way we lived and the things we did meant a lot to us, all of it functioned, and we loved it, none of it was for sale. But one trader figured all that out and found a way to even use that to his advantage.

A friendly, smooth-talking, lame-dog kind of man, this *historian*/trader *limped* his way up into our camp one evening, ostensibly to take a look at my so-called *period* horses, but whose real agenda was to talk me into leading a re-enacted horse ride of historical significance that he was putting together.

Somehow he knew a lot about me and Blue and where we rode and how we went about our lives, and I knew nothing at all about him. He said because I had the *right* historical period horses with the *right* historical look, and I knew the historical territory through which his *riders* had to pass, better than anyone else alive, I would be a perfect fit to lead his *period* riders on a short, day ride through the mountains from Pecos, NM to the Santa Fe Plaza, following an almost forgotten spur of the last bit of the Santa Fe Trail.

When Blue didn't like a person or what they were pushing, he was always right. Blue didn't like this guy. I didn't listen. Blue was right, again.

Assessing everyone and every situation according to how they could be made to feel indispensable and important, in order to be economically exploited by him, unbeknownst to me at the time, this dealer had invisibly researched my existence and had sized me up as a very interesting, honorable, historically knowledgeable fool whose good nature could be easily manipulated. By cleverly appearing to care about some of the things I loved: like the people and history of New Mexico, and the magic of my horses etc., The Trader labored to emotionally nudge me into position as a pliable prop in a bigger scheme he was concocting.

One of the scams by which this dealer survived was by organizing historical horse treks sponsored by big-money collector interests: galleries, museums, and historical societies, to demonstrate and iron out historical questions and doubts about *old trade routes* and trails, for which this trader could always produce a plethora of *artifacts* for sale once their validity had been established, or at least made more plausible.

In my case, this same Parasitic Trader had already organized a group of *riders* who were an already established club of mostly white men and women from Colorado and Wyoming, whose hobby had been to dress up in period clothing of the 1840's and in little twenty mile stretches, each weekend, relive and re-enact the lives of *American* traders and immigrant business families who plied their *trade* back and forth between the pre-1840's boundaries of the USA (the Mississippi river), and the northern capital of New Spain (Santa Fe, New Mexico), in which, when it was still owned by Spain and then later by the country of Mexico, Americans were considered foreigners and were required to have a passport and a local citizen as a guide.

A friendly good-talker, this man easily gained the interest of magazines, television, newspapers, etc., to report on his group as it followed the Old Santa Fe Trail on horseback. Dragging mules or horses packed with modern facsimiles of old goods and supplies and camping equipment, these re-enactors rode and camped—where it was still feasible—the many routes that ran from the point of entry to New Spain at Independence, Missouri overland the nine hundred miles to the *Barbería* (the Barbershop—what the old official immigration-stop was called), just outside Santa Fe, a location that is now privately owned, but still called La Barbería.

While this had been *re-enacted* several times before with wagons and such, this time he intended that I should guide this same group of riders on the very last day of their trek to re-enact a passage over a forgotten *back route*, an old alternate shortcut that spurred off from the last bit of the normal trail that carried the old-time wagon-trade running between Santa Fe and the USA. This rugged shortcut was never feasible for wheeled vehicles, but had been reputedly employed by horse and mule caravanners in competition with the wagon-trade. Pueblo Natives on foot, of course had established this route thousands of years past. It had been in general use until the late nineteenth century when its whereabouts were lost to general knowledge. If I agreed to it, I would guide them just that last particular thirty-mile stretch through the rough mountains into Santa Fe.

Because of my friendship with Mr. MacAllister and his trails, I'd stumbled upon that beautiful forgotten route by accident earlier in the year. When I found it, though incredibly overgrown, it was miraculously still in evidence for its ancient reliance on mountain sheep trails. There were parts of it that were very tricky, with some pretty steep going. Until then, nobody alive knew exactly how those sections of the trail had been originally traversed. When I first heard about this trail, people called it *La Vereda de Ladrones*: the Path of Bandits and it was known only by legend. I never told anyone I'd found it.

How this Mr. Trader, historian, ride-organizer knew I'd discovered it, he would never divulge, but he wanted not only myself, in my normal togs and tack, to take his team of *historically correct* trader re-enactors through that route, but he wanted to rent my horses too. Having done his research, he knew that the Barbs I raised were the horses that had been the only horses in use in that era and probably the only ones that could take the rugged terrain. Though I'm sure in those times traders no doubt relied more on burros and mules.

After luring me to his house/trading post only a mile from our camp, he further courted my participation by producing an old-looking, well-made, hammered-silver concho belt, and said it was mine if I accepted the job. Though passing it off as an *old* Navajo belt, I could see it was modern, but well made, an old fake made by one of his *forgers*, but it was great. Then he gave me my choice of one in a row of seven Mexican saddle trees from the 1830's with Santa Fe slot cantles. A home-cooked breakfast on the Santa Fe Plaza, of buffalo steaks, eggs, oven bread, and more all cooked on an open fire at the end of the trail was also promised, upon arrival, if I'd lead them over the high altitude shortcut of this last thirty miles or so of that very long trek from Missouri, to get them through the wild-forest-mountains and valleys into Santa Fe, to land at the Governor's Palace on the Plaza.

Scheduled for the end of June, this ride would be gorgeous and pleasantly cool up in those high altitudes, but not a little dicey for the ever present possibility of lightning strikes accompanying those high-mountain afternoon thunderstorms that had blown more than one high-trail-rider to bits when caught up on one of those ridges during a storm.

The chance of constantly discovering new little natural marvels, the clear air, and soul-healing beauty made me love summertime distance riding, but the thought of being compensated for such riding on top of it helped rationalize my joy, because then I wouldn't be just philandering around in the hills when I should have been earning a living for the family. If I had to, the concho belt he showed me could've been easily sold for a couple thousand dollars.

So I said yes, I'd do it.

Blue was disgusted. He mooned me for a week and wouldn't talk. But the good thing about him was that even though we could violently disagree, unless it involved a gas well or a yellow painted line, once we were already stuck in the stew, he generally never balked away from what we had in front of us. A good horse.

We were supposed to make the passage starting mid-morning, arriving at La Barbería by evening, camp the night, and start into town just after dawn the next day, to arrive on the Plaza mid-morning for our Big Celebration Breakfast. Sounded alright to me, I love breakfast. By this *shortcut* there were no flat places at all like where the normal Santa Fe Trail had been accustomed to run, just a rocky, slim trail at best that ran square up a mountain valley, straight up over a higher ridge, straight down into another narrow valley and right straight up, over and around the side of another really steep mountain, then down, down, down straight into the *Barbería*, not far from Bill and Bundy's headwater hideaway and Sarco's old herd rendezvous. From there it would be easy going, but then one would have to contend with the irritating issue of getting this crew trailing around mansion after mansion till we would meet up with the city's officially designated last mile of the modern paved road of the Old Santa Fe Trail, and from there ride down another mile into the Plaza, where the *news party* was supposed to begin. Considering all of this, I had a few conditions that had to be met before I would agree to this trader's proposal.

"First," I said "I'll agree to lead these people while we're out in the mountains, but you will have to take over once I get them to the edge of Metropolitan Santa Fe." He said that was all just as he would have wanted it. He actually did say that.

"Then," I said, "I will head up this group if you can vouch-safe that there will be no alcohol drinking while we are up in the hills."

"You're right, that wouldn't do," he said.

Then I said, "I'll lead the ride, but you must be responsible for making certain, beforehand, that all your riders have horses strong enough for scurrying up and down mountain trails. I won't rent you any of mine because I don't know what kind of riders your people are." Then I said, "For safety's sake, I want to make sure you've inspected their equipment for soundness and make certain everyone has some water, a little food in their bags, a blanket or a coat for a high-altitude ride, and fire-strike kit in case we are forced to camp." That was just fine with him, he said.

Then I said, "For the duration of the ride through the mountains between where we embark here in the mountains, to the edge of the paved roads of Santa Fe, you will have to have the people's solemn word that they will follow my lead and do as I say, and stay together as a group with me, and not break off into little groups and go wandering off at the whim of some individual who may not know the terrain and get himself lost." I wanted to avoid having to go chasing after disorientated folks.

None of these things would be a problem to ensure, he said.

Ironically, the historical cut off from the main Santa Fe Trail was located in our very camp, right in Juniper's corral! But the reenactment of this ride, over this old spur of the Santa Fe Trail, was set to leave from the Trader's store a mile from us. When the day arrived I didn't trailer, but just saddled and packed my *alforjas* and simply rode over on Old Blue into the crowd of horses and people gathering under that sweet smelling June's morning sky, over at the Dealer's house.

But when we rode into the milling crowd, except for four Quarter horses and one little Arabian, their horses were of a wide array of either worn out, wormey, malnourished, out of shape, or much too old. By my agreement, Blue and I should have resigned on the spot, and returned straight home right then and there just for this breach of agreement alone. Three quarters of the horses had been *rented* just for the *event*, from a dude ranch trail-string on their last season of service, all scheduled to be slaughtered (when that was still legal), and would possibly have arrived on the flat, but unlikely to have survived the strain of this particular type of mountain riding.

Their equipment was even worse. All of it had seen better days, for they were props out of gallery exhibits and some, no doubt, had probably been made in the historical *period* in question. The saddles and cinches, bridles and mecates, because they were legitimately *period* and over one hundred and forty years old were actually, of course, all worn out and needed renewing, at least with new rigging and rings, to be safe from coming apart and dropping a rider up on the steep mountain sides or cutting into the horse's withers. I loved riding in beautiful, old gear, but they always had to be periodically renewed and made sound. And then, because the saddles were from an earlier era, they would fit only horses like mine. The horses they had rented were modern horses, so the saddles didn't even fit the horses' projecting withers, which would be murder on these poor horses in the steeper climbs! But nobody seemed to know the difference and took great exception to being questioned or having it explained to them. All these people knew was they had to *look the part* for the media photos. They were historically correct looking, but historically unsafe! Without having to put the sweat and time into re-making something old into gear that still functioned as well today as it did then, they were risking a lot of accidents and damaged animals.

Blue and I rode from horse to horse reviewing the fitness of the *troops* till we located the organizer, himself looking very *period*, whose young Quarter horse looked healthy and capable, who sported *period* gear that actually fit, but still had a few weak spots too.

"Mister, with all due respect, I really don't mean to wantonly criticize, but most of these horses are too frail to do the mountains we have to ride through, plus a lot of the people's gear is liable to fail right in the bush, when they'll need it the most. Nobody's carrying water or warmer clothing, if we meet a high altitude hailstorm. And where's the food if people get stranded? And where, if I may ask, is your emergency kit, your first aid stuff?" I asked in as much a relaxed tone as I could manage.

"I thought you were a medicine man, Martín, you can take care of everything that happens right?" this fellow snidely replied. "Plus, everything they might need is on that pack horse over there." Pointing to a sparsely packed, black, grade gelding pulled along by a very tall, bearded, *period* fellow, who actually did look like he might know what he was doing, riding a red Quarter horse with a homemade *period* looking saddle that did fit.

"That's no good," I said, "what happens if some of these unruly riders lose their way and get separated, and all the gear is on that horse? Every individual should carry a blanket, water, fire-making supplies, and some modicum of food."

"What are you, a cavalry sergeant?" smirking, the organizer asked. "Don't worry; it'll be a good adventure; it's just a day ride."

What every male *did* have was a brace of flint-sparking pommel pistols over his saddle horn, a heavy, black-powder long rifle across his lap, a powder horn, shot-bag and belts bristling with a pretty impressive array of hand forged period

The Wild Rose

knives, one at the back, a machete in the saddle sheath, a neck
knife, and a tomahawk. But, no water, no blanket, no food. Oh
well, I prayed we didn't get stuck under a lightning storm at ten
thousand feet with over twenty guys carrying that much heavy
iron and steel, plowing over the very tops of ridges: the lightning
hitting that many guys, with that much lighting-attracting iron
and that much powder! It would blow every person and horse
to bits. They were definitely not New Mexicans!

There were about eight women riders, and all but one of
them were more minorly arsenaled with one gun each, and
equal amount of cutting implements. Though beautifully
dressed in ruched-up silk skirts and blouses, nothing was
strong enough for busting through mountainside brush! Then
the most unpardonable sin was that every man and woman
sported a really ugly, floppy, felt hat! The old-time people had
wonderful hats. I love good hats, but I hate cheap, floppy, felt
hats. One unarmed woman, not wearing a bad hat, had her
own good horse, wore silk and was riding in a side-saddle.
She made the whole ride smiling, and got to the Plaza without
so much as a squeak.

By now the organizer could see I had my doubts, and after
leading his horse to where Blue, with me in my saddle, were
standing waiting to decide whether to stay or leave. "Look
Martín," he said, "I'll take full responsibility for anything that
happens, you won't be implicated, it'll be on my back." I was
more worried what these people might need to survive the
historical inaccuracy of their movie-derived looks than who
would be held liable if they failed.

And just as I was weighing their fate and whether or not to continue, seeing as not even one of my conditions had been met, the organizer mounted his horse and lifted one of his *period* carbines and let off a shot, and called the group to order. Just like a movie!

He did have a little panache, in a way. Well, I surmised at least most of the guns probably worked, for whatever that was worth!

"Ladies and gentlemen, it's time for us to get on the trail, next stop Santa Fe, New Mexico." And they all started yelling.

While the Parasitic Trader was delivering his pep talk, a friend of mine, a Spanish speaking, Northern New Mexican named Randy, decked out in buckskins to the teeth, rode up beside me on his dark Arabian, along with a smiling, teenage, white kid wearing old-time suspenders and riding a sparky rattail Appaloosa. "How did you get conned into this?" he laughed, slapping me on the shoulders. "I'm sure glad you're the one leading the way, I have to say," Randy burbled out. "This fellow here is Josh, and he loves your horse," and we shook hands with the boy.

By then the Trader was yelling: "This is Martín. He'll be leading you through the hills."

I was still with one foot out the door, thinking I might just get them over the worst of it and come back home, but like I did at the beginning of anything I did, I began praying out loud, this time in various Native tongues, per my custom, to ask permission of all the Lord and Lady Gods of all these mountains, valleys and streams, asking plant and animal

Gods for their help to pass through their land. When I was almost done blessing, one short, well-dressed, mustachioed fellow with a big wide-brimmed hat that made him look like a portobello mushroom astride a pony bellowed from under his hat: "What the hell is all that racket, talk American you bastard, we don't want no prairie-nigger talk around here."

"Well, hello Sir," I retorted. "Nice to meet you too, but the truth is I *am* talking American, and 'around here' as you put it, these are some of the languages we use when we talk to the Divine through whose territory we're intending to invade. Look here, you're probably the grandkid of some immigrant turnip-farmer from another country whose people, once they got in the United States, were rudely forced to belch in English, but English isn't actually an American language. English is from England! Remember!? Learn some manners, Sir. I'm actually praying we all have a good ride, including you! If you'd rather, I can pray you don't fall off your unhappy horse in English, if it makes your royal highness feel any better?"

Which I did, but it didn't make him feel any better. On the other hand, the jug he was swigging from over the shoulder, (like he saw in the movies), apparently did.

Not even one of my qualifications had been respected: they were drinking, their equipment was dangerously in disrepair, their horses sad and frail, and with no food, water, or useful clothing I thought I should just leave the abusive, ungrateful, and racist to their deserved fate and ride home. But the capable, good-hearted, thirteen-year-old, freckle-faced boy on his little Appaloosa, and Randy, seeing my dilemma, both whacked me on the back and sweet-talked me into doing it anyway.

Blue cocked his head, looking back at me, rolled the one eyeball I could see and quoting the Mongolian national credo, said inside my blood: *"Avil buqui, kivel bueï.* If you're afraid, don't do it. If you're going to do it, don't be afraid. Come on, let's get going." He was smiling when he said it, and he was always right. So we went.

The aroma of the dew-soaked creekside air as we stretched out single file and pushed up the first canyon was bolstered by the heady smells of thousands of medicinal plants growing in thick stands, whose stems wounded by the horses passing hooves sent the olfactory mix of their mystic brew ripping up into the air. These powerful rotations of fragrances cut through the wounded thoughts grinding in my craw making a pungent salve to calm my pride.

Josh and Randy understood the situation and obeyed my every thought; Josh had all the fun of running back to the rear of the column keeping track of and counting up the riders then riding back to me out in front while I led the rest single file up the hills, to report on the gossip and state of horse and people stamina and the condition of their *gear*. Randy, I sent ahead to scout on the condition of certain of the forks and switch-backs I was worried about, for the overgrowth was thick from a season of very good rain, and sudden mud slides and downed trees were not uncommon, for that reason, and the fact that only he and I had brought little foldable saws and shovels with which to cut branches and dig if we had to. These two people made the morning ride a joy.

It turned out that the melodrama of a mutiny was a planned event in almost every one of these people's *Santa Fe Trail* rides and was now already getting organized, additionally fueled by the Mushroom Man's resentment and increasing drunkenness. These people had seen too many movies and had lived too few of their years in a life away from the desk. By intentionally searching for any excuse for a showdown, they felt it was part of the drama they were *re-enacting*. But this trail was no place to screw around on.

Knowing that some rough trail was coming up ahead, and the group would have to stay close to get through to the final approach together in one piece, in order to camp at the Barbería by evening, I began to think that maybe I'd been too hard on the Mushroom Man, and maybe I should apologize. Leaving Randy at the head of our column I ran with Blue back to the rear, to find and fix up any hard feelings with the Mushroom Man. But in all the column, he and seven others were already missing.

The ladies informed me that these *mutineers* had enough of the gradual motion of my caravan and looking for more action decided to take a shortcut that one of them claimed to have found on a map, towards which they had all flown on their own, in order to get ahead of us. Maybe this was not so bad after all, as no doubt we'd have to run into them somewhere up ahead and like the despondent sour horses they rode, maybe they could work off some of their grudge and take the edge of their alcohol.

To garner some energy just before the big-high-ridge push that was coming up, where we would lose the relaxing stream we'd been cruising alongside of, I asked everyone to dismount, have some food, rehydrate and let their horses recharge and graze lightly on the beautiful herbs and high mountain grasses.

Unfortunately, both the organizer and guy with the pack horse carrying their supposed provisions had all ended up with the Mushroom Man's contingent! I couldn't believe the predictability of the choreographed disaster of these people's need to fake adventure.

To counter this I knelt down and made a gallon of tea by boiling some stream water and handed out twenty mouthfuls of dried meat and chokecherries, supplying everyone with a little something from my own saddle bags, 'cause nobody else had brought a thing!

Blue was having a nice roll in the grass and I was taking a five-minute nap, when Josh woke me, in a rush to tell me ten more riders, thinking I was loafing, had gone on ahead to find the other guys!

Saddling in a flash, I got the remainder of the people and horses squared up and moving, all the time noticing how some magnificent cloud banks were building high-up, off to the northwest, and the thuds of their approaching thunder were already echoing up and down that high canyon we had yet to pass.

I knew we had to get ourselves in and out of the next arroyo, through which we would soon have to cross by this route, and the next one after that as well before the storm, or we all stood a chance of either being swept away in a flash flood, or isolated from our goal till tomorrow, as we would have to wait on high ground in between the two until the water level had dropped, both behind us and in front.

Because I'd known all along that at this point I would have to really push these people to get them up and over the ridge, and past the arroyos in question, I initially had stopped to rest their poor, tired horses to have enough energy to do it. But now with the prospect of rain, we couldn't wait. For when the promised rains finally let loose and the subsequent flash floods they caused were behind us, we still had one more relatively difficult rocky climb in front of us that would be harsh and exhausting if we had to do it over wet boulders in a storm, which would make the rocks all slippery and the lightening a tremendous hazard for unfit horses. Since most of the heavily armed guys with all their artillery had mutinied, it was a little less tense and weird a situation in my group.

Just then Josh and Randy came running back up from where I'd sent them scouting to check on the others who had supposedly jumped ahead of us, but who had never reappeared, to report that the first eight riders and their ten new additions had tried to climb a really steep mountain off to the side to get to the *goal* quicker. But misjudging the route, because even though by mileage on the map their *route* made this one mountain the only thing seeming to stand in their way to the

Barbería, by their drunken judgement they failed to notice the fact that this mountain was way too steep to casually scale, which is why nobody but Elk or mountain climbers had even tried. So to reconnoiter, these well-armed, historically correct, *period*, drunken re-enactors had all dismounted at the base of this mountain to have a confab and yet another drink! Three of them then tried to ride up the incline, but only one made it to the top, at which point everybody's horse broke loose and ran up to the mountain top scared to be away from their old trail buddies. This left the entire mutinous crew afoot in the ravine, because the two horses that didn't make it up were stuck in the middle of the climb having been lamed on the rocks in the process!

While they were busy doing that, I led my group up to the top of *our* hill in the lightning and rain and rapidly down the other precarious side, which was already very slippery and scary in the wet, but I succeeded in bringing my crew safely into the Barbería where the camp people were just barely setting up.

Reading my mind, Blue turned and gave me that look. "What? No way! You're not thinking of going and saving those hateful ingrates, those drunks, and lead them back here to the camp? In a lightning rainstorm?! No way! Don't be an idiot. Oh no, don't tell me we're actually going to help those guys. Remember what they called us…!" And he actually started stamping the earth in contempt.

With Randy and Josh, I rode back up and over to the *other* mountain to the south, climbed it in the rain from *our* side, and when we achieved the top, we found these mutineer's horses standing in a huddle. I asked Randy and Josh to gather two horses each from all those up there and ferry them back down the hill, the way we had come up, back down to the camp at the Barbería, knowing that all the other loose horses would automatically follow right behind, unprompted, including that funny, old pack-horse who miraculously still had his pack.

The one *rider* who'd actually made it to the top was prostrate and so raving drunk he couldn't function, so I left him there to deal with later, while Blue and I, in the storm, rode down the side the mutineers couldn't climb. It really was terrible and treacherous: when I got to the bottom, I hauled each of these well-armed, inebriated guys, one by one, up the mountain by forcing them to stand behind Blue, and with their hands twisted and twined into Blue's stout red tail, stumble and stagger their way up the hill. One by one, fourteen men in all, Blue dragged them up that two thousand feet of steep, trailless mountainside, in the sunset, over wet boulders, and in the lightning. Fourteen times down, fourteen times back up to the top of what none of them could seem to manage alone. Then, once they were all on top of the mountain, one at a time I rode double with a drunk seated behind the cantle, down the opposite side, then going back up and down fifteen times, like a mine-donkey in a coal shaft, until every single *rider* was in the Barbería. Except for one lost, angry person who'd wandered off too drunk at the very beginning of the ride, before the floods, and who having gotten to a highway on foot and hitchhiked was found the next day back where we started, still drinking, I got every rider into camp as promised! A Very Historical Ride!

That night at the camp everyone was tired. Though irritated that one horse had been unnecessarily shot and killed by the mutineers, and the fact that no one except my family and Randy and Josh, who stayed at our fire, would talk to me, we tried not to laugh too much about the craziness of the day. The food at our fire tasted better than God. To Blue, on the other hand, it was all in a day's work, and drinking from the trough, grazing nearby, he was ready for tomorrow's next episode of "I told you so."

The next morning, after combing out our horses, and dressing up in our *period* outfits (I just dressed like I always dressed, which was considered *period*), the organizer, the Trader, with not even one hint of apology, or good going, or thanks for saving our lives in the lightning, with no mention at all about the circus of the day previous, came to find me, brandishing a pair of rather wicked-looking, hand-forged Spanish spurs with long shanks, big star-like rowels and noisy jingle-bobs. With these dangling from his left hand, he said to me:

"I need you to put these on if you're planning to ride with the boys to the Plaza. You can keep them as part of our deal if you do."

"I don't actually use spurs," holding up my antler quirt studded with brass tacks and silver. "I ride with this instead."

"That's nice, but you have to wear these, so when they photograph us on the Plaza you'll look like we need you to."

Blue looked at me standing beside him, "Go ahead, wear 'em, they'll make a nice rhythm while I trot; you sing and I'll dance."

So I strapped them on my boots and adjusted them so they rang loud at every little jostle. I'd had some experience with spurs, but one rode differently with spurs on your heels than I normally did with my quirt riding, which relied on my toes. But the main issue was I had forgotten that for the sake of being *period*, my rear saddle girth was a fancy braided one, made from horse-mane hair, which was plenty beautiful, but a bit of a trap for spurs if they got caught up in one of the strands.

Since my part of the job was technically finished, and supposedly there was to be a big, open-fire cooked breakfast on the Plaza, and there would be no more of my chasing these melodramatic drinkers and actors around, I thought I'd go down with them the three or four remaining flat miles into town, eat a good breakfast then come back here, load up old Blue with my contingency and drive back to our own mountains.

But we couldn't move most of the riders from the day before. They were too beat up, bone-sore, and hungover to ride, except for one. The lady's dresses were all shredded and ruined, so the riders we rode into town with were mostly well-rested newcomers dressed up for the part, who just showed up to swell the ranks! The organizer, the pack horse and his tall driver, Josh, Randy and two of the ladies who both had new cool outfits, and myself were actually the only riders of the original thirty left from yesterday's strange adventure to ride into town!

Blue had ferried all those people up and down that big mountain (what not one of them could even manage once), making more than thirty journeys, and he was sparky and all prancing and ready to go. I had my charcoal just in case we hit a rash of yellow lines!

The ride should have been as simple as it was for those that stayed close to Blue and I out in the hills. For people used to riding like that all the time, this was just going to town to do a little business or pick up supplies, it was not a ride, just going to town. But I always remembered what Admiral Byrd so accurately stated, something to the effect that a "sure recipe for extravagant adventure is bad planning!"

Once arrayed in our buckskin jackets, decked out and ready to ride, the jingle bobs of our spurs tinkling, the ever present arsenal, even on these new characters, bumping alongside us, with Old Blue prancing away, we avoided the mansions and travelled a couple of easy miles on a dirt road until we met the official edge of town. And on the pavement of *upper* Old Santa Fe Trail, that ran into the city proper before we began trotting our way down to the Plaza, there waiting for us were:

Two gigantic street sweeper trucks!

Yes indeed.

When they saw us coming, these two gigantic street sweeping trucks switched on their rumbling motors just as we trotted by and taking up the entire road they followed right behind us in roaring tandem. Then, two city cop cars entered in front of us, their lights flashing to clear the road.

Because horses and riders were illegal on public thoroughfares in the city limits, the New Mexico Museum sponsoring this *ride* had obtained a *parade permit* for us. This parade permit required that even a single rider and horse had to have a *poop scooper* behind them everywhere they went, and more than two horses required a big-old street sweeper with its big rotary brushes, and more than ten horses required the full regatta of two or three or more! This was a comical surprise for me because as a child, flocks of sheep and herds of cows, shepherded by men and women on horses, were a common sight moving along right through town as they drove their flocks and herds from spring pastures to summer grazing up into the Sangres.

Now the racket of two street sweepers groaning and rumbling behind us, never mind the flying gravel and dust they spit out, was bad enough and definitely removed any semblance of the romantic effect this entrance of *period* riders was intended to conjure, but the sweepers behind and the cops rolling in front with their flashing lights and intermittent siren blasts at intersections would have made most horses more than a little edgy.

Most of the horses had been so out of shape when they started that they were too tired to be crazy and needed a rest before they could act up. But Blue! Well Blue, like he always did after extreme exertion, was increasingly, day by day even more and more charged up, so he pranced and we jingled the whole darned way.

When we finally got past the Capital Buildings, over the river and up to the Plaza, the organizer, in the moment he'd been waiting for, had all the riders fire off their arsenal of shotless black powder rounds into the air while they kind of *attacked* the Plaza and tried to run dramatically around the kiosk on the pavement around Plaza Square, for a picturesque entrance. They had choreographed it for all of us to run clockwise once completely around together, then parading slowly around the second time, holding their carbines up in the air and then coming to a halt, stand mounted right in front of the Governor's Palace, where this group was to be greeted by the museum director and given a breakfast, which I was really looking forward to because I'd forgone my camp breakfast to have room for the promised celebratory repast being prepared for us here at our destination.

When the guns were done shooting, and the noisy crowds around the Plaza had pressed and gathered to see the action, the organizer and his troop of mountain men began their tired parade around the Plaza intending to show off a bit. The poor, exhausted pack-horse who'd been off on the eternal drunken detour the day before could barely manage to wearily galumph along, but when I put my spurs lightly to Blue, we really hit it.

A movie crew was standing off to the side. They'd been filming a modern western on the Plaza, for which they agreed to politely hold off until we were done with our *entrance*. Blue and I started slipping around the square corners, cantering much faster than the rest, sailing past all the other mountain men and ladies on their second slow-parading-go, and when they slowed to pull up in front of the veranda in front of the old Spanish Governor's Palace as planned, old Blue and I were not with them.

No, Blue could not be slowed down and so I decided we'd just continue circling the Plaza alone a third time at this speed. Now Blue, who was usually a very good listener, had for some reason, instead of slowing down, decided to increase his speed and uncharacteristically refused to obey any of my suggestions. This was not his doing, but on account of the fact that I, not being used to six inch long, period, Spanish spurs, had managed to get the spur rowels on both sides equally tangled in the braids of the fancy rear cinch and which were now locked into the cinch and goading old Blue into action. For the life of me I couldn't seem to pull those damned spurs out of the cinch! Both my heels were locked tight, and the rowels, were of course permanently and increasingly with every hop, jammed tighter into Blue's gut, sending a signal that only said: faster, harder, let's go... and man, go we did.

We were speeding around the corners of the Plaza at breakneck speed, the crowd was cheering thinking it was a special exhibition of mountain man horsemanship. Blue almost washing out, slipping out on the pavement as we rounded every paved corner at such a speed, after one complete circuit learned to leap and slide at the corners, fishtailing on purpose just to recover in time to do the same thing at the next corner. It was terrifying and I was utterly aghast. But both of us making the best of a bad situation, with my reins loose, I just waved my quirt victoriously in the air over my head while the crowd went wild, as if it were all planned and we weren't just heading to our doom, moving so damn fast to crash onto the slick pavement!

After circling the Plaza some fifteen times, just as if we did this every day before breakfast, by some miraculous divine intervention, my spur rowels, of their own accord, suddenly dropped out of the braided, horse-hair cinch just as we came around the last corner, at which point I aimed old Blue straight toward that pile of tired horse bottoms with disgusted riders looking my way, and for a full thirty five feet I reined Blue in hard to slide on all fours, to which he added a perfectly executed three hundred and sixty degree spin, bringing us into a twirl that landed us totally still, and standing facing squared up right in front of Tom Chavez, the Museum Director, who clapping and laughing emerged to meet us.

Lifting my hat, the crowd screamed and whistled, clapped and cheered and went crazy. I turned Blue around, who was definitely smiling, to face the crowd. A handsome elderly cowboy, came shuffling across the Plaza right up to us, in his black hat and grabbed Blue's bridle with one hand and my buckskinned arm with the other. "That was the most incredible riding I've ever seen in my entire life and let me tell you I've seen a lot of stunt riding, where in the world did you find this horse? That was just heart-warming, I thought guys like you were all gone."

Not having the heart to tell him it was all an accident, and I'd only intended to roll into first, not slide into a perfect, swirling, ice-skating standstill, it was still good to hear Richard Farnsworth's praise. It made up a lot for the lack of thanks from the day before and ever after.

Feeling betrayed and outdone, the rest of the riders were glum and full of hatred, except Randy and Josh who kept squinting their eyes and slapping my back, baring their teeth and howling until they had to look down shaking their heads, 'cause of course both of them knew full well I'd just gotten those infernal spurs locked underneath. But still, we'd done it and came sliding in to home plate without a scratch. Blue was smiling, but disgusted with the other riders.

Not a single cooking fire, or anything resembling breakfast was in evidence to my nose or that I could see anywhere. But after the director had presented the organizer to the crowd and made his smiling speech about the forgotten spur of the Santa Fe Trail that we'd *all* rode in on, he finally yelled, "come on ladies and gentlemen, your breakfast is waiting for you around back." Finally, thank God! I'd been hungry to begin with, but all that running around the Plaza made me so hungry I could've eaten the director himself, cooked or uncooked!

He had us dismount (per city rules) and walk our horses to the west side of the Palace and tie up at the old carriage rings on the bronze posts, still there for that purpose from the 19th century. I took off Blue's fancy silver bridle, hung it on my shoulder and tied him to a post with my mecate, and went inside to find out what was for breakfast, and eat it.

We were all shuffled off into a side office of the museum, just off the corridor with its very highly waxed floor. There, two friendly museum officials with aprons started handing us little folded white takeout bags, each containing an Egg McMuffin and a small styrofoam cup of bad black coffee.

That was it.

That was our promised home-cooked breakfast and all the thanks "me and my horse" ever got from the museum or the Parasitic Trader. So hungry that I swallowed it in one gulp, I tried hard to like it, because I'd lived in a lot of places where people had died for lack of food and I knew that all food, no matter how bad it was, had to be regarded as Holy. Food was life. But, it was after all, a big disappointment, albeit I was ecstatic to just be alive enough to be able to even eat it.

As a horseman, and knowing my animals, I always kept the policy during rides, to be on the safe side, to eat and take breaks right alongside the horse I was riding, so as to be there if anything broke loose. Tying our horses where I couldn't keep an eye on them in the unconscious tumult of a city had me feeling very nervous, so I had my ears tuned and perked for any horse trouble that might flare up outside.

While the *historical period*, attention-mongering riders were all lining up in the other room to be photographed, I thought I could hear the footsteps of a shod horse casually clip-clopping on a hard surface somewhere not too far off. Worried that one of our animals might have gotten loose, or been maliciously untied by some passing prankster, exiting the office, I went off to check. I arrived just in time to see

275

Blue's rear end, his tail and a dragging rope disappear out of the corridor and into the rear entrance of the main exhibition hall of the Governor's Palace Museum, too early yet to be opened to the public still waiting out at the Plaza. Having untied himself, I figured he'd come tiptoeing into the building, sauntering down the slippery waxed corridor looking for my whereabouts.

As a little kid I loved museum dioramas, and my mother took me to all the history museums within five hundred miles. In this very room stood one of my early favorites: a remake of the original Santa Fe Plaza during colonial times exhibited under a wide glass case that stood in the middle of the hall like a table.

As I entered the room, intending to grab Blue's lead rope and take him back out, before I could do so, he very quietly and gentlemanly spun away from me, instantly lifted his tail and pooped out a big, steaming, gooshy plop of mountain grass manure, causing it to land with great aim square on top of the horizontal plank of glass of the main diorama. Then just as quickly he stretched himself out to half the length of the room, and before I could stop him, proceeded to forcefully piss out all the waters of half the world's rivers in a hot, acrid, foamy, yellow flood that filled up half the floor. He would not be moved until he'd finished.

This was the one and only time that Blue was led to the extremity of actually pooping and peeing inside any house or building whatsoever. It all came from his extraordinary intolerance of promises made to manipulate, fake personalities, and social cowardice. His big dump was just Blue's commentary on the fakery of the whole damn thing that insulted the lives we led, which were real. Blue could act as well, but his reasons were always real. His indoor poop and piss kind of said it all.

People were so tied up with being important and photogenic that nobody noticed us walk out, and once I had him bridled with his silver, and I was mounted up on his back into my homemade silver-conchoed saddle, then by pure miracle, with no street sweepers or parade permits or spurs, we successfully dodged all the police. Leaving bad breakfasts and all parasitic traders behind, together Blue and I rode back a different route into the beautiful mountains behind the town, picking wild medicinal plants along the streams, until we arrived at our camp at the Barbería and from there trailered home hungry, but this time when we got there, we were well fed and welcome.

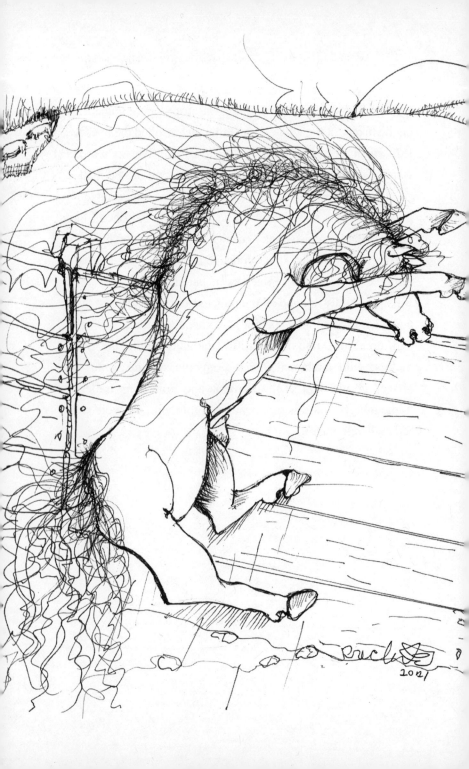

Chapter 15

Rewa

Before the *historical* ride, the Parasitic Trader had commissioned me as a silversmith to make a pair of *period* silver men's earrings, two heavy men's bracelets, and an old-time necklace, just like the ones I wore every day. But after that crazy ride, months had gone by and there was no sign of the promised concho belt, the precious old saddle tree, and he'd neglected to pick up and pay me for his commissioned jewelry, so I headed on over to the Trader's house/store to gather up what he owed me, on horseback of course.

But when I got there, the cupboard for me was bare. The beautiful *old* silver concho belt he'd shown me was nowhere in existence. Instead, the Trader handed me a badly approximated nickel *silver* remake of a Plains Indian woman's belt with screw rivets. I would later customize this belt and add a good silver buckle and a new row of silver trailers on the tab and it has served me well, both to remind me not to fall into so many traps, and even when you do, that beauty can always be conjured, if you just know how to work with what you got.

The old saddle tree, though, had been one of seven rare, wonderful trees someone had rescued and taken from old saddles made from whole tree crotches in the 1830's-1840's; but the special one I had picked out and he had promised to have re-covered with new rawhide had been *accidentally* sold to a *mountain man* for good money, supposedly while the Trader was out! So instead, he handed me a tremendously dilapidated looking tree, of very old but undetermined history, which the Trader no doubt knew was pretty much an unrepairable piece of old junk.

But the worst evidence of his dishonesty emerged when it came time for him to pay up for all the *old-time* jewelry I'd newly made per his request. He rejected the entire *ensemble* as not what he really wanted. What he had been hoping for, he said, was to get the ever-present silver bracelets off my own wrists, and the man earrings I daily wore, and my own old necklaces, as he put it, "warm off your body," as if I was a freshly killed enemy whose corpse he was robbing. This gave both me and Amarillento the shivers, to say the least, and though he was offering decent money for such an outrage, and I needed the cash, I had to refuse on the principle of self-respect.

So wearing the nickel belt, and tying up my poor, substandard saddle-tree behind his saddle, Amarillento and I prepared to set out again for home with the jewelry left unclaimed and unsold, when this Parasitic swindling Trader ran out of his historical adobe home/store and stopped us:

"Martín, I almost forgot. I saw what you and your little blue-eyed paint could do on that ride, and I need you to find me a *period* horse like that, a horse descended from the old Spanish Indian horses like all yours, but I need the strongest, most durable Barb you can find, the best one you've ever seen. I'll pay you five thousand dollars 'cause they're going to do a big magazine article on a ride I'm preparing to do solo from Chihuahua City in Mexico all the way up to Calgary and Banff in Canada. He's gotta be tough 'cause that's close to three thousand miles and straight up the Rockies. This will prove to everybody that Spanish speaking traders brought weapons, horse gear and horses to the Blackfeet, Stoneys, Assiniboine, and Cree much earlier through Santa Fe than historians presently surmise!"

What a manipulator! I knew he would sell the horse for fifteen thousand dollars afterwards, arrange to be compensated five thousand dollars by his sponsors for riding, and then write a guidebook on the collector value of certain artifacts that corresponded to those his ride and book would legitimize as collectible, which he would just happen to have come across during his travels, (but actually forged by his talented, minimum-wage sweat-shop of company-stored, drug-addicted forgers).

What audacity! The "hot off your body" thing alone was too sick and weird to begin with, but being swindled after saving so many lives in his fiasco of a ride with no thanks and then having the audacity to petition me to find him a real horse…!

Once home, I couldn't stop fuming about this raw treatment.

While I licked my wounds, confiding my contempt for the Parasitic Trader to Blue as I cleaned out his hooves. Blue always saner and more clever than I would ever get, spoke up in my heart:

"Why don't you just go get that one tough little horse with the long silver mane and tail for him out of Iowa? Maybe some good will come of it. As far as that saddle tree goes, don't be a droopy drawers, make the best of it. Strip off all the old rawhide and take a look at how it's really made. Then go make a new saddle out of it. I think it will fit me perfectly. Put silver on it. It can be all mine and we won't have to keep using my sister's saddle.

"Then as far as all that jewelry is concerned the answer is simple."

"Is it? What do you mean?"

"Come on Martín, wake up! That man is proud to be a parasite, a user, and a swindler! It's not like he's hiding it. He thinks he's doing history a favor by keeping alive a traditional, historical career of taking everybody for a ride. Everything he sells or trades will always be less than what is declared, and no promises need be kept as far as he is concerned. He never legitimately delivers what he offers. His motto, he thinks, is from the Old West, "If you let yourself be swindled, it's your own fault. It's an honor to be taken by a historically correct period trader!"

"So, what you do now is you tell him you've reconsidered about the jewelry. Then you take off all your own everyday jewelry that he covets, put it in the box, leave it here in your cabin. Then put on the new bracelets, the necklace and the earrings you just made for him, ride over on top of me and give him his, "warm off the body jewelry:" the jewelry you just made. He'll never be able to tell the difference. Then when you've got your money, and you're back home and out of his sight, put your own old jewelry back on like always. That's what needs to happen!"

Who knew Blue was capable of that much devious inspiration?

Life in our camp went on peacefully and in less than six weeks I had built a new saddle on the base of what turned out to be a very well made and preserved saddle tree crafted from a single trunk of some kind of jungle hardwood hiding beneath a worn out one hundred and fifty year old rawhide exterior. Blue was right, the tree was excellent and once re-rawhided, layered with leather and silver, it turned out beautifully and fit him perfectly. It soon became our favorite.

Though I was doing everything in my power to keep the Parasitic Trader and his requests out of my consciousness, and finding a powerful horse for him was definitely not the first thing on the list of my rational mind, what Blue had said about his cousin, the silver-maned gelding, kept nagging at me before I slept each night.

I had actually seen that horse in Iowa running in the herd of Barbs on open land in the farm neighboring that crazy pig farming couple out of which Blue had been liberated. That horse was fast and *arisco*! People had tried and tried, but nobody could ever seem to conclusively catch or contain that long-maned gelding beyond pushing him into a big corral with sixty other Barbs. He was elegant and swift for sure, a true beauty, and no doubt durable beyond most any other, but he didn't like people.

This shiny copper gelding was only eight years old, and rumored to be *half-broke*, if you could catch him. Like Old Blue said, he would be just the right animal to be ridden by a rider of equivalent capacity the three thousand miles from Mexico's northern deserts to Alberta without wearing out.

The owner of the land and the herd that was running on it was an architect who didn't really pay much attention to the horses. As he hadn't struggled to get them and they had just been handed to him free of charge, he was basically ignorant of the treasure he'd been handed, a treasure he took for granted and by which he was daily surrounded, but a treasure he daily cursed, and one of which he was now trying to rid himself. This became the secret mine from which the Owners hauled all their amazing Barb horses. As the emissary from the Owners, the Rich Kid had played it to become this man's friend and over the decades almost every one of those one hundred horses would end up in the backlot horse facilities of the Rich Kid's family. But they had never been able to catch this long-maned gelding.

When I heard through the rumor mill that the Rich Kid was preparing to drive again to Iowa and fetch three more horses from the same architect's herd, against my better judgement (Blue thought it was fine), I put it to the Rich Kid if he wouldn't like to *go in* with me on that copper gelding, if I could manage somehow to catch 'em?

I proposed that he, the Rich Kid, who now identified himself as an official horse trainer, could green-break him, then I could ride him into form, and then we could sell this beautiful Barb gelding to the Parasitic Trader for five thousand dollars and split the profit fifty/fifty, each of us receiving twenty-five hundred dollars.

Without waiting to think, he agreed and away we drove one Monday morning in that same infernal yellow Suburban, dragging a slightly more reliable, but really ugly stock-trailer whose lights pretty much all functioned, to avoid any friendly policemen.

Mona had never bothered to communicate, so even though I figured I was safe, I was still pretty nervous when we hit the pig smell and rolled right down that country alley, past the Dirigibles, into the architect's gigantic dairy barn, all lit up end to end with fluorescent lights.

Next day, after corralling the architect's remaining herd of over sixty mares and foals, the kid, the architect, and I took turns manning the gate as we let loose all the horses we didn't come to buy back to the open grazing, keeping back the four we'd come to fetch.

When the three friendly, big-bellied mares the Rich Kid came to fetch were left, the copper gelding I came to get, by a ruse of having ducked down and walking side by side, leg by leg with the last horse we set free, slipped magically past us unseen, merging back into the herd again, out on the loose! Very *arisco*, very awake, very crafty.

I don't think anyone had truly registered how wild and majestic a being he really was, which was only intensified up close when you saw his very long, bright silvery mane and tail, both of them corkscrew curly, the mane just two inches short of the ground when he ran, and his tail dragging *on* the ground. With a bright red stripe down his back, all black legs and copper body, the strange dent in his face only added to the intensity of the smooth motion he made across the earth, looking almost like some fast ocean-going fish with long silky fins.

Right away I nicknamed him *Rewa* or Swift, in my hometown dialect of Keres, without even possessing him. The original owner of all these fabulous animals, which had included Blue as a foal, had been a very kind-hearted, buckskin-wearing, wealthy man, who when all these horses of his were still in their native New Mexico, and the registry had become overly bogged down with the bureaucracy of *in your face* high school politics, he resigned his membership, and pulled out all his beautiful horses.

One by one he began diminishing his herd by giving a few to deserving people. One of these was a teenage girl from the Jicarilla Apache Reservation to whom he made a gift of Rewa as a stud colt. But when this girl decided it was time to geld her elegant young stallion, she had the misfortune of hiring some inexpert cowboy, who roped him out of the herd, threw him down, haltered him very tight, and unceremoniously slit this horse's scrotum with a pocketknife and removed his testicles, doused the wound with wood ashes and in a bad nightmare fashion, untied the colt, and kicked him to his feet. This young woman, realizing she'd made a mistake letting this guy at her horse, started a tussle, for which the man was unprepared, during which Rewa, seeing his chance took advantage of their brawl to run back to the herd to heal, but was determined to never be catchable again, while the gelder wandered off unpaid with a broken rib!

Because no one could catch Rewa and the halter remained tightly buckled on the colt's face for at least a couple of years, the horse grew to adult size around it. Very good with horses, after years of patience, Alice was able to slowly catch her horse again, remove the horrible halter and actually saddle and ride Rewa for nine months. But the strange indented band from that halter would ride permanently over his nose the rest of his life.

When this young person's life took some hard turns and she left her home for a career in nursing, she let the horse go back to the original owner. When the herd was later divided: one half was shipped to the northern Cheyenne in Montana, the other half with Rewa in it was shipped to Iowa, right where we were standing that day.

Rewa was beautiful and though, understandably, he had a blanket policy of not being caught, still I noticed, like all my other Barbs, he was a horse that thought things out. He was only eight and his only crime was his extreme power, speed, and the strange ridge on his nose. The Iowa architect really wanted to get that proud gelding off his land.

After Little Richie had loaded up his relatively friendly-old, pregnant mares into the trailer, I convinced everyone we should go back out and chase all the range horses back into that dairy corral of big planks again and try one more time to catch Mr. Rewa. Nobody really wanted to, everybody grumbled that it was futile. But I talked them into it and we went ahead and tried again.

This time we were more careful. When Rewa was the only horse left in the corral, he grew very uneasy. I asked everyone to leave me alone with him for a while. When they left, I began singing to him and after an hour he almost cottoned up. Then, just as he was about to let me put a soft lead behind his ears, and scaring the fleas off both of us, that blessed architect came roaring up through the gate driving a forklift bearing, yes... an eighteen foot, welded, steel panel with which he intended to mechanically push and *crowd* this powerful scared animal into a corner! I couldn't believe it! What timing! What stupidity!

I was so livid I could've eaten a bucket, and I wanted to hammer that gate straight up that turnip-eater's rectum, for of course the horse gave up on me. Who wouldn't? Rewa turned, and with no open gate to run out of, and the heights of the fence too great to leap, and with no other obvious means to escape the gate, Rewa stood straight up and threw his sternum square at the planks of the corral fence, and with his front hooves, like a karate expert breaking two-by-fours with just the right center of balance, Rewa with all his weight perfectly poised behind him and a speed calculated to do it, he smashed open a horse shaped hole right through the planks, through which, in one motion, he dove and sped away leaving in his wake a shower of splinters and split-lumber shakes that hung in the air behind him, just like a lightning-strike on a big tree, before settling to the ground.

Rewa was definitely gone. Goner than gone. I was sure he must've fractured at least his breastbone.

I'd been so close and focused and then... It took me another hour to reel my rage back into my heart and to sizzle it down in the waters of my sorrow over human stupidity to the point where I could fake any degree of civility.

The three of us walked back the quarter mile to the barn so the Rich Kid could pay up for his three new mares and get us going-on-down to the highway and the hell out of this land of pigs and gate wielding imbeciles.

Because I had been busy in the enclosure with Rewa, I hadn't watched the Rich Kid load up his newly acquired, very tame mares at the barn. He had all three isolated together in the back compartment of the trailer with the middle partition closed, while they peacefully stood eating the hay we had brought along; he'd thought to leave the rear swinging gate open just in case I'd been lucky to actually catch that wily gelding and load him without having to fiddle with opening the rear while holding a wild horse.

I was so despondent, disappointed, and furious when we got into the barn that until my eyes adjusted to the light I failed to notice, what to my great delight, there standing rather calmly, like Blue two years before, was that wild-tailed and mane-dragging monster-beauty of a gelding, both sad-eyed and fierce-eyed, self-loaded right into the rear compartment, just as if someone had put him there for us!

Unlike Blue, he hadn't been kept in a hog pen eating hog food, but had been grazing really excellent grass with his old herd, drinking water from a creek, but just like Blue, he was saying, "Close this door dammit before I change my mind, but don't let that guy with the gate get close to me, and let's get the hell out of here!"

He didn't want to be tricked any more. He didn't want anyone where he couldn't see them sneaking up on the trailer and slamming the door, 'cause he'd panic and force the door before it could be latched and be gone for good. So before I tried to close the door, I politely asked the architect if he could please go to his house and fetch us a bill of sale for the horses, and told the kid to continue standing in plain view and not to move while I, singing to this incredibly beautiful warhorse, who almost did flee, but then calmed when I walked straight up toward him and slowly closed and bolted the rear gate of the trailer, still singing. He was in. He'd let me catch him! I reached between the struts and stroked his powerful, wild-smelling withers. He was really solid, his heart was really strong and full of grief. Nothing was broken or even cut. He was really something. Thank the spirits, the architect didn't return driving his forklift.

The kid and I split the price of that horse, we split the gas, and when we got home he trained Rewa. Meanwhile his family, without a hitch, registered all four horses within three weeks. When it was my turn to ride him down and I had brought Rewa up to our camp in the mountains, Blue remembered him when he came in. Amarillento couldn't believe his luck, but couldn't convert this tail-dragger to his method of mischief, for Rewa had his very own brand and had Amarillento cowed for the first time in his life.

Incredibly lithe and strong, he was a joy to get up on top of, moving over the hills and through the land, mounted in my church. And for once, Blue mysteriously didn't play dead.

Blue was the most magical horse I ever had, Amarillento the fastest and bravest horse on earth, Ojo Sarco was the most solid and creative, but Rewa was a tragically magnificent warhorse, fierce and fast and ready for all comers.

I liked Rewa a lot and he liked me I believe, but it was hard to know because unlike Blue he didn't communicate in the same way. I would have definitely conspired to have kept him for my own, but considering only *half* of him was technically mine, I would have had to pay the Rich Kid his half of what we would've made selling him to the slippery trader, which I couldn't economically rationalize doing in those days.

The day came when I thought it must be time to buck up and call the magazine-article-mountain-man-historian-re-enactor and let him know I had the toughest historically correct, most perfect *period* horse, broke and ready for his highness.

But of course I dallied, and Blue started talking. "Look man. Try to make your thinking bigger, make it clear like big mountain air does on a little mountain. Use the head your mother gave birth to, to look farther: do you remember that brush-necked stallion colt Little Richie has running out on the range? The one with the long tail and a mane like a twelve inch broom that won't fold? The one whose coat is the color and marking of a strawberry-colored coyote, a roan with a red stripe down his back, black legs and hooves like turtle shell?"

Who could forget that little horse? I'd been trying to buy him as a colt but they would only sell him gelded and he hadn't been old enough to cut yet.

"That's the horse you *should* want," Blue intimated in his way. "Trade your half of my dent-nosed cousin here for all of that stud colt, so you can make more of our kind. I can tell they're going to try and cut him soon, get him now, take him home."

Blue had a real good idea! If I could only pull it off. I knew those Owners had done everything to make sure I would never get a Barb stallion, as they wanted themselves to be the only breeders around, but it was worth a try.

As I started to move toward calling the Parasitic Trader, Blue read my thoughts again and called me back "'*T biena*', wait friend!" (Sometimes he talked in Mayan, sometimes Spanish or Keres, or sometimes he talked Mongol, very occasionally in Navajo. Like me he was multi-lingual.)

"Remember how that guy refused the beautiful jewelry you'd made even though he'd commissioned it, because what he really wanted was the silver jewelry "hot off your body?" Now remember this is the same guy you're thinking of calling about selling him my dent-nosed cousin. Don't you dare do that. No! No! No! Remember how I told you to leave the jewelry you wear everyday at home, and put on the ones you are selling? Then call this swindler up and tell him you've changed your mind and are coming over to give him the jewelry that he wanted all along. When you go, saddle Rewa with my cool new saddle and without once mentioning what you went through to find this horse to sell to him, ride

Rewa over to his den of thieves to deliver the jewelry hot off your body."

"He is not an honorable person. Like so many manipulative people, he's damaged in the soul, he doesn't want to help you by graciously accepting what you are openly trying to give him, he just wants what you have. He only wants to possess everything you are, not just what you own. He wants to obtain *you*. He is a hungry ghost whose hunger cannot be satiated. He will consume everything he can get, but he'll never get full. Because he's so jealous and covetous of what he can never ever be, he wants to take *you* away from *yourself* and leave you just as empty, hungry and desperate as he is!

"Like a feral dog who won't take a gift of meat face-to-face from your hand, but instantly steals what you are not guarding, behind your back, he'll try to get Rewa for himself if he thinks you don't want to part with him. You know, just play hard to get, and then sell him for more than you were going to."

"Blue. That's pretty damned conniving. Pretty trader-like." I said.

"Well, if you bring Rewa over there for him to look at, he won't buy him because he'll think that you, like he would be, are trying to swindle him. Like your jewelry, he only covets what is rare or he cannot have and only wants what you don't want to sell. He'd take your land if you owned any, and if your wife weren't sharper than he is, he'd find a way to ruin that too. He's a settler, he's re-enacting one of those lying, cheating settlers from the past, and proud of it.

"Do it all. Do it just like I tell you. You watch, it's going to turn out different than you think, anyway!"

So with that advice firmly under my sash, I called the Parasitic Trader and told him I'd changed my mind about the silver and needed the cash and could I come over and sell him my own jewelry?

When I got to his house/trading post, five other Old West, antique-art dealers and two hobby *mountain men* were sitting outside drinking and passing around a beautiful, old, 19th century, southern Apache, beaded, buckskin jacket with bands of zigzag lightning beaded down the sleeves, and lined with mattress ticking. This was an *insiders* game of trying to price a *precious*, rare find that as far as Natives were concerned should have never hit the market in the first place, as no doubt it came from some nefarious source. This jacket was not a forgery, it was real: these kinds of coats originated in the 1870's during all those terrible years of warfare and imprisonment for the southern Apaches. The juju had to be tremendous on that coat and indeed when Rewa, who like Blue could really see ghosts and spirit attachments, and I came upon these men, he arched his back like a porcupine, bulged out his eyes and insisted we walk a good distance around that knot of *famous* gallery people. They really were all just a bunch of ghouls rolling around in the spoils taken from the dead.

But the Parasitic Trader remained the worst of the bunch, for he was delighted with his *body warmed* bracelets, earrings and necklaces, adding them all to *artifacts* he was salting away for the future, to sell when someone like me was the subject of some book or movie and he could make a killing on the collector's market.

One of the men there held a grudge against me. He'd been the fellow who had taken off with the original saddle tree I'd been promised, switching it for that dilapidated wreck the trader gave to me. Though he still had to pay a lot to the Parasitic Trading Post Man for the original tree that I had reserved for leading his ride, he reckoned that my expertise on the subject made it so he'd gotten the best tree of the bunch. But once the tree was rawhided, it disintegrated, splitting into three pieces and was rendered useless to make a saddle. This man felt somehow I'd magically swindled him, even though he'd swindled himself, and the Trader, who was the real swindler, got still richer from the deal, no matter what.

Though both he and the Trader had knowingly cheated me, this man who everybody called Raf, short for Rafter, because he was a professional construction welder on high-rise buildings and bridges, held me irrationally responsible for his bad luck, especially now, since he'd heard Rewa was wearing the saddle I'd made from the dilapidated tree he'd discarded, which obviously ended up functioning very well and was looking quite stunning!

Rafter said something raw and unkind about me as the Parasitic Trader handed me the cash for the "warm off the body jewelry," still none the wiser for the switch, though it was not a swindle, for he'd ordered that very jewelry to begin with.

Forrest, a big older fellow, very well-known and one in the knot of these traders, spoke up: "Raf, you're just pissed off 'cause this man's incredible, little-paint-horse had to drag your big, drunken rear-end up that mountain to save you from being dragged down the gully to your death in that flash flood. You're mad 'cause he saved your life."

Which was true, but he was just one of fourteen. Then the others, including the Parasitic Trader, started enumerating Old Blue's other legendary deeds, all of which pushed the welder's pride over the edge. Loosening his neck up he yelled over them: "You really think an awful lot of that horse of yours, but I don't think he's all that!"

"I think you're right," I agreed. "That horse already thinks an awful lot of himself without any of us adding to his big head."

Then to make things worse, the other guys started listing off even more highly embellished accounts of Blue's more outlandish deeds, and when they got to the point again about having to drag the welder back up the hill he cut them off: "I bet you wouldn't last three seconds without getting arrested if you and your *super paint horse* tried to cross through that Baptist Center," whose entrance was situated not a quarter mile right in front of the Parasitic Trader's center of operations and almost in plain view, and in whose membership Rafter had relatives.

I had no intention of taking that bait, for I was pretty much in agreement with him. After all, the police and the gate guards, cattle guards, and the electric fence were all pretty formidable. Then again, the northside was forested and unguarded and only lightly hemmed in with just a simple four-strand barb wire range fence. I started imagining how one could do it. Then I imagined Blue looking at me about now, grinning. What would he say? I had to do it!

"Okay, so what are you betting we can't do it?"

"I'm not betting anything 'cause you're not that good, you couldn't do it."

Then all the other men started to heckle the welder for refusing to complete his challenge.

"Okay, I'll bet you one hundred bucks you can't ride into the Baptist Center and out without getting caught."

"A hundred bucks?" I hissed and laughed. "Look, I'll bet you two thousand dollars I can do it, against that fancy-beaded Apache jacket you guys are passing around there!"

"It's not my jacket, I couldn't..."

Then Forest, who claimed he was the jacket's rightful owner stood up: "I'll take the bet. You get the jacket if you can get in that place on your horse and get back out without getting caught, and if you do get caught you owe me two thousand dollars."

Blue's soul got into me real intensely, and I was fired up.

"Alright," I said, "we can do better than that. I'll ride across the Baptist Center grounds on Sunday morning in broad daylight, ride into the church building while in service, and still mounted, kiss the preacher at the pulpit and get away. If we can do that without being caught, I get the jacket."

Everyone jumped to their feet applauding and cheering. We shook hands on it, except of course the welder, who now felt even worse and more diminished than when we started.

Intending to remount on Rewa and making motions to move off and head back downstream to our camp, the Parasitic Trader stopped me, "What horse is this one? I haven't seen you ride him before."

"No, I've been kind of just keeping him to myself, as a kind of secret. I'm working him up for bigger things." I said, not really lying yet.

"He's a good looking Barb, boy look at that mane and the tail, is he strong?"

"Oh yeah, he's my strongest, nothing can stop him, he's one of those real, old-time Indian Ponies." Still not lying.

Forrest interrupted, "Yeah, he looks exactly like one of George Catlin's paintings of a Comanche riding a horse identical to this one, coming to parley with the American dragoons in like 1850 or something." It's nice when traders pitch in free of charge.

"Where did you find him?"

"I can't divulge that, it's our secret little source. He's one of Blue's cousins, out of the same herd." Still not lying.

"Hey, don't you think he'd be perfect for my ride, remember the one I was telling you about."

"Oh yeah right, I've been looking around and I've seen a lot of horses, but none of them are as strong and old-time as you want." Still not lying.

"What about this horse right here, Martín, don't you think he could do it."

"Oh yeah, no doubt about that, but he's mine. I couldn't let him go. I'm too attached to him and spent too much time on him. Don't worry, I'll keep looking, sooner or later I'm bound to run into something, there's got to be another good old-time Comanche horse out there somewhere." All of that could be true.

"Well, look, I got to have a horse like him soon 'cause this ride is only six months off. Come on Martín, help me out; sell me your horse. The more I see him, the better he looks."

"No, I couldn't sell him, I'm too attached." Not really untrue.

"Is he as good as your *paint*?"

"There's no comparison." Which was true, Blue was a magician, Rewa was a warhorse.

"Come on Martín, sell him to me."

"I just couldn't." This line of bargaining was really something, Blue was right as usual.

And I went to mount again, "Look, I said I'd give you four thousand dollars, so I tell you what, I'll give you five thousand dollars for this boy here."

"Sir, with all respect, you offered me five thousand dollars to begin with." Blue was right.

"Okay, I'll give you five thousand dollars."

"No, I just couldn't. Come on, let me go before I change my mind." And I went to mount.

"Okay, take six thousand dollars and give me this horse."

Six thousand dollars, wow. I mounted and we stayed standing for a minute. "Six thousand dollars you say."

"Yeah, I'd have to give it to you in two payments."

"Forget it," and we turned to go…

"Okay, I'll go get the cash," and he did.

I asked Forrest to drive me, my money, my silver saddle, my fancy bridle and the empty feeling in my stomach home after leading Rewa into the corral at the Parasitic Traders.

It felt peculiar and unjust somehow to leave noble Rewa in that man's corral. He shone there like a gorgeous turquoise stone in a bucket of bolts, and only stayed in its confines out of sheer loyalty to me. As Forrest drove me away, the feeling of sadness and self-defeat I had in my stomach for having outwitted the Parasitic Trader at his own game turned to heartbreak when the whole unhappy thing began to descend over me like the night's darkness on our camp. Rewa was gone. I'd sold my jewelry; I had my money. I felt horrible. I'd never make a good businessman.

Now I had to figure how to kiss a preacher and run!

Chapter 16

Mounted in Church

After a couple of days, the initial, small, elusive odor of shame and guilt that nagged my heart over the stupidity and flagrant flippancy of being willing to discourteously interrupt anybody's discussion with their God grew inside me until its overwhelming stink threatened to stop me in my tracks. Even if, while professing to be a *Christian*, this particular preacher openly endorsed a racist hatred against Guatemalan immigrants, and had publicly railed against me during his services, and his congregation really did feel that their God was opposed to my own spirituality, a spirituality of the Divine Heart of Nature with whose magic I was so deeply in love, I nonetheless made it my personal credo to *never* diminish anybody else's sincere love of whatever Holy beings they might love, even though they might berate my own. So, at least unto myself and for the calm in my own heart, though in the end it might have all *looked* the same in action to anyone who'd been watching, I rewrote the definition of the bet I'd made to now read:

"Instead of simply *invading my enemy's* fortress, uninvited, to rudely kiss the preacher, who openly despised us, and escape somehow with our skin, I would instead make a mounted *Love Raid*: a deliberate foray of blessing, whereby Blue and I, as unexpected guests, would charge in among that preacher's praying, polyester republicans, right inside their own church, during next Sunday service, and openly bless the preacher and his people with Health and Life, kiss his pulpit and run, hoping not to be arrested!"

And with that I felt a little better. Whereas Old Blue could've given a pig fart for how we worded it, he just couldn't wait till he could attack the mediocrity and hypocrisy of the settler-brain with his intact, ice-hatched soul, and bless their hate into dust with the beauty of our raid. He was ready.

For as far as Blue and I were concerned, the Wild Land was our church, and we were already mounted in Her, and kissed Her every day. All her Caves, Rivers, Canyons, Mountains, Drifting Sand, Cliffs, underground Streams and hidden sacred Springs, whose spirits filled the Sky with all her Clouds, Rain and Fog and Snow, Hail, Sleet, Heat and Cold and Light and Dark, all the Wild Land and all the Wild Sky and all the creatures that lived in both, all the Water Birds, and Summer Birds, and Winter Birds and all the Birds, and Dragonflies, and Bats, Squirrels, Deer, Weasels, Elk, Antelope, Beavers, Otters, Skunks, Martins, Bobcats and Lions, Bears, Snakes, Lizards, Turtles, Frogs, Toads and Salamanders, Trees, Coyotes, Berry Bushes, Foxes, Insects and Bees, Wasps, Bears, Grasses, Fungi and Drone Flies, Oak trees, Alders, Badgers, Piñon nuts, Pines, Firs, Cactus, and Saltbush, and Estafiate, Gophers, mountain Prairie Dogs, Chipmunks, Spiders, Whirlwinds,

Breezes, every little Plant and all the big Plants, all the rolling Stars and spinning Galaxies whose seasons and mystic winter dreams that conjured summer into view, where the immensity of what had once existed, was married to what someday might come about, lived in a tiny universe waiting in a blind beetle's antennae, where they powerfully dreamed each day, waiting in every molecule, into life anew: all of this *was* the church inside of which our hearts daily prayed, a church of Nature's wildness inside of which I always went mounted and singing on a horse, who fed the world by the beauty of his going.

But still, inside that much bigger church of Nature, there off to one side, the harsh white spire of the square, white, settler-church imperiously rose, looking strangely defensive, it was very small for being so isolated from the blessing of the majestic immensity of the forested hand into whose wild palm this angry, unidirectional spike had been so violently hammered.

Though their church and retreat center had been injected into the grandeur of the Church of the Wild, the people who worshipped there hid from Nature's vast and humbling deliciousness, safely armored inside their enshrined white spike, while their own real natural souls, unrepresented by anything they did there, rustled painfully beneath the crisp exoskeleton of the veneer of their assumed superiority, only achieving the depression, repression, and hate that such a dull, gray existence enforced on its adherents by the shame and limited imagination of its tradition.

Out of the wild and into that narrow-minded milieu, I would try to make a warrior's charge to bless, not to kill, to bless, not to maim, to bless, not to defrock or diminish, to bless, not to possess, not to derail, not to discard it or destroy it or endorse it, but to simply Bless. Of course, this was all a grandiose and young thing to even think, for while most likely nothing at all would truly change for having done it, and it would have no support from any faction whatsoever, the fact that such a thought could be thought and put into action, and that it had actually happened, in that alone it would sustain the exuberance of appreciation that people should exude for being given the opportunity to have lived, and therefore it all praised God in the biggest of ways.

Together my horse and I could be just as vain, just as brave, just as glorious as any fighting warrior of the past had to be, and without endorsing the mindset and meanness of what hated us, or any hate we ourselves might have hiding, we could, unarmed, actually risk our necks to give what little blessing we could carry, to make more life, just by the fact that we could do it. In modernity, most people are so misspent and ungrateful for their lives, that I was under no illusions that any of this would be received with any spiritual intelligence whatsoever. But like a chokecherry tree who only makes delicious chokecherries every year, and is not involved in who ends up eating what she creates, I was a maker of blessings and so I must bless no matter how well the blessing would be received.

Then the day of blessing came.

I knew the Bears, Elk, and Weasels heard us coming, for if anyone had been listening on that morning in the local

Church of the Wild, they probably heard our riding-songs echoing steady and strong up the creek canyon at the bottom of the mountain. After Blue and I jumped the back fence of the Christian's fortress into *their* grounds, still singing, we fast-walked up to the church, in service that Sunday morning, where inside, they too were singing.

This was a white Baptist church, so the singing was pretty square, but still, it was singing and it was that great sound of people singing together that we, who too were singing, outside their door, were hoping for. Not only did their singing cover the sound of our mounted entrance through the double doors and our clip clop past the atrium with all its cork boards fluttering with propaganda, but with me ducking down to fit right through the church doors once we got inside, Blue loved the sound of the singing congregation so much, and the swell of the organ, that he danced and bounced right down the aisle, smiling as if they were all just singing for him!

As we approached the pulpit, I too was singing as loud as I could manage, with full lungs, in our own Native tongue, to be heard above the din of the settler's invasive tune. Not expecting a horse and a rider, singing Indian songs, to be sauntering down the aisle, we made it all the way to the pulpit before anyone noticed. At which point the startled minister and the dumbfounded choir came to a halt. I switched to English, made my prayer to the Wild on their behalf, beseeching the Wild Flowering Jade Water Earth and all her animals, waters, dreams and plants to give them all life and heal any hateful thoughts and sicknesses any might bear. When I strewed a fistful of turquoise beads as a gift, everybody ducked, and when we spun around, I grabbed the preacher's hand, pulled him toward us and kissed his little-ripply-bald-head. Releasing him and still singing, we calmly turned around and rode back out of the church, walking slow to ensure that no one, especially any little kids, would be trampled.

But the second Blue cleared the church door, we hit the ground running, galloping like sizzling hell off into the forest. I knew no imperialist could ever forgive being blessed by a heathen, on his own terms, right inside their own imperial house.

The minute we'd entered the church, I noticed an usher rush right out to call the guards, and so they had a good head start. I had planned it all to be very rapid, and indeed it had all been so quick that more than half the congregation never actually saw it happen, and never looked up, and had no idea we'd even been there! But when the entire retreat center was audibly saturated with those air-raid siren alarms they'd installed for forest fires, the settlers went wild, people everywhere started running in every direction, while the police, with their dogs and golf carts, started searching the grounds for us.

But, by the love of the Holy in Nature, by the time they caught our scent, we had already jumped back over the fence, where thankfully, earlier I'd left a tarp draped over the top barbed wire, and we were safely out of their district and out of view, Blue grinning and trotting proudly right inside the little creek, sloshing downstream to throw off the scent for the dogs, and to leave no tracks for the men, hidden by the Holy Wild.

With Blue sweaty and tied out of sight up the mountainside aways, I sat at home in one of our tipis drinking tea and eating lunch, pretending nothing had happened, for I knew the sheriff, my friend old Pete, would soon come around to check on us. No doubt he would have divined it was yet another one of my horse antics. But since no true crime had been committed, besides the fact someone had come into a church to bless the people uninvited, he couldn't really be bothered to ruin the rest of his Sunday chasing down a blesser, just to let him go with a warning for trespassing. Thank the lord Blue hadn't pooped in the church! After drinking coffee with us, Pete was grinning and shaking his head when he drove off.

Blue and I had tried to bless a preacher and his followers, who wouldn't bless us, at his own pulpit, and in land where none of us were even allowed to walk, so we'd had to gallop and sneak up on 'em to bless 'em. It's hard to bless people who invade your land, that don't want your blessing. You gotta have a fast and brave horse.

A brave horse is a dangerous, stirring thing to a heroic soul, for as much as such a horse is an inspiration to always do mad things that assault mediocrity, it all flies in the face of common wisdom. After all, do we really want our children to grow up thinking that my crazy ideas are what they should aspire to?

I still have that beautiful jacket, but I don't wear it, 'cause it belongs to someone else in the past, it is theirs, not mine. I simply wanted to liberate it from the "Period Traders" by attacking the same mentality that had caused its original wearers to lose their natural ground and life ways and this jacket by blessing the descendants of the settlers who took it from them with the powerful force of life from that same natural ground! A force of Indigenous Nature that remains unconquered, giving life to all.

That evening, after the world had calmed down a bit, the sun beautifully golden, the smell of food grilling on the fire outside, just as I was fetching Blue out of hiding, back down to his home corral, who else should come streaming back up to us in a sweat, still smiling, through the woods, down to his corral with Amarillento, but Rewa himself, saddled and bridled, with no rider and his reins all snapped off! What a day!

Worried that the Trader might be down and hurt somewhere, I called his place to find that Rewa had just run away while being saddled. These things happen with puppies and horses, who sometimes keep running back to the herd or their old home until they feel they can accept their new owners place as a place they want to be.

The Native people where I was raised have a small naming ritual for dogs, tools, and horses to help them accept their new homes, but I hadn't shown the Parasitic Trader, because I knew it would end up in one of his brochures as a selling angle on the label of a fake artifact! When a new horse or puppy comes, you have to give him or her a new name, not a public name, a secret name between you and the horse. You have to spit this name three separate times into your horse's mouth, and on the third time explain to him or her that this name makes your horse part of you and your land. Then you tie a precious stone onto their mane or tail, as a gift.

The Trader sent someone to fetch his horse.

Two days rolled by. On the evening of the second day, Rewa, with a plebian cowboy saddle on his back, a bad bridle and no rider, came thundering up to where I stood, mounted on Blue, returning from the ridge behind.

When I called the Parasitic Trader, he said he'd been riding along the railroad tracks that ran opposite his store/home and Rewa, from no known stimulus, had gotten him off and ran away.

"How did he get you off; was he bucking?"

"No, not really."

"Did he rear up and drop you?"

"No."

"Did he sidle and you rolled off?"

"No."

"Did he spook, then bolt and you bailed?"

"No."

"How did it happen, Sir?"

"I'm not quite sure. He's really slick. We'd been out for a couple of hours and were just coming in along the tracks, and all of a sudden I was on the ground and he was gone!"

"How strange." I said, squinting my eyes and probably sounding perplexed.

At our place, Rewa had never kicked, bucked, reared up or anything. He could certainly run and jump, and get going but... this was all rather peculiar and a mystery.

I went outside and asked Rewa what it was he thought was happening. But Rewa was still not much of a talker. So I adjusted the stirrups on the Trader's own saddle, and after adding on some new reins, using the same *bad* bridle he came in on, I rode Rewa up and down and all around, experiencing no untoward motions whatsoever. I saddled up Old Blue, pulling him behind, as I rode Rewa back to the Trader's house and dropped him off, intending to ride Blue home.

"What do you think I should do about this horse?" the Parasitic Trader whispered in a desperate tone.

After thinking a while, I spoke: "For starters, maybe let's get you to stop feeding him that straight alfalfa hay and absolutely no grain. He's not a Quarter horse. These horses are easy keepers and don't need such high protein, they get too hopped up. They stay very fit and a lot calmer on good grass hay. That's why this horse will stay strong all the way to Canada, just grazing the grass you find along the way. Just like the old-time Natives' horses.

"Also, I think you two have to grow into each other, learn each other's ways. This horse is not just a sit-down, four-wheel drive lawnmower you can climb up on, crank the key and ride. He's a warrior and has his pride. He is flesh and blood like you. You said you wanted a powerful, spirited horse, one strong enough to carry you through to Canada. That kind of horse has to have a rider who can ride that kind of strength.

Maybe you're not really ready for a strong Native horse with a broad, old-time *horsality* instead of just a shallow modern personality!"

"No, No, No. I'm ready, I've ridden solo for thousands of miles all over the US, I've written books and articles all about those rides! What I meant was, can you give me some pointers on how to deal with one of these old-time Spanish horses?"

I thought I had. Then I tried a little harder. "Look Sir, you've got to think of this horse as if he were a flooding river with white caps in the wind. You can't *force* a river to calm into a friendly surge; a horse of this kind is very special, and you have to learn to ride that surge. Ride him just as he is, and then you have to like riding him as he is, then he will like *you* riding *him*. This means you have to stop thinking Rewa is just there to take *you* for a ride. You have to put the same equivalent energy and motion of your own body into him as he puts into yours while you're on his back. You have to work as much as he does if you want him to pull you across the Earth.

"After you saddle up and before you go out on the trail, ride him in a bunch of figure eights, both tight and loose, and then around in some double-volute spirals, and then in circles in both directions, then back and forth in straight lines, like you're sewing the East to the West: you're the needle, he's the thread. Like two molten metals, the river of his spirit force and the action of your spirit force have to begin to alloy into a new kind of substance: your spirit has to kind of wear a good groove into his motion, and his motion has to wear a groove into you. Do that until, together, you both fit into each other. Then both of you can take on the world!"

I thought this was all good advice, but soon realized talking to him was like playing cards with a scarecrow, or debating with an answering machine: for I had to do all the work. Just like him riding Rewa, he didn't want to learn how to ride him, he just wanted Rewa to learn how to carry him as he was, and make him look good. His only response was:

"Do you think he needs to be lunged around a bit? That's what my neighbor thinks he needs."

"Sir, I have never lunged horses to train them, but that might be a way to get his edges a little smoother before you head out on your daily ride."

"Could you teach me how?"

"Oh, I could, I guess, but truth is, this horse is ready to go as he is. You just have to somehow hit it off with him and it'll all be fine."

"Okay, tomorrow, I'll bring him over and you can show me how to lunge this horse, okay?"

This horse was fine, but his new owner was determined to get his money's worth.

But as it turned out, he didn't have to bring Rewa over, because by dawn Rewa was looking in the window, watching us eat our chaqueue, green chile, tea, and eggs. I asked him through the open window:

"Rewa, is that guy really that much worse than Iowa?" But he wasn't talking... yet.

The Parasitic Trader showed up faithfully ready for his lunging lesson, which coming from me was a little like trying to get a cooking lesson from a bear, for we had no round pens or arenas, upon which that European training method depended. Nonetheless, though totally unfriendly to my home-grown, Reservation style of training, since this big-city method basically involved accustoming a horse to move around in a circle, while attached by the nose to a long leash held by a *trainer*, who, by signals with a long *lunge whip*, causes the horse to walk, trot, canter around her/him in circles, and thereby impart the voice signals to teach turns, stops, right and left leads, and more, from the ground, and because I was fairly certain the Rich Kid's training methods had involved lunging Rewa plenty, I figured I could teach a lunge-like exercise to the Trader, which might enable him to get a little closer to his new, powerful, little horse.

The truth is, I had lunged horses a bit here and there, but I didn't care for it all that much. Nonetheless, when he showed up, I took the Trader and Rewa down to a grassy flat area by the little creek where its cut bank formed kind of three quarters of a circle, to give the illusion of an enclosure some sixty feet across, where a curve in the stream closed the remaining quarter of the circle. This would be our *round pen*.

I asked the Trader to loan me his lunging whip, which he'd borrowed from his neighbor, and with the Trader watching beside me, I let out the lunge line like a fly-fishing line. As suspected, Rewa knew exactly what to do, responding perfectly to every command. With me in the center, Rewa dutifully walked, trotted, cantered, and reversed, as I let out what I'd figured had been the Rich Kid's commands, then after changing hands and doing the same in the opposite direction for some twenty circuits, I turned the whip and lunge line over to the Trader and asked him to take over while I watched.

Though a little clumsy at first, the Trader actually got him started, and Rewa was still going around the Trader and the Trader was giving the signals when I left. Giving them their privacy, I walked out of sight back up to our cabin to begin storing the many dry bunches of medicinal plants I'd been gathering all through the late summer.

My young kids and a couple of their little cronies were giving me a hand by breaking up the dry plants into storable sizes, which we then stuffed into various cotton sacks and arranged them in the wooden chests we used just for that purpose.

Though we were a hundred feet up the hill, and out of his sight, some loud sounds of frustration and some general, run-of-the-mill swearing reached our ears through the rustle and crack of our industry with the plants.

"Come on Rewa, come on boy, come on boy."

"Giddiup, Giddiup."

"Let's move, come on, let's get going."

"God damit Rewa, let's go. Come on alright, alright we can do it. Come on boy, come on."

"Reeewa, shiiiiiiit! Man, come on, let's go."

I said to myself, "Well, Rewa is his horse and maybe this is the way he can get more of a relationship. Accustomed to horses who were shallow, uncreative servants, a real thinking-horse meant the Trader had to get himself thinking even more than his horse. Maybe by struggling with each other on the ground, without actually having to ride, they could come to some common ground without the Trader having to keep hitting the ground!

But when the whip started cracking and cracking incessantly, and the swearing got more and more vehement and creative, and harder and harder to translate to the kids, with all my nosey little helpers, we made our way down toward the lunging *circle* to investigate what all the noise was about.

After cautioning my assistants to be very quiet, we laid on our bellies and snuck up on the bluff. Each of us, one by one, slowly peeked over the edge of the little bluff to see if we could get a look at what was going on with the swearing Trader and his new Barb.

But what met our eyes had to be one of the wonders of the world; something I'd never actually seen before, and definitely was not anticipating. For right smack in the middle of the little bluff-held-crescent, Rewa was standing, all squared up, calmly gyrating, the lunge rope taut off his nose, attached to a very red-faced, sweaty Parasitic Trader leaning forward, swearing and puffing with the whip slashing the air out in front of him, who was sprinting in complete perfect circles around his horse! Rewa, shamelessly smiling, stood there and turned in place like the hub on a wheel, and appeared for all the world to see that he was lunging his owner!

I'd never seen a horse lunging a man before! But there they were, as plain as Mercury orbiting the Sun. This man was hooting and yelling all sorts of encouragement as he ran around and around, strangely unaware that he was now the only thing moving, mysteriously thinking he was somehow still chasing his horse into motion, while Rewa having slowly and slyly engineered a reversal of roles, just grinned, and did his part to keep the Trader moving.

Biting our lips and tongues to keep from laughing, the kids and I rolled back from the edge of the little bluff. When we had pulled as far enough away as we could hold it, we all dropped and rolled around on the grass and red earth laughing. The harder we tried to stifle our mirth, the worse it bubbled up and out of us, so hard we had to hold our stomachs.

Though pitiful in a way, and viciously wicked for any of us to have prized the obvious presence of natural justice in the sight of the Parasitic Trader completely outfoxed by his own would-be-slave, where he, by his own instigation, with great vehemence, was running himself to exhaustion in beautiful perfect circles, ironically unaware that he was obeying his own commands as he orbited the warhorse he would dominate, who rotating in place still smiled very politely the whole time. On a more banal level, it was nonetheless somewhat reassuring to those of us who'd been repeatedly exploited and manipulated by this man's ruthless business angles that something bigger than man and horse was in charge of the river of life, in whose rough current all of us must find a way to swim!

Chapter 17

That Song Really Makes Me Soar

Laughing for joy is good all the time, no matter what you're doing, but while riding, often times singing is the best way to express that joy; for in horses joy manifests as a musical thing.

In everything they do, real horses have a lot of music in them, even as they move. They love it when someone sings in the rhythm of all their sounds: to the sound of their grunts at different gaits, or their hoofbeats at every gait, or their nine kinds of whinnies, wails, nickers, snorts, and more. The Mesta horses were made of music. Not only in their souls, where there really is a huge amount, echoing and rattling about, always just waiting to surface, but in the everyday reality of their very presence, horses are very deeply made of music.

The music they make, if allowed its voice and rhythm as we ride with them in the open land, feeds God as Nature and stirs the heart of humans to freedom, inside and out. This has been especially evident in those cultures where all music comes from horses.

Remember that the origins of all modern stringed instruments, both bowed and plucked, come from horse-culture peoples. All the violins, violas, cellos, contra bass, and guitars come from more ancient stringed instruments: rebec, comancha, qobiz, citole, lyra, morin khuur, and many others, all of which descend directly from horse-riding nomads, who developed bowed instruments long ago by restringing their hunting bows (as in bow and arrow) with rosined hair from the luxurious tails of their little horses, played against strings made by stretching the same horse hair in bundles of twelve and nine across rawhide-covered, long-handled milk ladles, as far back as the bronze age! These instruments are still popular and increasing in popularity worldwide. But even so, it's a known fact that *all* western symphony music originally descends from horses and the utensils used for cooking the food of horse people, long before there even was a Europe.

But the ancient, horse-nomad origins of the music we today take for granted doesn't only lay with the vast array of musical instruments, but with the actual music itself. The music that people today have, and to which we have always sung the stories of our origins to, is very often not recognized as having originated from music made in horse rhythms. In some a trot: dut dut dut dut dut; others a walk: kalump a dump a dump a clump; many, many at a canter: tada dunk tada dunk tada dunk; or a gallop: dug-a-da-ta-ga-ta-dug-a-da-dug-ata etc. And even more.

Horses *are* music. Like birds, they are by their nature, musical. On occasion you even find a horse, that, like some people, learns to appreciate the music, rhythms and sounds of other people's languages and their culture's songs. While all horses love music, some horses really love the music of people. And then, there are some horses who love *all* music.

Blue was one of the latter: he even dug the white-noise of the heavy metal at rodeos, or the obnoxious ice-skating music people play during their monotonous horse show routines. Above all, Blue loved the sound of a single person singing their heart out, or a guitar, or a flute, or a ranchera band, or Beethoven, or the Canyon Wren, whose song cascaded behind his digs up at our camp all summer.

When we finally figured out what to do about yellow lines, and we began to show ourselves off by riding in local parades, once it was known about Blue's love of music, I was usually lucky to get a position riding behind a float with a live band chugging away as we went along.

Once the parade got under way, like Shindai, Blue would rock back and forth and shimmy to the band, but, unlike Shindai, it was beneath his dignity to rear and dance like a dog begging for a bone. Instead, Blue could grapevine, or dance gyrating in a circle, or even dance moving backwards. The people loved him and would cheer as he rocked himself through a *ranchera* or swayed away to the waltzes; plus he was so handsome he always took the prize.

On one occasion during a lull in dancing, waiting behind the Blue Ventures float to start up again in the annual July, Española parade, an angry spectator jumped out of the crowd and grabbing Blue's silver headstall yelled, "If I had a horse that ugly, I'd shoot him."

To which affront, Blue wound up a juicy sneeze and immediately blew a big horse snot onto the poor man's face, and then kept sneezing for three times more.

Furious, this fellow dug his way around and out of the crowd, who were cheering for Blue's comic revenge.

But twenty minutes later, farther down the road, while we danced away to *La Mosquita*, the same guy, to get back at us, pushed his way out of the crowd and whipped three long belts of lit firecrackers under Blue's dancing legs.

The firecrackers snapped and cracked, jumped and popped, but Blue didn't jump or panic, but just kept shuffling to the music, his powerful sloped croup rocking back and forth to the rhythm, right in with the racket and sparks of the fireworks. All the people clapped even more, thinking it was all just part of the parade.

Blue was indomitable.

As a boy, my parents, my brother and I lived on the school compound in housing provided for teachers who taught at the Pueblo elementary school on the Reservation. Though four miles from the actual Pueblo, in the middle of otherwise unpeopled Pueblo lands, it formed a tiny pueblo of its own.

Only a few of the teachers actually lived there, and mostly Native Pueblo people from surrounding Pueblos rented the houses around us. Though four hundred miles from his tribal home, a Diné Navajo gentleman named George Sandoval, who was our beloved history and shop teacher, lived not a hundred and fifty yards away from us. In my teenage years, on the summer weekends, I often visited him, and he would teach me to sing all kinds of old Navajo songs. I tried to be a good learner, and could sing pretty well, and he became my friend.

Occasionally when his Diné nephews would visit him, we'd wander the Pueblo reservation, walking and sometimes riding. It was from George that we learned to sing Diné *riding songs*. While Native culture everywhere is deeply held alive by singing, and anything sacred in Diné culture has always been kept alive through a deep liturgy of sacred song, Navajo people were also famous for their horse riding songs. George showed us that besides the usual riding songs, any reliable ceremonial song that was commonly known to his people at large, could become a good riding song. You could also make your own if you knew the phonetic formulas. Like horses, songs were prized possessions and maintained as living jewels, and only handed over to someone else with the same great reverence and worth as you would hand over your horse.

The one song I prized the most was one he taught me as a corn-grinding song, sung communally on the advent of a young woman's coming-of-age-ritual, that when sung out of context as one rode out in the old days, would ensure that you were recognized as a safe visitor when coming toward another Navajo's home. Traditionally, strangers showing up silently, without singing, were always suspected of being an enemy or livestock thieves or worse.

But even better still, George showed us younger guys how it was that when riding a long ways over varied terrain, the position in which one unconsciously kept one's body while singing in tandem with your horse's rhythm, helped both horse and rider.

It was pure magic to see how little stress your horse's back and girth sustained if one sang certain songs, out loud, in a certain beautiful way, to the shuffling *long walk* gait of one of these old-time Reservation Barbs! No saddle sores, no galls, or cinch sores, nothing. Singing was good for the rider too, because he/she had to maintain a graceful pattern of breathing to fulfill the phrasing of the song. So riding-songs of the proper kind saved the horse's back and the rider's circulation and gave a power to the riding, whose particular relaxed posture necessary to sing, fed the world by the beauty of both the singing and the way a singing rider and horse moved across the Earth.

They had to be the right songs though: songs with a certain togetherness with your horse's motion. Such knowledge was ancient among Scythians, Mongols, Native American nomads, some Gauchos, and real tribal horse people worldwide. Though most people today are settled peoples, our souls have not forgotten that we too are a musical species, and horses have loved humans because they can sing with the horse as the accompaniment.

Eurasian horse nomads, Mongols in particular, often designate distances, not by mileage, but songs, by music. On the steppe, in particular, where trees are very rare, and where every subtle landmark, every hidden valley and rolling hill needs to be remembered, or one can get dangerously lost. In these stretches, the distances from place to place was calculated not by mile marking, but by the singing of certain well-known ballads, at a certain rhythm of one's horse: a walk, a trot, or a canter! If one asked, "How far is it from here to the upper fork on the Orkhon River?" Someone might reply: "Two complete singings of the Altai Magtal at a trot, and a full song of Erke Mergen at a walk!" One actually arrived safely by the song.

Our indigenous relationship with horses always has to have singing and music in it, the songs going from the heart of the horse, to the heart of people, and together to the heart of life, who is fed by women and men singing with the orchestra of the sound of their horse's motion. It is stunning and beyond beautiful to hear the proud sound of a hundred men and women singing together, coming to a ceremony on horseback; the sound of the horses making the rhythm, to the sound of the song. Horses are music, organic music, sung music.

On occasion, though, a horse can be rather particular; after all, some music is better for them than others...

The Parasitic Trader, feeling that he'd more or less gotten the hang of chasing his new horse around in little circles, *boarded* Rewa at our place for a couple of weeks, during which time he showed up every other morning, and for a half hour *lunged* his new pony down by our little stretch of the Glorieta Creek. We never dared to look, never sure who was lunging who!

Then one afternoon, returning to our camp in our old red Ford from a day trip to town and seeing that Rewa was missing, we were relieved to find a note *nailed* on the hay shed that read to the effect that the Trader felt he and his horse were *meeting up* pretty well now, just like he'd seen in all the *horse training* videos, and so he'd taken Rewa back to his own house.

Rewa and the Parasitic Trader were well matched when it came to inter-species deception. Though the Trader was actually good at seeming to praise his horse, what he was doing all that time was just a theatrical investment: something he'd read about, or seen on television. Instead of courting the horse's nobility and friendship to carry him across the land because he deeply felt that way and couldn't live without his horse, everything he did was an empty, liturgical equation, a technique designed to *seduce* the horse into giving him what he thought he deserved for the purchase price.

It was probably too optimistic to hope that Rewa would one day let that man ride him, unless the Trader got a Scrooge dream and somehow truly changed. And I knew the Trader expected the horse to make all the changes, and if in the end the Parasitic Trader couldn't ride the "strongest, toughest southwestern *period* Barb," he would try to get his money back, blaming his own inadequacy on the horse.

But all this being said, I had taken Blue's advice early on: for I actually no longer owned any *piece* of Rewa when he was sold to the Trader. I had already transferred my *half* to the Rich Kid, who had been the sole owner when the Trader bought him.

Once Rewa had been riding well, I had traded my half of ownership of him to the Rich Kid for a different horse: a two-year-old, strawberry-roan, Barb, stallion-colt cousin of both Blue and Rewa, who I'd always loved since I'd first seen him at only three-months-old. For years I'd been trying to buy him, but previously the Owners had never been willing to sell him to me.

So, if the Trader decided to give up on Rewa and wanted his money back, he'd have to deal with Richie.

I sincerely hoped it wouldn't come to that and the Trader and Rewa, dragging his silver mane and tail, would find a way to ride it out together in magazine-story glory all the way into Alberta!

But after only two days away from us, and still considering our place his home, one afternoon, while we stood around a big heap of cottonwood embers, moving from here to there to dodge the smoke of some cow-elk and sheep rib racks we were broiling for a little feast with some friends from Nayarit, with whom we were happily singing off to the side with our guitars, Rewa came quietly sauntering up to our fire, still saddled and riderless. Looking like he'd like a tea, I let him drink up mine, which had cooled, and I asked him sadly: "Rewa. What happened this time?"

Unlike Blue, Rewa was still not a talker. So, I went to the cabin to phone his owner, but put the receiver down because the Trader drove in screeching, dropping out of the cab holding a *period* rope.

And before I could even ask, he volunteered: "He got me off again. It was like magic. I didn't even feel it; I didn't even know I wasn't on him, till I hit the ground. What's wrong with this horse Martín? He's so beautiful, do you think he just doesn't like me?"

Finally a real question, with an easy answer, but I couldn't just tell him for once he was right.

But still, none of this was really making sense. Every other time when Rewa showed back up, I'd ride him all over and he just became more limber and better all the time.

"Okay," I said. "Let's go riding together. I have to find out what's causing this to happen." I was going to watch every detail, ride with this man and figure this all out, and then come home and we'd all eat ribs! They were smelling awfully good.

So at the edge of our camp under the Pines, I saddled up Amarillento with the Trader's funny, fancy, old saddle, put my bridle on him, and I saddled Rewa with mine. I told the Trader to mount little Amarillento and I'd ride Rewa.

I had the Parasitic Trader mount Amarillento, because he was the only horse I owned that could walk as fast as Rewa.

Riding side by side, the Trader on a much humored Amarillento, and myself riding Rewa, we fast-walked straight up our famous log-skid, up and up into the mountain side, the smell of smoke and ribs on the coals following us all the way up, making my stomach rumble. We returned by the more precarious ridge route.

Both horses rode spectacularly, the Trader kept saying how totally stunned he was that both horses could even walk that fast. Obviously the Trader had ridden a lot over trails, but probably never on the backs of truly small, strong, old-time horses. One had to actively *ride*, these little Barbs, practically standing in short stirrups to stay tight with them on all the turns and changes, to work together, moving together with horses, as we are meant to move in a way that frees up the horse's physique to be able to do what they're meant to do with us on their beautiful backs.

After sharing our meal of ribs and baked sweet potatoes with the Parasitic Trader, we all sang songs together, Indian songs, old hippie songs, Mexican songs, American folk-songs, and made up songs, the Trader even singing a few of his own favorites about the Northwest Passage and all that *period* trail-blazing, imperial, white guy stuff. But we sang everybody's songs together and were all happy, even Rewa and Amarillento, neither of whom, because we were so hungry and salivating, had we bothered to unsaddle, but who stayed close by after being hobbled and left to graze freely.

Finally, with full bellies and a peaceful feeling, while the Father Sun was still a little bit up in the late afternoon sky, I had the Trader saddle up Rewa with his own tack. I scrutinized his every move, and his every method, to see if anything he was doing would inspire this horse to somehow jettison the Parasitic Trader. But nothing strange could I detect.

Similarly, I saddled up and bridled Amarillento with my gear, and this time with both of us mounted on our own horses, we set out to repeat the exact same route we'd fast walked up two hours earlier. While I kept one of my eyes vigilant on the Parasitic Trader and Rewa to see what I could see, we pushed up the skid once again, side by side. But the evening was so grand, and we were having such a relaxing, luxurious, late-summer, after-dinner-evening ride, with all the beautiful smells and no flies, the sounds of the Canyon Wren off somewhere cascading away that I was lulled into a less than objective mode.

Halfway up, the Trader asked in a friendly tone as we rode, "People say you like to sing when you ride, is that true?"

"That's true, actually. If I'm at a walk or a slow, Indian shuffle, I love to sing Native riding songs."

So I slowed my pony down to a sensible walk and started up singing one of the old songs Mr. Sandoval had given to me years past. Using the horse's rhythm and the sounds of the bit jinglers, I sang in a low pitch at the beginning and then moved up to the fall of falsetto notes, which for the first time, I realized were actually the same notes as the Canyon Wren's cascading song.

As I sang, both horses ears began to relaxedly flap and mark the time, and the horses started surging intentionally to the rhythm. Tashlunk, tashlunk, ta shlunk etc...

Singing right along with the Canyon Wren, the horse's heads swaying to the beat, the *coscojos* on their curb chains jingling and slushing, the sound of their hooves making the song's cadence; all the world was beautiful. I stopped singing for a little while as we continued in the same luscious rhythmic sway walking up the incline through the forest. Rewa seemed fine. The Trader was fine. The world was fine.

The singing made us all relax and I forgot I was supposed to be scrutinizing the Trader and Rewa out of the corner of my eye, and as we walked up the mountain, I allowed Rewa to drop a full horse's length behind us to the right.

Then, all of a sudden, startling us out of our peaceful rhythmic reverie, a loud, ugly, croaking howl emerged from behind me, which I eventually realized was the voice of the Parasitic Trader feeling the euphoria of the afternoon, who now decided he too would sing a song as we rode.

He was a big fan of old western movies and especially those starring Fess Parker, and so it seemed that his favorite song to sing as he rode along was almost always the theme song from the 1950's TV series Davy Crockett.

But songs are powerful, and when that Trader sang his song, he dropped into a fantasy trance: I was no longer Martín, nor he the Trader, but we were now two old-time heroic mountain men, riding old-time horses into the Rocky Mountains in some movie from his childhood. His singing commenced in very low, kind-of-rumbling, hound-dog-like voice, rising to enunciate every syllable and holding vowels quite long, and with all his ruthless heart and an ecstatic look on his little kid face he sang, "Daveeeee Daveee Croooockett, Kiing of the Wiiild Frontieeer."

For some reason, both horses, at the sound of his tune, started nervously marching and arching their necks, as if to bolt from the scent of a lion. By the time the Parasitic Trader was at that place in the song where he says, "Killed him a Bear when he was only three," both horse's necks hardened, their ears gyrated everywhere, and separately, and they wanted to run so badly, they both had to be forcibly reined in.

Then as the chorus came around again:

"Daaavy, Daavy Crockett, King of the Wild…
Frontieeeeer."

The long word Frontier came up from behind me in a split second and flew right on past my right ear, at which point, doing all I could manage to hold Amarillento from bolting, I chanced a glance to my right and there was the Trader, himself whizzing by me mid-air, with no horse, flying like Superman horizontally, four feet above the ground still singing! He landed *kablamo*, dropping mercifully right into a stand of mountain madder bedstraws and ferns when the inertia of his trajectory finally played out and the flying singer hit the earth!

I looked back to see about Rewa, and there, head down and still plodding right along, very mildly, like nothing had transpired, no longer wanting to bolt or run away this time. Riderless, he pulled right up alongside Amarillento and I as we rode up to where the poor Trader had been chucked. Getting to his feet and rubbing his kidney fat, he seemed to have survived alright.

"Dammit, you see what I mean Martín? All day we're having a nice ride, everything's great, and no matter how hard I try, or whatever I do, out of the blue, Rewa just drops me in the end."

The truth be told, I don't think Rewa actually dropped him, or even bucked him off, but somehow chucked him like a spear! I had no more idea than the Trader himself exactly what sly move that tough, long-maned, little horse used to propel this man flying so cleanly and horizontally through the air and into the bushes, but at least now it was pretty obvious why.

"Well, Sir," I tried really hard not to laugh or smile, "look on the bright side; we've made some progress, 'cause look, your horse is still here and didn't run away like usual, and we now know why he sends you flying."

Although, understandably reluctant to climb back on deck after being so rudely and unexpectedly catapulted, I finally cajoled him into getting back in the saddle. Rewa was just fine and looked a little sad actually.

"Look, the only thing between you and a beautiful ride from Mexico to Canada is that you just have to promise me you won't sing that song while in the saddle!"

"Are you telling me Rewa doesn't like the sound of my voice."

"No, I think he likes your regular voice just fine, but he doesn't know what to do with the vibe of what you turn into when you start singing about Davy Crockett." I stopped short of giving him a short history lesson about how Mr. Crockett was a notorious supporter of Black slavery, a killer of Indians and died killing Mexicans, trying to create an illegally gotten slave country, and that Rewa was an Indian/Spanish/Mexican horse. Horses like him had principles. He was sensitive.

Instead, I explained. "What I think, is you just need to learn to sing a lyrical ballad, in Spanish, in your regular voice, without going into a movie-glaze-out-fantasy and he'll ride you wherever you want to go." I told him I could teach him, but he wouldn't take it seriously.

Horses are made of wind and songs.

Horses love to sing, and they love singing.

Songs are powerful. Some songs are life-giving, some songs fill life with trouble.

Real horses are honest.

They know the difference.

Chapter 18

The Wild Rose

Just like Blue said, Rewa wouldn't stay gone.

The Trader would saddle up, ride out from his horse trailer or his historic house, and lulled by Rewa's beautiful shuffle, soon enough the Trader's eyes would glaze over and he'd slide effortlessly into the persona of some imagined storyline where he was a western movie hero on the trail again. Goose bumps would come over his whole body then bumping and chugging along in the saddle, like a little kid, he dropped into a trance out of which sooner or later the song of Davy Crockett or the chant of the Northwest Passage would come bubbling up, singing out from his chest, and before he could stop himself, *kazanggo,* away he'd fly, catapulted from his horse, who would then bolt back to our house without fail, every time.

The Trader couldn't curb his instinct to sing that crazy song, and Rewa couldn't keep from stiff-legging him off when he did. So, just like we had all surmised, the Parasitic Trader, unable to ride the "most powerful Barb" I could find, finally asked me for his money back.

Luckily, since Rewa didn't actually belong to me when the Trader bought him, he had to approach the Rich Kid, who was totally nonplussed. But the Rich Kid wasn't rich for nothing, and in the end he succeeded in buying Rewa back for one thousand dollars, leaving himself with a five thousand dollars profit and still in possession of the horse! Wow.

After this, the Rich Kid cut Rewa's mane to a mere six inches, trimmed his tail and tried to use him as a lowly packhorse in some of those three-day horse adventure treks he had organized with city people. But the kid's habit of leaving the pack mules or pack horses loaded up, but loose, to follow untied, never functioned in Rewa's case, because he walked so much faster than any of Richie's animals that in the end, Little Richie remanded Rewa to pad the ranks of his recently concocted personal Mesta herd, on over six thousand acres of rolling grass land and diminutive sink hole canyons he leased at the very western edge of New Mexico's eastern plains.

Though it took Rewa three years to grow back his mane, during all that time he was on the range, he'd managed to rise in the ranks to where he was a sight to see; heading up the uncut, young stallions of the *stud colt* band, who like rows of streaming quail rolled single-file out of view into the canyons and back up over the grama covered hills with Rewa, his mane and tail dragging, chasing them all from behind.

In a motion that initially seemed positive and useful, Richie opened up the range to anyone who wanted to breed their *blood* Mesta Barb mares, if they would share the work, breaking winter ice at the water wells and patrolling fences, and gathering and separating horses in the spring.

Like a co-operative of sorts, it operated not unlike an old-time Spanish Mesta, and was ironically located only eight miles south of where the original Mesta of the Spanish Colonial Viceroy had kept their own horses during the 17th and 18th century. Horses that were the direct ancestors of all of ours! When the nation of Mexico was formed and all Spaniards were deported, their horses were either divided up, lost to the wild or absorbed into Native herds. That was exactly where all of our own horses descended from, right there.

At one grand moment, our Mesta grew to where together we grazed over seventy horses: a stud-colt band, a mare-single-stallion-foal band, and a yearling-and-two-year-old band.

Those years were good and there had been the blessing of summer rain. The native grasses were excellent and of the most powerful nutrition, and along with the good wild air and the wild water with no pollution, the horses, totally back in their element, really thrived. Not wild, not feral, but owned, just not strictly contained, they were very well exercised by the instinct and the eternal wisdom of their mare leaders and stallion guardians, who always made them move to new grass, while watching for danger. They all grew into truly majestic beings.

Richie's self-styled Mesta became popular with a number of us as a fine place to keep young horses we were not yet actively riding, and to renew grown Barbs that had been worked hard. It was not only much more economical for the owners and healthier for the horses, but we could have our mares give birth in the open land where they originated and the foals had a chance to actually grow beautifully into what they were meant to be in a herd, at their mother's side. Several of my mares and a foal stayed with the mare herd and I took my turns driving my truck the forty miles to fulfil my obligations, as we all had agreed to do. Lasting only a couple of years, its communal success was unfortunately short-lived, but while it operated it ran entirely like a medieval Mesta, complete with Mesta horses.

The Rich Kid's family had always used their horses as a tax write-off from the time they were little kids, but as adults, after inheriting a very large amount of money from the break-up of some ancestral estate, the question of how to economically get the most out their horses made their horses the motivation for a strange war amongst the family. Whereas previously, the twelve members of the Owner family felt they had all owned the horses communally for tax purposes, these Barbs had nonetheless always been the favored project of only three of the family members, and even then all the horses were legally registered in the name of only one sister.

The following year, after coming into yet another, even larger inheritance from the distribution of another ancestral estate, the Rich Kid's brothers and sisters revived their old arguments about everything, about who should get what, or about the tax advantages of a communally held this and that, whether to distribute money or to keep it in one chunk, invested, etc., and so on.

All their horses, of course, ended up in the middle of this family war. Though I preferred to live in the fantasy that our Mesta had been devised for the horse's sake, I guess we all knew that it was mostly just a way for Richie to separate himself and his own horses from his family's horses, especially his older sister, between whom there ensued a bitter quarrel! Their city place had become a battleground.

When the Rich Kid, as a tax write-off for *his* personal cut of the inheritance, went about hauling off the horses he considered his own and setting them loose on *his* personal Mesta, his older sister, in whose name all of his horses were registered, claimed she and every other sibling owned a portion *of every horse*, including those Richie had out on the range.

As far as I was concerned, all of this nonsense would have added up to nothing more than a teaspoon of flea farts, except for the strange and cumbersome detail that when I traded the Rich Kid my *half* of Rewa for *all* of a stud colt that I really loved, it turned out, according to his sister, I'd only traded for *half* ownership of the stud colt, because she claimed little Richie didn't own all of him, the family owned the other half! Sister maintained that the other half of Punk, as this legendary young strawberry colored stallion was nicknamed, was not yet fully paid for by me from the family, for which this sister claimed to wholly represent, because Punk was registered in her name!

So without knowing it or wanting it, and having done everything to keep my distance from it, I had nonetheless landed square into a bubbling pot of some rich family's B.S. While we really had shook on it, and I'd been led to think I'd completely owned Punk, when I found out I'd been given an unclear deed, I took it in stride and accepting the sister's premise, I headed in to talk to her and in good faith buy the *other half* of the young stallion from the family. Now this was the same person who years past had gelded Amarillento in a fit and who had called ahead when I tried to buy Blue as a stallion and got him gelded, so when I approached her about Punk, she would not allow me to buy *her half* if I didn't have him castrated, so that he would no longer be a stallion when I owned him! She refused to sell him intact!

Since I couldn't just go and pick up my *half* of Punk and take my half home with me, when I conspired to at least get *all* of him out onto the open range on the Rich Kid's Mesta, the sister stepped up her campaign to cut off this young stallion's testicles.

Twice I headed off a vet friend of mine and his tech, who I'd serendipitously come upon at the Owner's conveyor-belt horse facility, just readying their anesthetics and tools to carry out the operation to geld Punk without my permission, the sister having ordered it.

Because our camp lay thirty five miles east into the mountains, it became a hideous, nerve-wrenching game to save Punk's testicles. I spent all my time driving and no one knew where it would end. I had to get him out of there somehow, without getting arrested.

Finally Punk performed a magical act. Though he'd been *sheath squeaking*, like stallions do with a full set of two testicles, for six months, all of a sudden he no longer had two testicles showing, but only a single nut in one scrotum on one side, the other having disappeared, pulled up inside somehow. So each time the sister called in her vet, he preferred to wait until both gonads had descended, surmising that Punk was not yet fully developed, and though there is a way to *dig* such testicles out, this good vet felt it was a bad policy. Punk was only two-years-old by then.

But I knew better, Punk was like Blue, and playing with us.

For as soon as Punk knew it was I that owned one half of him and that I wanted him to stay as a fully male horse, a stallion, my half of him stayed a stallion! The other half was nutless just like the Rich Kid's sister wanted. Punk was always very obliging for a stallion.

Then in all the kerfuffle between the brother and his sister, the brother, during one of his raids to gather up *his* horses from his own family's conveyor-belt horse facility, Punk literally jumped out of his ugly pen, and just as they were driving off, he leapt up, miraculously squeezing his pushy stallion self in through the upper space of the closed rear trailer gate and somehow wriggled, Houdini-like, right in with the rest, to be hauled fifty miles away, out to the good grass of this Richie's self-styled Mesta! They didn't even notice he was in there until they unloaded.

At least for now, all of Punk was running free with Rewa, streaming over the grass and through the chollas, racing with antelopes, who were much faster, and though they always won, they daily trained the horses by pushing them into their top speeds. Antelopes loved to run in those horse herds. It was a majestic sight.

I could breathe a little easier for now, but not for long.

                            ♦ ♦ ♦

The land upon which we had our camp had finally been designated as a historical site commemorating an American Civil War battle by the Federal Government. The woman who owned this land who had been letting us stay there in exchange for our caretaking various buildings and other so-called historical *features*, began preparing to sell the whole area to get top dollar before the Park Service condemned it and converted the whole into a national monument. When we'd first landed there, she'd originally agreed to give to us an unstipulated *acre* as a bonus if she ever contrived to sell her land. But now that acre had disappeared.

In a down to earth response, Blue told me to ask her if she wouldn't like to have a horse. I was to tell her that in appreciation for so many years of having been allowed to carry on living in these wild mountain cliffs, alongside the friendly little creek, I would buy her a horse of her own choosing, within a certain range of price, I would care for her horse and she could ride whenever she felt the desire!

This daughter of wealth loved the idea, and immediately agreed. For she claimed that in her youth, her years riding Thoroughbreds, wearing a helmet, wellingtons, and sporting her crop, were the best years of her life. With a great groan and much to my chagrin, she had me buy a temperamental Thoroughbred mare who was a *Secretariat* granddaughter and was reputedly ready to be ridden.

Blue conspired that if our landlady got into riding her gift-horse over land that she owned, on a horse for which she need not labor, that I would care for, albeit she would pay for the feed and farrier, then she would be more likely to hold onto her land a little longer, to have access to the mountain trails I'd so thoroughly established, and we should have our home camp we'd come to love and trust as our life a bit longer.

I have to say I'd never really been that big on Thoroughbreds as a kind of horse I'd personally want to own. But that's the kind of horse this woman said she wanted and since I had offered, I was trapped by my honor. To keep my word, I bought *Rose*, who by Thoroughbred standards was not a large mare, some sixteen hands tall, but she looked like a Giraffe in our corrals, standing next to my little fourteen-hand Mesta Barbs!

A city horse for sure, this horse had been born, raised, and housed in a box stall, and only exercised on a hot-walker, and never let out to roam with a herd. Everything in her life had been aimed toward racing. At four-years-old, after never placing in a race, she was put up for sale right off the track for her slowness, and was now here at our camp, totally outside any of her previous life experience.

While she actually could be easily saddled and ridden, and the landlady did so for a while, Rose had demonstrated very little horsality and seemed to have no instincts whatsoever for how to be alive, much less how to be a horse. I'd never met such an animal.

My hopes were further pulverized, when, predictably, the rich landlady became quickly bored with her free toy, and losing all interest in horses period, totally abandoned poor Rose to me. "Go ahead Martín, you can have Rose, I give her to you. I've decided on a Buddhist life, and I will not cause a horse any suffering by having her carry me!"

Which is how I ended up with a sixteen hand, surly, Thoroughbred mare, who didn't know the first thing about what being a horse actually meant. She would even sometimes get her head stuck in the watering trough and almost drown herself, or get her head wedged under the corral rails and lift the whole fence up and walk around, pulling the entire thing, until she collapsed under it, and thinking she was dead wouldn't move until we had disassembled the entire section of fence, and, after three hours, finally convince her she was still alive and get her back on her feet! She was certainly alive enough the next week to break the femur of one farrier and the arm of another the next month, for which ill-behavior nobody could be found in the entire state willing to trim or shoe her feet, never mind that her hoof wall was as thin as a piece of matchbox-cardboard and could hardly hold a clinched horseshoe nail anyway, causing her to drop shoes every two days!

Unlike all my other horses, big bay Rose had no common sense, no horse instincts and was addicted to having everything done and thought out for her. Rose was totally human and owner dependent. For me to work with her, she had to be a horse; there was no *horseness* I could get a handle on to bring her out of that human-dependent trance. In the end, this became no good for us or her: for I tended, at our camp and at the makeshift Mesta, over sixty-two other horses with less feed, drama, time, and hassle than this one self-spinning bay mare took all by herself!

She was not really my horse, for of course I hadn't chosen her and never would have. But she'd been thrown away on my shift and I knew I could not in good conscience just sell her to an unsuspecting party. At the same time, I couldn't continue to keep Rose, since her refusal to become an actual *horse* was not something training could remedy. Horses reflect their owners and her original owners had abandoned Rose when she didn't make easy money, and her second owner abandoned her when it all became work. Rose herself seemed to have abandoned living because it was too much effort for her as well. Just like the people who had created her kind of horse, she was spiritually lazy. I couldn't just destroy her, as many suggested, for that would have been too much for my soul. I decided to enlist the help of the horses of the Mesta and meet her weirdness halfway.

One afternoon in the midfall, before the heavy snows, when the wild grama grasses were grown, and their grain heads full, the water still thawed and the wind fairly still, I trailered this spoiled, cranky, city-brained, four-year-old bay mare to the six thousand fenced acres, in the middle of 700,000 other open acres, at the makeshift Mesta of the Rich Kid, out on the rolling hills before the plains.

When we got there, I waited and listened a bit to the Piñon Jays massing for the fall. When I heard that same bird imitate an eagle to scare the little birds off the trees, only then did I call in my own mares, with my own snorting sound of a stallion salute that always brought them up in less than an hour or so. When they first showed, they came streaming to the east, then disappeared, then rose up again thundering straight for us, then two hundred yards out, went wheeling into their own dust and back down some arroyo to reappear to the west, then far to our right, a quarter mile off, they appeared running behind us and then they split up, half of them staying back, while the rest ran right up to the trailer. Eventually the entire bunch thundered in, probably sixty two of them, all sniffing, squealing and snorting, and taking rude turns fighting to get a peek into the trailer at this new arrival.

I explained to them all, "Unlike yourselves, this mare has no idea how to live." Then after a silence, with every one of them ears-forward-listening, I continued, "She hasn't learned how to graze on the open land, what to eat and what not to eat. She has weak hooves from not having to negotiate hard terrain. She is high born among people, arrogant and lazy, badly built and spoiled, and like the people who cause such creatures to be born, she's been denatured. But none of this is her own doing. Her own creators have thrown her away."

I explained to the herd that out of desperation I was at a loss as to what more to do, "So," I told them, "I've brought her to you, Lords and Ladies, who know exactly what Life and the Wild Land charges its natural equine citizens to live on her breasts and in her womb. Will you please accept her as a kind of cultural exchange student, at least for a while, until she makes it here or doesn't."

When I finished talking, the Piñon Jays in a raucous array flew over us heading west. Then the world was quiet, except a couple of snorts. At some signal, a sudden wheeling and raising of choking dust ensued and the horses all threatened to run off again.

I opened the trailer's rear gate and pulled that thin-skinned, gigantic, solid-bay horse to the wild pebbled ground of the Mesta and set her loose. All the horses stopped, turned and stared. After they'd had their look, three quarters of them just left, disappearing back into the range. The quarter of the herd that remained, weirdly, paid no attention to the presence of the big mare: they didn't sniff her, they didn't run up and challenge her, most did not even look at her. It was as if she wasn't even standing there right in front of them. They all just started grazing in a kind of nervous insulted fashion, purposely ignoring her presence.

A blanket of deep sadness dropped over me to realize the vast width of the abyss that exists between all over-domesticated beings: animals, people, and plants on one side and our Indigenous souls, who, unfettered, run in the inner bigness of the wild, infinite, open grandeur inside us, on the other side of that canyon.

I think the heart in any of us can still feel the anguish of the longing to at least just once touch that wild Indigenousness we are really made of. But that evening I wept to see this mare, so big, but so lost without a pen, without a friend, without a human butler to show her how to drink water, so afraid of that open space, that to any other horse should have been a hope and heaven, who just like a kid locked away for years in a boarding school, who finally comes home to her backwater family, finds her family won't recognize her denatured form as even legitimate enough to greet, much less accept. Rose had been truly abandoned by both those that made her and by Nature.

But still, I left her there and as I drove away I stopped to watch the mares kicking her and driving her off like an enemy, allowing no one to let her drink or even graze. I was certain in the end she would perish, but this was her chance. This way she was not pent up in a box stall, spoiled, self-spinning, and brooding herself into weakness, eventually lame, steroid-dependent, and then dead, like so many of modern civilization's horses.

Whereas, in the city, it was as if she'd never even been born, at least here, under the stars and sun in the wild, if she found a way to live, she would be alive for the first time. If she died, her molecules, after death, would re-mix back in the great sub-molecular awareness of the wild land and eventually find their way back into the blood streams of other wild beings, and at least in that never truly die.

She was the husk of a horse, the appearance of what horses had become.

That winter during my turns cracking ice in my visits out on the range, when horses came in for water in the blowing snow and the bitter wind, I never once saw Rose with any of the Barbs and surmised in the springtime we'd find what the coyotes, ravens and magpies had left of her presence somewhere, when on horseback we went to gather the herds and check the perimeters of the fences.

Punk was supposed to be out there too, but I never saw him either. All and all, whatever happened for him, it was a better life than having to constantly dodge the knife. Not that I don't like geldings, 'cause I do, and for most male horses, gelding is alright. I have always ridden geldings more than mares, for mares can make more horses and when they are busy raising their soft-nosed foals and grazing to get milk into their beautiful sueded udders and teaching their youngsters how to be horses, why bother them with being ridden, no matter how good they are? Punk, who was only two-and-a-half, was going to become a perfect old-time stallion and the very reincarnation of his legendary great-grandfather: a Ute horse, miraculously saved by white sympathizers during the American Army's Ute horse extermination program of the late 19th century. What Punk would become, and the offspring he might cause to be born, was rare, and not a good thing to lose.

The next spring, when everyone who had wintered horses in the herd on the *Mesta* went down together to count their horses, we didn't have to round them up, because two days earlier a couple of us had thought to build two connected portable corrals around the only water on the land. When we arrived to count them, most of the herd were already waiting, thirsty for the doors to open, the rest thundering in a half an hour later, at which point we opened the gates and let all of them into one corral without letting the rest out.

With so many animals all churning about in constant nervous motion, it was hard to count them and make sure everybody's animals were present. There would be no new foals, because in Nature few mares would have been bred to foal in winter when they have full furry coats. By horse tradition, mama horses always started foaling from spring to midsummer, about the same time the stallions would breed with them, and since horses have eleven to twelve month gestations, this usually meant spring and summer babies.

In order to see if everyone's ponies were still there, and to generally calculate how many expecting mares there seemed to be, one of us dropped hay into the adjoining corral, whose gate, between the two big corrals, had been closed. Then two people with push button counters sat on either side of the gate, straddling the middle fence, while two others of us opened and closed the gate. This way the guys with the *counters* tallied each horse that rushed through the gate to get to the hay. When every horse had passed into the second corral, we compared each counter's tally. Both of them came up with sixty-three horses, mares, stallions, geldings and yearlings all together...

This was one too many. Before we commenced counting, we had all looked through the herd for a half an hour and none of us had seen, in or out of the corrals, any sign of the big Thoroughbred Rose. With sighs, we all knew we'd find her remains in the next few weeks as the ground thawed, when we went out checking the fences. But still, without Rose there was one horse too many, for we only had sixty-two horses here, and they had counted sixty-three.

So we changed roles, I took a counter and the Rich Kid took one, and the former *counters* manned the gate and drove the herd, one by one, back through the partition, returning them to the water.

Again we came up with sixty-three, one too many. How could it be? The day was just slightly windy, we had our coats on, the Father Sun bright, the earth still mushy and barely beginning to green, and small patches of snow still lay at the edges, on the north sides of all the clumps of *eyebrow* grasses.

So we counted them again as we let them, one by one, back on the range. But this time we began the tedious job of writing down the name of each horse, with his or her owner's name, before we tore down the catch pens.

All eight of my mares left the corral, Punk was definitely alive, pushy and causing trouble, and Rewa was there, and when all were tallied and written down, everybody's horses had been let out and accounted for, nobody was missing; all of our animals had survived the blizzards of that bitter winter. But there remained, pacing in the corral, trying all the gates and panels to get loose, and unclaimed by any of us, one little, restless, bay mare with a wind-tangled, dreadlocked mane and tail.

Nose to the ground, with chipped hooves, and cocklebur-encrusted belly hair, a few bite scars, and dark burning eyes, this mare desperately searched the perimeters for a hole to flee off with the rest, spinning and raising clods and flying stones. She walked right into the low-edged water tank, fiercely sloshed the surface, splashing water everywhere in rage, and after making the reflected clouds ripple, took a nervous mouthful but didn't drink, just enough to moisten the dryness of her mouth, then nimbly hopping out, never took her suspicious wild eyes off any of us. Like a second hand on a watch, she kept rotating, from panel to panel in the corral, where outside some hundred yards off all sixty-two released horses stood in a row, waiting and watching, not running off.

Of course it was Rose.

They were waiting for Rose. The new Wild Rose.

Not one of us expert, horse-know-it-alls even recognized her inside the herd, and even now, all by herself, it stretched the mind to make what we saw in front of us somehow come out of the memory of the form we had remembered the spoiled Thoroughbred to have been. It was like trying to imagine how an Eagle used to be a chicken, or making your head turn a bathroom shower into a hurricane storm, or a corgi into a Wolf. But who else could this be? She used to be tall and gangly, lanky, thin-skinned, uncreative and dull, and now she was compact, scraped-up, and just as fiery and full of life as all the rest. Her coat was molting off patches of dull, muddy fur, under which shiny dapples and a red sunglaze had begun to emerge.

Rose had actually become a horse!

I wept and laughed through my tears 'cause I'd wanted it so badly to be true, but I hadn't even dared to think it could truly happen. For if a spoiled, lost, self-centered, instinct-bereft horse, so badly raised she could drown in a horse tank, or couldn't even stand up on her own, could Indigefy and find a real horse in there somewhere, maybe the over-domesticated, self-spinning, shallow, modern husk of what people have become could also molt into real, indigefied, natural, decent human beings as well.

The miracle had happened.

If it happened with horses, it could happen with culture, and people, and history. This Rose had not only found her Natural Wild Soul again, but even that had been further hammered and shaped by the fierce, patient, windy regulations of all the tribal mares who now stood there, loyally waiting for their *sister* to rejoin their ranks, a horse, who six months before was basically invisible dross to them. But this Rose was now a Wild Rose, and Wild Rose now had a place; not first, not last, but somewhere in the matrix of the mother herd!

When I finally lifted the gate latch to set her loose, she crashed the gate right out of my hands, and coursing like an antelope, let herself back into the wild herd, who having seen her escape and fast approach had already turned on their heels to run before she got there, and by the time she reached them, she merged as a tributary into an already moving river, flowing into and indistinguishable from the rest, part of the rest, another surging white cap in the flood of horses thundering back out to the range.

Chapter 19

Into The Flames and Out Of The Mire

After a year of relative calm, while none of us were watching, or even suspected that members of this family were still quarrelling, and would conspire to do such a thing, little Richie's big rich sister, in a quiet unannounced raid, designed to quickly repossess horses she considered *family property*, drifted out to our happy, wide-open, make-shift Mesta with two large goose-neck stock-trailers into which she had her day workers indiscriminately scoop up at least a half of all the horses we kept on that range and carted them back to the conveyor-belt horse facility of the family, i.e. the Owners headquarters.

In the confusion of her hurried and chaotic seizure of screaming Barbs, she made no effort whatsoever to separate other people's animals out of the herd, my own mares and a foal having been rudely rounded up and loaded, resulting in a very dangerously combative Punk. Though she felt she still owned Punk, he was too fierce, and the sister was too intimidated to catch him. But Punk, unwilling, as all stallions are, to allow *his* mares to be separated from him in any way, forced his militant way into the trailer in which my mares were riding and rode back to the city with the rest.

When the Rich Kid found out what she'd done in a fury, he wasn't sure what to do, but postured like he was heading into battle. Luckily for me, one of the associates of our little Mesta found me to tell me about my mares and that *my half of Punk* was back in the city, in a pen, still fiercely guarding his mares and wouldn't let anyone within thirty feet of them without dangerously charging at them!

We were worse off than before. But since there was nobody contending my ownership of my seven mares and the foal, I drove into town to see what I could see and do what I could do, and at least load them up and bring them back to our camp. Seeing as the Mesta was no longer really safe, I thought maybe I should load up Punk too, who would follow my mares anyway, and finally take them all home with me!

My stock trailer could only hold seven horses packed tight, and I kept calculating how to get them all in there, and of course what to do about my half of young three-year-old Punk, for that would make eight horses. Even so, if he did come home with me, our camp had no *stallion* pen strong enough to hold such a fierce, young, male horse.

The name that the crazy sister had given him when he first arrived at four months of age was at least a dignified name, and so he was registered in the Barb *registry* as Bashkiri, for the curly, strawberry-roan coat he sported as a yearling, reminiscent of the original Bashkiri Nomad, curly-haired, milking horses of the southeastern Ural mountains, in what is now Russia. But even so, no one I knew had ever called him Bashkiri, or even knew that was supposed to be his name, because his foal mane, as he matured, became at least five inches thick at its base on his massive stallion neck, and grew straight up off his neck like bristles on a new broom, until it reached a height of a complete foot! Because this vertical quivering crest was so stiff, it would not fold over like most horses do, so all the little neighborhood kids thereabouts called him the Punk Rocker, because of his *Mohawk* hairdo!

Like a Zebra mane times two, it trembled very impressively when he screamed or did his *pig honk* stallion grunt, and every time he stomped or jumped it was like he was brushing the teeth of the sky with his mane! Punk was a handy name, and he was pretty punky too, so everyone just naturally called him Punk, and Punk was the only name he listened to or that anyone ever knew him by. His mane wouldn't actually begin to fold over until his Lordship, still a stallion, turned four and by the time of his sixth birthday in August, his mane, like Rewa's, would end up dragging in thick, black, sausage curls right to his cannon bones, and his curly tail did drag on the ground, grinding off the tips as he ran. But as I drove my rig into the south Santa Fe district where Sister had taken my horses, he was only three, and his mane still stiff and half grown.

Somebody's house must've been on fire, for black flowers of thick smoke rose frantically up and over the whole area, and when I neared the conveyor-belt pen facility, two fire trucks sirened me off the alley to get past me. They rolled screaming into the Owner's horse lot where they joined three other trucks already deployed in battling the fierce flames of the loft in the second story of the Owner's hay barn, which was already swallowed in flames! Constructed entirely of creosote-soaked railroad ties and rubber conveyor belting, the smoke was black, like used oil, and the stench toxic and dense.

I left my rig up in the alley and walked down to the pens to check the welfare of the horses, for most horses would be instinctively trying to bolt to get miles away from the harsh heat, the demonic ear-splitting crackling of such a massive fire, the sirens, the hoses, the yelling, and all the walkie-talkie racket. Some horses are known to even freak out enough to run hysterically straight into fires and die there consumed in flames.

At first I surmised that the Owner's notorious habit of purchasing wet, sub-standard hay bales had finally caused some to heat up and explode into flame in the haystack, as sometimes happened in big stacks of hay not carefully dried and baled, which accounted for most barn fires, but then again, maybe somebody disobeying the rule in every ranch of, "no live cigarette butts stamped out around the hay barns," had sparked it up. Authorities would later show that neither of these were the cause, but that some angry person had intentionally set the barn ablaze.

But right now in the urgency of it all, none of that mattered, for after checking all the horses, I found Punk missing. My mares were more or less safe, but I'd searched everywhere and Punk was nowhere to be found.

To get a look at the burning barn, I pushed hard through the fire fighters wetting down all the surroundings with their hydrant hoses. A fist of horror slugged into my tightening stomach: Right in the middle of the hay-littered bottom storey of the burning barn, in between the ten burning pillars that held up the barn, beautiful Punk stood calmly guarding one of the sister's terrified mares. There, he was circling the stunned mare directly beneath the burning loft and the roof, engulfed in the bolt-melting flames. His mane was smouldering and his eyes all smoke glazed and white. The wall of firemen would not allow anyone to attempt to rescue them for the real fear that no one could predict when the burning loft would come crashing down on whoever went in to chase the horses out.

The mare had freaked out when one of the Owners tried to move her from the pen she was held in adjacent to the fire. Hysterical and disoriented by the sirens, the smoke and the fire and all the yelling, she pulled loose and ran straight into the barn, where even more confused, she just stood there unable to act.

Punk, who had been in a pen a couple doors down guarding my own mares, saw it all, and considering all mares *his* mares, turned into a frantic, screaming maniac. He jumped his own pen and, with no one to stop him, barged past everyone, right into the barn to fetch her out. But once inside, Punk found the mare too tranced out, smoke-brained, and unwilling to be driven out or follow him. So he stayed and was calmly pacing to avoid totally burning up.

Without a thought, like a fool, I ran to my truck and with my knife slashed an old dusty army blanket down the middle, then jumped with both halves into a three hundred gallon horse trough of water and rolled around to thoroughly soak my clothes, the blankets, my head and my felt hat. Then dragging the heavy water-logged blanket halves and myself, I ducked and ran like a bull through the firemen's barricade, and by leaps and bounds, managed to make my way into the barn with Punk. He was looking at me with a proud smile, calmly ready to die I guess, 'cause the mare wouldn't move, and glad for the company at the end of the world.

The firefighters were furious with me and yelling away as they should have been, but I was moving fast and had already instantly slung a wet blanket, already hot and half-steaming, over the mare's head so as to block her vision and one over Punk's smoldering back. I started pulling the mare with the blanket, and unable to see all the fright, she finally started to follow as I pulled. Punk, still awake, very usefully, in a split second, took up the rear and began biting her hard on the butt to drive her forward, which was of great assistance in getting all of us moving. His whiskers were all burnt off, his mane all but gone, my boot soles instantly melting, and with every step over the loose burning hay, flames and smoke shot out from under every one of our hooves like dragon tongues trying to lick our knees and burnt off my pant edges and the horse's long hairs.

There was nothing to breathe in there, so I almost fainted, not because of smoke, but because there was no oxygen left, for the fire had sucked it all up into the funnel of flames overhead, so once we thankfully hit the air at the edge of the burning barn all three of us gasped and the people cheered, and the firemen tried to grab me, but Punk just kept pushing that crazed mare and pulling me along with him. Right then and there I decided this stallion was the best horse on earth, and we needed more just like him and that nobody was going to cut off his testicles or take him away from me anymore.

Removing my belt and knotting what was left of my scarf to form a neckrope, I led Punk straight to my trailer, and miraculously he followed, though his eyes were milky looking and compromised. Punk just got in with no fight, despite his mares not being with him. He was definitely a keeper. Tough, not hysterical, full of calm thinking, he could reason and be reasoned with. When the chips were down, he kept his nerve. Very rare among horses, who are prone to flight as a cure all. Even rarer in people. Those are the things we should want horses to pass on to their children.

Right then Little Richie's big sister, without having lifted a finger and having watched the whole affair, and with no thanks for having saved her mare, came running up, viciously yelling and waving her arms to protest my taking of Punk, but then stood back when I turned around and she saw I had no eyebrows or hair left, and Punk no mane, and the look on my face must've had some old Mohawk, Lenape, Cree, Irish ancestral fierceness, and she kind of staggered back in horror. Realizing she'd gone too far, she began to praise instead. But it was all too little too late for me, and I was in no mood to negotiate with people who had caused me and my animals so many detours with too much uncalled for spoiled behavior, so I was on edge to say the least, and absolutely finished playing footsy with such self-serving demons.

"Ma'am, do you see that mare of mine over there with the white flash on her side and the four month old foal?" She did. "Well, I'm giving them to you right now. They are what I'm paying you with, for my half of Punk. I'm buying your half of Punk right this minute. You can take the mare and baby right now. Now, I want you to get me Punk's registration and a bill of sale for him right this minute. Not tomorrow. Do you understand?!" She did.

And in that very tense moment as I so uncourteously laid out my case, the entire roof and loft of the barn burnt entirely through and careened to the ground. With a loud bone-curdling crack, an over-all hiss, and a long drawn out groan, tons of furiously burning ties and hay all crashed down exactly where Punk, the mare and I had once been standing, throwing millions of sparks and red-hot nails, like darts, in every direction. What was left of the barn turned into a real bonfire in hell, melting conveyor belting and starting up spot fires in hay piles and pens as far as two hundred feet away, towards which every extra person ran to douse with water buckets out of the troughs. Some of the more thoughtful people began dousing the horses too, like one should, many were blistered and singed.

No one there dared to argue with me, no one even watched or helped me as I loaded all my mares in with a very tired, appreciative, but nonetheless screaming, demanding, stallion Punk, still on the job of watching out for them all. It was pretty tight, but without the mare and baby, there were now seven horses, where seven fit, and none of them or I complained as we thankfully drove away from that burning rubber hell. None of us ever looked back or ever once again came near to the Owners on purpose.

Tom and Vera Romero had been right. But then again so was I, for though Punk and I had both lost our eyebrows and our manes, he still had both his nuts and I had him, my mares, Blue and Amarillento, and we were out of there for good.

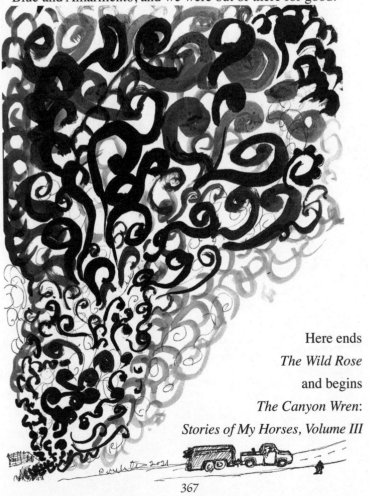

Here ends
The Wild Rose
and begins
The Canyon Wren:
Stories of My Horses, Volume III

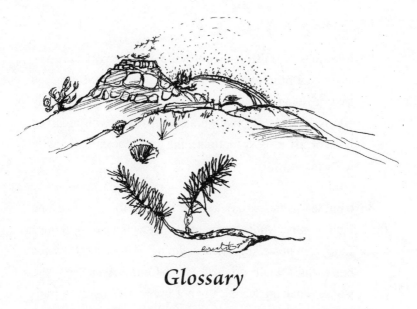

Glossary

Alforjas (Arabic descended Spanish; pronounced Awl-for-hahs) – common Southwestern word, even among Anglo cattlemen, that signifies the double saddle bags spread over a pack frame on a pack horse.

Arriéro (Spanish; pronounced Ah-ree-err-o) – a drover. Person who manages a string of pack or baggage animals: mules, burros, horses, etc. A well-established career throughout the Spanish speaking areas of the world, especially traversing mountainous areas where no wheeled traffic could pass. Like sailors, they have been famous for their songs, poems, stories, and their knowledge of knots and the stars.

Arrisco (Spanish) – common term for a horse that is very alert, elusive and difficult to catch.

Barba quejo (Spanish) – signifies the chin strap that keeps a rider's hat from flying off in the wind or the breeze caused by fast riding. Originally, this strap could be considerably adorned, made of ornate braided goatskin with a carved bone or silver slider for tightening under the chin. Literally a "beard stay."

Barb horse – at present day, a confusing term for more than one kind of horse whose meaning has been clouded by various European horse registries claiming Barb ancestries for horses that actually originated from Central Asian Nomadic stock, which are technically not *Barbs*. Originally, a Barb horse referred to horses historically belonging to any of the many diverse Berber peoples, both nomadic and settled, both inland and along the *Barbary coast* of Morocco, Algeria, Libya, parts of Egypt, etc.

    The famous Spanish horse of the Middle Ages and Renaissance no longer truly exists in Spain due to devastating horse epidemics during the Napoleonic Wars and the 19th century Spanish Civil War, but was originally a fine Barb-type horse. The original *Mesta* horses of the Americas, the Cow pony of the American Southwest, was often called a Barb by 19th century American cattlemen, and Moro (Moorish horse) by Spanish Americans, who very intelligently recognized these powerful, small, beautiful horses for what they were: a North African Spanish horse of mostly Barb descendancy that were brought to the

Americas before they largely disappeared in Europe during the terrible horse epidemics.

Bramadero (Spanish) – from the word *brama*, meaning the fertile period or sexual heat in a female animal. A bramadero is a very sturdily built breeding pen with a stout post buried in the middle where a bull and heifers are brought together for mating. But in the Spanish speaking Americas, a bramadero more often refers to the post or *brake* where horses begin their training. See *breaking a horse*.

Breaking a horse – bad pulp fiction about horses has confused the notion of what breaking a horse actually means in English. A horse that is broken is not *broken* like a twig, but tamed to be ridden. While there are horses that have most certainly been wrecked, destroyed, their souls reduced to sulky bitterness, and this is all atrocious and uncalled for, none of this has anything to do with what people mean with the term *breaking a horse*.

Breaking a horse arises from an historical semantic mix-up and orthographic inconsistency. Originally the word *breaking*, as in breaking a horse, was written *braking a horse*, referred to *softening* or *suppling* something, as when softening an untanned hide to turn it into leather. *Braking a hide* was part of the old European leather tanning process and was carried out by two individuals who, from opposite sides, pulled a previously *cured* skin back and forth over the top of a smooth stake to soften it. Looking like a five-foot-high, gigantic polished baseball bat set deeply into the ground, this stake was known as a *brake* in German, Celtic, and eventually English. When hide tanners went about softening a skin, toward the end of the tanning process, they called it *braking a skin* not *breaking a skin* i.e., softening a hide on a brake. Training a *raw, green* horse properly, stage by stage, over a period of time, to slowly make a suppled, tame riding horse was likened to the many stages of courting a raw, freshly-removed skin of a large animal, called a *green hide*, to slowly turn it into a beautiful, pliable, strong, good smelling, and very useful piece of leather. The last stage of hide-softening and horse-gentling was also called the gradual *braking* or suppling of the horse, like a calf skin, into a pliable and useful riding horse!

While a *horse braker* was originally a person who could *gentle* a horse, a horse *breaker*, on the other hand, was a term invented by pulp fiction writers to designate those people who used rough methods to *dominate* strings of green horses for quick sale by bucking them out till they couldn't move and selling them as *broke*.

A horse tamer was a person who *bucked* horses out. A horse gentler was a person who softened horses and accustomed them to the saddle or harness. It's good to know your own history. But in the American West, a *broke* horse still means a horse that's been gentled, softened, and made pliable to ride, not a horse ruined and dominated into submission.

Bozal (Spanish; pronounced bow-sáhl) – horseriding equipment. In the Americas, a braided leather or rawhide noseband set in a headstall. Shaped like the frame of a Native snowshoe, the *bozal* is used instead of a bit to train a horse to respond to being steered with reins by pressure on the nose, without the danger of ruining a horse's mouth. Usually, once the horse rides well on the *bozal*, a bit is added and a very thin *bozal* replaces the original noseband. The theory is that the horse learns to respond to very subtle rein cues without having to be cued by any direct pressure on the bit.

Cabestro (Spanish) – means different things in different parts of the world. But generally it refers to some type of horse halter, a rig that fits over a horse or donkey's head, running from behind the ears to a noseband and fastens under the jaw. In some places, *cabestro* refers to a headstall. See halter.

Chaquegue (Tewa Pueblo language adapted into New Mexico Spanish – pronounced chah-káy-way) – this is a mush made of Native blue flour corn, toasted, then ground fine and mixed with cold water, then added to separately boiling water and stirred until cooked and smooth. The ancestor of the modern Italian polenta, which of course originated in the Americas under many different names. Chaquegue is one of the most ancient foods throughout the American

Southwest, Mexico, Central America, and South America. Served variously as a base of many sauces and proteins. In Northern New Mexico this is the traditional breakfast, often served sweet with honey and goat milk, or savory with chile and eggs.

Chimajá (Spanish from the Native Keres Ch'm'aa) – referring to a dwarf, wild-desert celery whose leaves and roots are locally prized and eaten fried, fresh, or dried and crumbled into all types of traditional food among all old-time New Mexicans: Pueblos, Diné Navajos, and Spanish speaking. Also used to make a famous *digestivo*, a kind of liquor. By soaking the fresh leaves of this plant in *mula* (native corn moonshine), the resulting liquid, after a year, is used externally as a liniment for contusions and sore muscles, and internally on Christmas and New Year's Eve, where a small *shot* is consumed by each member of a family to insure good health.

Chicken snare saddle – in the old American West the word *chicken*, in settler-English and the corresponding *gallina* in post-colonial Spanish, did not always refer to a domesticated chicken, but more often than not to some species of Grouse or Prairie Chicken. Thus, even on a map today, the Gallina Mountains, Gallina River, or Gallina Canyon, Chicken Creek, etc. all refer to the wild galliformes, not Leghorns or Barred Rocks. The early Spanish and the first Anglo-Americans in the West learned to trap and eat these wild ground birds from the original Native peoples of the area they invaded. One type of these traps had two bars connected by two bent branches and a net stretched over the whole that would snap shut like a clam when tripped by a bird trying to eat the corn with which it was baited.

The quick-to-make, rawhide-covered, antler and wood-slab saddle made by many tribes for riding or packing was likened to a prairie chicken snare: thus the name chicken snare saddle. Very useful, actually difficult to craft, and with a good furry sheepskin or pelt, not too bad on the bottom. Native American women's saddles were for the most part exquisite works of art and, although made of elk antler as well, they were very tall and a different thing altogether.

Coloratura (Italian, Spanish, English) – opera singing term for the improvisational trills and ululations at the ends of phrases in old Italian operas.

Coscojos (Spanish) – little jinglers or tiny silver bells hanging from curb chains in tiers, sewn onto men's pants, or suspended from *anqueras*: the hip straps that run under a horse's tail. This very ancient horse adornment descends from the Caucasus, Central Asia, and North Africa. Many medieval European knights had these sound makers all over their outfit. Very rare nowadays, but still a standard part of Native bridles in some places.

Coursing – an unofficial term for a very official horse gait. People think that saying a horse is *coursing* over the land just means the horse is galloping fast, but *coursing* is a particular way to cover land. Some people think horses have only four gaits: walk, trot, canter, and gallop. But horses around the world have all sorts of gaits associated with types and breeds. There is the tölt, paso fino, amble, marchalarga, walk-run, the rack, not to mention unfortunate, synthetically enforced gaits, to name just a few.

While individual foals are often born with extra gaits unknown to the parents, for the most part in my neighborhood, our horses move in the following gaits:

1. A walk, which has a two-beat rhythm.

2. A trot, which has a single, alternating staccato beat.

3. An Indian shuffle, which is a cross between a trot and a rack that is a smooth motion through sand that rocks from side to side.

4. A lope is a slow canter in three beats, lovely and fast enough.

5. A full canter, a fast three-beat motion, the best gait of all.

6. A gallop, a fast four-beat divided into two.

7. A run, a smooth, very fast, reaching gait.

8. A *course*, just like a Jackrabbit or Leopard runs, by reaching forward past the ears with the hind legs and pushing powerfully forward, while reaching way forward with both front legs and powerfully pulling forward. Once well established, its just like a fast-moving river and feels

pretty much like flying, because the horse is in the air three times longer than his feet are on the ground. So coursing across the land, a herd of wild horses can look like a flash flood of flesh, fur, and dust. Very majestic to ride and see. Called a *full career* by the stuffy.

Crop (English) – a thin, semi-flexible, short whip used to cue a saddle horse. A constant presence and fetish of status in northern European horse riding. Originally made of a thin piece of dried bull penis covered in braided black silk, but later made from whale baleen and braided silk, nowadays most are fiberglass and polyester. Any European-derived, saddle riding tradition is always done with a crop, often a symbol of gentry, imperial domination, and European cavalry. While all horse cultures have some sort of riding whip to urge their horses, more often they are beautifully adorned, more whiplike, and works of art in themselves. Worn more as a piece of tribal jewelry than a functional tool; compared to these, an English crop is a rather anal, puritan-looking, sneering twig.

Delicia (Spanish, Southwestern "English") – the lusciousness of something, the deliciousness.

Diné (Diné) – a Diné word for themselves. Also known as Navajo. The actual meaning of the word Diné in Diné language is complex. It is now politically proper to designate any Navajo person as pertaining to the Diné tribe. But the word Diné doesn't actually imply Navajos, or humans. It refers to the living form of anything. For instance, Lightning Diné, or Fir Tree Diné, or Corn Beetle Diné, or Rain Diné. Different tribes are *Paiute* Diné or *Taos* Diné, *Mexican* Diné etc. To distinguish themselves, the Diné of today generally say *Ta'á Diné* to signify their particular *Navajo* Diné.

Dinétah – old Diné word for their tribal homeland. A euphemism sometimes used by non-Navajos for the landscape where one *belongs*.

Doings (Native American English) – signifies an important ceremonial ritual with a large communal attendance.

Dorsal stripe (English) – a type of horse marking, used to signify the dark narrow line (red, black, grey) that some horses exhibit that runs from the mane down and over their withers, right on top of their spine, to the tail. Considered by veterinary science to be a primitive horse coat pattern from before the Pleistocene era.

Ergot (Latin/English) – the strange English language term for the little bony protuberances at the rear of the fetlock on a horse's foot, which, along with the *chestnuts* found on the insides of the horse's forearms, constitute what remains of the original three other toes of the pre-historic horse ancestors of our now single-toed horses.

For a lot of tribal horse people worldwide, these ergots and chestnuts are considered to be very powerfully charged with medicine.

Gallo and gallo horse (Spanish) – The word gallo (pronounced gah-yo), means literally a rooster in Spanish. But a *gallo* is also the colloquial name for an ancient game played on horseback that has far-flung origins among horse people throughout North Africa, Europe, Central and North Asia.

When the Spanish colonial culture came to what later was called the American Southwest, they brought with them a lot of their animals, cultivars, tools, and methods for taking care of all that, their religion and a lot of customs. Not all of these things flourished in their new setting, but some things stuck and became so much a part of Native cultures and Hispanic post-colonial life that people sometimes forget their origins.

Horses, long-horned cows, Churro sheep, Angora goats, big red hogs, rabbit hounds, steel knives, axes, hoes, pulleys, shovels, pliers, scissors, nails, wheat, barley, grapes, peaches, plums, cherries, radishes, haba beans, parsnips, carrots, oats, peas, floor looms, spinning wheels, playing cards, chess, to name just a few, all combined with the amazing plants and minerals, tools and methods of other people the Spanish had overrun farther south; when all of these things merged in turn with the equally rich and capable cultures already in place in what is now New Mexico, the resulting culture became the unique phenomena it is today.

One of the things that really took off was the raising of chickens. With chickens, one doesn't only end up with eggs and delicious chicken recipes, but roosters. You only need a single rooster to breed forty to fifty hens, but with a lot of broody hens you end up with a lot of roosters. Just like horses, unless you castrate them, you end up having to deal with a lot of fighting males. Like stallions, roosters are very fierce and jealous of their females. A castrated rooster, called a capon, is an eating specialty of certain peoples, especially the French and Italians and formerly the English. They grow real big and taste very good.

But in our area, the yearly over-population of roosters was annually dealt with by their part in an ancient horse game, brought by the Spanish, which was then further finessed into Pueblo spiritualism. In our area of New Mexico, on the Saint's day of San Antonio on June 14, San Juan on June 24, and Santiago on July 24, great contests and exhibitions of horse riding expertise were carried out, called the *gallo*: the rooster.

In this game, after villagers donate a great number of live roosters, up to three hundred Native riders and their little horses line up to have a chance to pull a live rooster out of a hill of sand where he has been buried up to his neck. Riders canter past the rooster, just to the left, then without stopping, and leaning way over to the right, attempt to pull the entire flapping bird out of the ground as they pass. Most fail to grab the wily dodging head of the rooster, but when one is successful, this rider then grabs the bird tight so as to avoid the rooster's wicked spurs, and in the same moment, with a knotted cloth for a quirt, the rider starts his horse galloping as fast as he can, and in any design of motion to avoid the thundering mass of the rest of the three hundred riders chasing him and his horse and the flapping rooster, who are all dedicated to rudely wresting the rooster away from him by whatever means possible. At break-neck speeds, the riders dodge and hit, ride sideways, and do all sorts of maneuvers, the rooster often serving as a club to beat off assailants.

The flapping of the rooster only served to make all the horses go faster.

The goal, if you got a rooster out of the ground and got away, or succeeded in taking it away from some other rider in the thick dust and swirling milieu of horses, was to ride like hell to the house of the girl you loved the most and throw the rooster in through her adobe doorway, at which point the rooster was already dead, or killed by the lady of the house, and all pursuit was called off and the next round of riders went after the next rooster in the very long line of buried roosters. The *gallo* could go on in this way for eight to ten hours making it a test of tremendous endurance for both man and beast. The roosters thus distributed were plucked and stewed and taken, by the sweetheart, all dressed up, to the parents of the young man who had tossed the bird into her house as a kind of courting gesture.

In this game a lot of expert riding techniques were used, but riders often toppled from their horses, losing their seat while trying to retrieve a rooster. Newly proficient young riders, the heroes of the game, were always emerging to take the day, but a lot of big, rowdy, middle-aged Indians, veterans of many *gallos*, were the admitted masters. Church bells were rung and bugles blown every time someone was fleeing with a rooster. And after a while, all the previous winners had to ride single-file between two long poles, each maneuvered by two men on the ground. Between the tops of these poles a rope was stretched in whose center a live rooster was fastened. The idea was to stand up on your horse as you rode underneath this rooster that was held between the poles as he dropped and rose, grab the bird, jump back down into your saddle and once again run like hell to avoid a hundred riders on your tail trying to get the bird away from you.

To ride in the *gallo* you needed a really good horse and the short little *Mesta* Barbs were made for it. Like polo ponies, they had to be able to stand, but then respond in a flash, turn on a dime, move sideways and feint, stop and jump out, charge undaunted into other horses, and into a huge rush of animals, then light out, like a Hawk with a chicken, in a second without biting or striking, and never tire. It was extremely rugged, very exciting, and very heroic. There were a lot of broken noses, dislocated fingers, broken ribs. Sometimes riders were maimed in the fray and every few years someone was killed, usually dragged, caught in the stirrup, and smashed into a wall. But everyone riding in a *gallo* came out a little beat up and bloody, but smiling and excited. The horses loved the *gallo* with all the herd-like free-for-alls.

But a good *gallo* horse was always a prize animal. Funnily enough, when American-style rodeos began to dominate the *Western* scene, they were all called *gallos* by the locals, not rodeos. In some Native languages, such as Diné, a rodeo is still called *hoohai*: chicken. When I was a little kid it took me a long while to figure out why Navajos always called their much beloved rodeos the *hoohai* or chicken. "Hey, let's go rope at the chicken, Martín!" It makes sense once you think about it, for at least where I grew up, in a full-on *gallo* there was a lot more wild horsemanship involved than any rodeo or horse event. Anyone who's seen or ridden in one can attest to the accuracy of that statement!

Of course when it comes to the Native ritual aspect of the *gallo*, there's a lot more to tell than the Spanish bugles, the bellringing, painting of the horses, the communal gift giving, the feasting, the anger contest, and a thousand more beautiful components, but in my experience, all the charm and excitement that a large *gallo* inspires in New Mexicans and Natives seems to be lost on most modern, urban people, so I'll just leave it at that. You get the general idea. Anglos call the *gallo* a rooster pull.

Gelding (English) – a castrated stallion. Supposedly devoid of the testosterone driven fierceness of stallions, and the unpredictable craze of mares in heat every twenty-one days; geldings are the world's most common form of riding horse. Most cultures geld male horses, keeping only a few intact stallions to further the line.

Granny gear (American slang) – compound low gear in old-time trucks. Those vehicles had four forward gears and reverse. But first gear was so low and powerful, most people started their trucks in second gear, using first gear (granny gear) only for slow, very difficult terrain. Before four-wheel drive was common, granny gear was all we had.

Green horse – an untrained horse. See *breaking a horse*.

Grulla (Spanish; pronounced grew-yah) – horse color from the Spanish word *grulla*, or Crane, as in Sandhill Crane. Typically a kind of holographic coat that reflects red or blueish overtones with dark legs, dark dorsal stripes, dark tail, muzzle, and mane. Crane colored.

Halter – a horse's headgear made of rope, leather, or webbing. Goes over a horse's head, behind the ears, buckling at the throat, used with a tie-on or clip-on lead rope to guide a horse to where you want, and for tying up to hold a horse still while saddling. Not made for riding, just for moving a horse on the ground, though there are people who ride with halters and reins these days.

Hand – in old Europe, comparative heights of plants, animals and people were generally communicated by the human hand, in positions.

By lowering or lifting an extended hand held horizontally, palm up, the height of a young sapling, or a crop of wheat would be conveyed.

The height of one's children was shown in the same way, but by holding the palm down, to distinguish.

To express the height of a farm animal: a cow, or pig, a lamb, or goat etc., the hand was held sideways, and represented the animals head, with the thumb up, standing for the animal's ears. By lifting or lowering the hand, the relative size of an animal could be expressed to a person watching or listening.

A horse, on the other hand, was and still is measured by the distance of how many of these sideways hands, with the thumb held parallel, measured across the knuckles, it takes, from the front hoof, up the leg, past the shoulders, to reach the tip-top of the horse's withers. Four fingers equaled a hand. Thus a horse could be 14 hands and 2 fingers or 15 hands, or 13 hands and 3 fingers. Eventually the *hand* measurement was standardized in most of European countries to be four inches, and each finger an inch.

Thus a horse that stands fifty-six inches from the ground, at the front hoof to the top of the withers, is said to be fourteen hands tall. A horse that stands fifty-eight inches to the withers is said to be 14.2 hands, or 14 and a half hands high, etc. Thus a 16 hand Thoroughbred is sixty-four inches tall at the withers.

Hashmarks (Western American cowboy slang) – horse color term for any number of dark, parallel stripes that sometimes adorn the fur of a horse's forearm, like the chevrons on the shoulders and cuffs of military uniforms that signify rank. Along with *dorsal stripes*, *spider webbing*, and *smokey withers* or *cross, hashmarks* are thought to be throwback markings from prehistoric equines.

Headstall (English) – the leather head gear that holds a bit in a horse's mouth, or noseband, in place. Used for riding with reins attached to bits or noseband.

Horno (Spanish; pronounced o´r-no) – a wood-fired, outside oven. In northern New Mexico, horno signifies a large beehive shaped oven made of tufa or adobes plastered with mud; used to bake bread, biscochitos, cookies, prune and peach pies, to roast meat, squash, and sweetcorn. Everyone loves to eat what comes out of the horno.

Horsality (New Mexico, cowboy English) – term used by horse lovers to signify the natural core reality of *horsiness*, where a horse's manner, politic, moods and reasoning don't derive from their generational exposure to human expectations. Where a horse's reactions and sense of self-respect retain all aspects of having a natural *horsality*, instead of the neurotic, boring, in-your-pocket, idiot horse who only has a *personality*!

Hozhro or Hozho or Hozhon (Diné Navajo) – term that implies the condition of wellbeing where every being is living according to his or her Nature and all life flourishes. The deepest definition of health.

In hand (English) – a common EuroAmerican riding term that signifies that a horse ridden, or horses driven, are responding to the signals of the rider, or their driver, by means of the reins held in the rider's or driver's hands: i.e., the rider is in control.

The common spoken English expression denoting a situation that is out of control: things "have gotten *out of hand*," originally meant that a rider's horse was not listening and responding to the handheld reins, and the horse was therefore *out of hand*, going berserk, ready to bolt, out of control.

Thus, things are *in hand* or *out of hand*.

Jinglebobs (Western American English) – refers to two small iron, silver, or brass pendants which dangle, free-hanging, from a hole in the rowel pin of a spur with a large rowel. An inheritance from Latin America and Spain and ultimately Medieval Europe, in which the spurs are made to really *jingle*. I don't use spurs, or like them, but I love jinglebobs on spurs to walk around feeling musical at every step.

Lance-side – an old English horseman's term for what in all of
Europe, in their own languages, is the original designation
of what today is called the offside on a horse: the right side.
Because medieval European knights, and earlier North
African and Arab knights, kept their swords belted to the
left, to be drawn with their right hand, and their lance-butts
socketed on the right side in a sheath-like holder strapped
onto the front cinch or stirrup strap, they always mounted
from the left, holding onto the lance to get into the saddle.

While horse cultures worldwide taught their children,
boys and girls, to mount and dismount from either side (a
very good policy), European descended riding traditions
mount only from the left, this being *the on-side*, and the
right being the *offside*, all motions militarily derived.

Mecate (Mexican Spanish; pronounced mek-ah-tei) – from the
Nahuat *mecatl*, originally an Indigenous Mexica term for
rope or cordage, usually expertly twisted from the fibers
of the blades of certain species of maguey or lechuguilla
plants. But, in Spanish, it gradually gestated to mean a
three or two-ply rope, one inch thick, made of the mane
hair of horses, and about twenty foot long. When used in
conjunction with the *jaquima* and *bozal*, it binds the whole
headrig in such a way as to provide both a set of reins and a
lead rope, all in one. American cowboys call it a McCardy.

But the word *mecate*, used casually, usually signifies a
twenty-foot rope used to halter horses *old style*, without a
halter, by a couple of configurations, to tie up a horse while

saddling and bridling, after which a loop remains around the horse's neck, and the slack tied up to the saddle while riding. This slack can then be let out while resting a horse, or tied to a tree while the horse grazes and the rider boils up some tea or coffee. Just like tying up a boat. I grew up with the *mecate* and not halters.

Mesta (Spanish) – originally a co-operative of Spanish stock-raisers who graze their animals in common and take turns watching over them and come together to co-operatively round up, move the animals, doctor them, and train them in the case of oxen or horses.

A kind of ancient Iberian grange where members met and voted on leaders, and what to do with animals, and who communally shared expenses. Because the livestock was generally herded in wild-open areas and not held in fenced paddocks or pastures, some herders had to always be on the job.

Any animal raised in this style of open, wild grazing was called, in Spanish: *Mesteño*. The word *Mesteño* eventually gestated into the American English word mustang. But originally a *Mesteño* horse was never an unprovenanced, ownerless, feral animal, but a horse raised in a *Mesta* herd, watched over by *Mesta* rangers. Colonial Spanish horse raisers spread the institution of the *Mesta* to their colonies, and Native populations continued raising their cattle and horses in this same time-honored way after Spain no longer claimed the area. We still did so in my youth.

It is interesting to note that the word mustang, even in standard American English dictionaries up until WWII, signified a "small, narrow-chested, Spanish horse of great endurance and steady temperament from the American Southwest": basically identical to what a horse of the *Mesta* had always meant.

But mustangs as *Mesta* horses disappear from the American consciousness after the 1940's, and ever since any large clump of unowned, feral, American ranch horses, draft horses, and ponies running on public land have been called mustangs. Though some of these are interesting, they are not the same animal in the least.

Mare – mature female horse.

Oregano de la Sierra – a variety of Monarda, a mountain mint treasured by Northern New Mexicans for medicine.

The Owners – As it occurs in the *Stories of My Horses*, the Owners refer to various wealthy, white families and individuals who for several decades, starting in the 1970's, were those who purported to be rescuing the Spanish Barb horses, the Native Mesta horse, from extinction, but whose practical motives were more deeply vested with the sizeable federal tax exemptions their horse-saving operations garnered for their inherited money.

To do this, these Owners joined a registry dedicated to the preservation of this famous American horse. This registry predictably schismed when several quarrelling Owners, each of whom *owned* sizeable bands of horses with particular traits, claimed that only their animals had the real original traits and therefore the original bloodlines. This in turn caused many registries to sprout up, each with their own breed of wealthy founder: i.e., Owners.

There were a few sincere people, both wealthy and not, who loved and rode these horses, who purchased horses from these Big Owners, but the gene pool became so absurdly reduced by all the fracturing into quarreling camps that it became impossible for regular people to keep their interest in this beautiful animal thriving without getting immersed in a pointless war of high school factionalism in which they had no vested interest.

When the federal tax laws were changed in the 1980's and again in the 1990's, all these tax shelter registries and all these Owners disappeared into the ether. Their horses were still around, but as a recognized breed they fell into total limbo and were scattered to the winds.

All the Barb Spanish Mesta style horses these Owners had ever *owned* were horses originally gathered up by a couple of old-time Westerners way before these Owners ever existed, mostly from Native Americans and Reservations.

When the Owners first entered the scene, they felt they alone possessed what was needed to save Native horses, and felt that they alone had the funds to do it, and that all the lesser non-monied people should be thankful to contribute to the cause in the capacity of laborers and advisors in the actual *work* of feeding, trimming, breeding, doctoring, gelding etc. to maintain the Owner's tax shelters. A kind of feudal mentality.

All the Native Navajos and Pueblos with whom I grew up have the time-honored tradition of developing nicknames for people based on some overriding trait, or something they might resemble in their folly. This is a fine science among most Natives and ends up becoming the name people know each other by. In this tradition, we facetiously called these wealthy people the Owners.

In *Stories of My Horses*, a specific division of the Owners is meant by the use of the word the Owners.

Our particular, local branch of the Owners, having no real experience with hands-on ranching or horse breeding to begin with, themselves fell prey to many *helpful shysters* whose *cost cutting* schemes resulted in a number of bad decisions made by the Owners, i.e.: badly designed barns, corrals, training pens, purchases of sub-standard hay and feed etc. Entrepreneurial opportunists can always be found on the fringes of any family with money, and one of these dreamed up a way to use miles and miles of conveyor-belting discarded by some failed assembly line facility. After convincing at least one *horse authority* on the more *humane* stretchy qualities of pens and corrals made by stringing heavy, three inch strips of rubber conveyor belting between creosote-soaked railroad ties, also discarded by the train companies, several wealthy horse people adopted this form of horse housing. Following suit, our particular Owners made so many runs and pens, including a double-story barn, of these materials that their horse operation was locally known as the *conveyor-belt horse facility*.

Unfortunately, the fiberglass and nylon-fiber-reinforcement-webbing running through this conveyor-belt rubber was always stripping off, causing colts who accidentally ingested these to experience severe intestinal obstructions and colic. The multiple accidents to frightened horses trapped into the stretchy fencing, combined with the constant exposure to heavy metals ingested by the horses chewing on the rubber, mostly lead, not to mention the arsenic in the treated railroad posts, caused tremendous health problems, several deaths, and a general unsettled character to all this would-be *horse rescue*.

What most people who just loved these particular horses didn't grasp was that the Owners throughout the country didn't actually want to have viable businesses with these horses. They wanted to have a money-losing operation that allowed a few of them to look like saviors, while saving taxes for their families, thereby *making money*.

Unlike the beautiful Native Spanish Mesta Barbs, the Owners were a specific breed of people who are still very easy to find and certainly don't need rescuing. The horses they said they were keeping vital have practically disappeared, yet again, back into the matrix of the world.

While there are people who still love, keep, understand, and ride these animals, most have learned to lie very low and maintain what they do hidden away in their own unflamboyant existences. Ironically though, many of us in New Mexico, not so very long ago, grew up riding these exact types of horses on the Reservations. After the horses evaporated into the incoming *white American* lifestyle of the 1950's and 60's, in order for any of us to gather up even just a few of these old-time animals in the 1980's, we had to turn to these same rich people who were ruining them by claiming to save them for their tax write-offs, because, by then, only the Owners had them!

Platica (pláh-tee-cah) – Spanish for conversation. In New Mexico, and other parts of the Americas, *platica* can mean the distilled central meaning of what someone is trying to get across.

Proud flesh – when a horse experiences a gash, like cats, their bodies quickly self-bandage themselves and try to cover the exposed flesh by naturally producing a kind of thick, gooey, very frothy, white substance that seems to keep out flies and dirt, but sometimes solidifies and cracks. Though it's part of the natural healing process, we generally wash it off to keep the wound filling with real tissue, which if given a chance horses do admirably.

Quirt (Southwestern American English) – cowboy foreshortening of the Spanish word *cuarta*, signifying a short riding whip that can take any number of forms.

The classic Mexican quirt has a wristband that attaches to a semi-stiff, tapered, braided shank about ten to fifteen inches long that has two, twelve-to-eighteen-inch latigo lashes attached at the bottom. Usually very ornately braided leather over rawhide, but sometimes five multi-colored strands of rawhide braided over a rawhide core, or even different colors of sorted horsehair braided over a braided rawhide shank, quirts can be quite beautiful. Different Native American tribes in North America made extraordinary, customized quirts from pieces of moose antler and skin, elk antler, wood covered in brass tacks, buffalo or mountain sheep horn, all with lashes of stiff, brain-tanned neck leather or braided lashes and fancy beaded wristbands.

All over South America, particularly the Gauchos in Argentina, some Spaniards, various North African peoples, Turkmen nomads, Bashkir and Kyrgiz still make beautiful quirts covered in silver. Except for Gauchos, Chileanos, and American cowboys, who ride with quirts and spurs, most quirt-riding traditions don't use spurs to cue or motivate their horses, preferring the quirt to direct signals. The author is a quirt rider and quirt collector.

Rateros (Spanish American slang) – means thieves or pick-pockets. From the word for rat.

Roan (Anglified medieval Spanish word) – signifies a horse who is covered in two or more distinct colors of hair in tight formation, so as to appear as a single color from a distance, but changes in tonality at different angles of the sun. There are red roans (white and red mixed), yellow roans (yellow and white), blue roans (reflective gray black and white), and grulla (black and red and white tightly mixed). A lot of color variations occur in roan patterns, some horses sporting five or six different coat-color-moltings of roan annually. There are many local terms for these, like: coyote roan, strawberry roan, buttermilk roan, etc. The research is not all in on the real dynamics of roan coloration, because, in my own experience, a totally different follicle function happens in the old *Mesta* roans that has seemed to defy veterinary science to date.

Round pen – self-explanatory. Looks like a circular corral, about sixty-five feet in diameter, but with no troughs or horse furniture, in which horses can be rather easily trained. The theory is that since horses run to get away from what scares them, if they flee from a person on the edge of the circle by running away, since the fencing is circular, the horse ends up right back where they started next to the person. In this way, when employed properly, a horse can be slowly made less wary and learn a number of rudimentary lessons on the ground, before being mounted to become a saddle horse. Round pens are very useful for helping rejuvenate convalescing horses, or taking the *sparks off* of an edgy animal: for exercising animals into a more reasonable mood.

Sabina (Spanish) – the One-seed Juniper tree, whose very fragrant, durable presence covers most of the area of Northern New Mexico from five thousand to seven thousand feet. Most people from tall tree or forested parts of the world have no respect for our little New Mexico *Sabina* tree, but it forms a belt running the entire circumference of the Earth's land masses, all the way from Manchuria and Mongolia, through parts of Northern Europe, into a lot of North America. Where it grows, it is universally considered very powerful good luck and health. The word *sabina* is also a modern horse color phrase.

Side saddle – this is a pretty strange rig invented for European ladies, in that period when dress styles interfered with straddling a horse, and when a woman straddling a horse was considered too *barbarian* and unladylike. All nomadic tribes had incredible woman horse riders, none of whom were stuck riding side saddles. You have to see a side saddle in action to understand its function. But in short, it involves a rather bulky asymmetrical saddle with only one stirrup on the left, upon which a lady mounts by plopping her bottom into a tall side-facing cantle, after which she wraps her right leg around a kind of cushioned post protruding at about ten o'clock from the pommel, so that both legs are essentially hanging from the left side of the horse. Very hard on a horse's back and strange looking in motion, but I've seen women who can really ride in one. Running from the 12th century to the 20th, where along with the riding habit (a gentlewoman's riding *costume*), wasp-waisted-baleen-corseting, slave-ownership, and of course a crop, it's part of European gentry horse history.

Snaffle/snaffle bit (English) (*filete* in Spanish) – a basic bit used worldwide, in which pressure from the reins is directly on the bars of the horse's mouth. Developed by proto-Scythian, Indo-European pastoral nomads three to four thousand years back, it was often the only metal (bronze originally) part of all their horse's harness. Composed mostly of two cheek-rings that are attached to the headstall and reins, the rings are connected to each other through the horse's mouth by two loose-sliding, metal bars jointed in the middle that runs over the horse's tongue. Considered the most gentle type of bit by most.

Saddle tree (English), or *fuste* (Spanish) – as used in this book, the core frame of a Southwestern saddle, upon which are mounted successive layers of vegetable-tan leather, rigging straps, cinches, stirrup leathers, and stirrups. Different cultures do it different ways. The Spanish use a basket frame, the American Southwest a wood frame. The saddles, as described herein, fit a horse only as good as its tree fits. A bad fitting tree is a bad fitting saddle.

Sangre de Cristos (Spanish) – literally Blood of Christ. The main Northern New Mexico mountain range that is the southernmost part of the Southern Rockies. Running north to south, this beautiful range divides Northern New Mexico ecosystems. To the east are the old-time buffalo plains, and to the west are the Jemez mountains and extensive canyon, desert, river land.

Strangely, the name was never originally used by New Mexican Spanish speakers, who called these mountains the *Sierra Nevadas*, or the *Snowy Saw*, or *Snowy Range*, as they called many ranges throughout their colonies.

It was a bunch of white Americans in the New Mexico Tourist Promotion Bureau trying to drum up business for New Mexico, who in the early 20th century, invented this romantic name and passed it off as an old Spanish settler term for the range, stating that New Mexico Spanish speaking Catholics likened the red glow that shone on the slopes during many of New Mexico's spectacular sunsets to the *Blood of Christ* on Good Friday! Of course every hill and mountain in our area is red at sunset. But these mountains really are wonderful, and the heart of all the land and people who lived around them, and now they are the Sangres.

Shinny – an Algonquin term used by Anglos for all the field hockey type games among all the Native tribes of the Americas. There are hundreds of styles and varieties. In New Mexico Pueblo culture, shinny is a ceremonial game played at only a certain time of year by two large teams, whose players each wield two curved sticks and a special stuffed hide ball. It's loud, rowdy, never ends, and a lot of fun. There are man-forms and lady-forms.

Smokey withers – a Southwestern cowboy term for a horse with a dark, smokey patch of fur covering both sides of the withers, also called a smokey cross.

Sorrel (English), *alazán* (Spanish) – horse coat color. Horse coat colors are impossible to describe accurately in short words and in the end are so thoroughly infused with the biases of the cultures of the people talking, the ambient light, which changes not only the horse's coat, but its appearance, that names of horse colors are vast. They totally change from climate and sun saturation and language. Plus, people are just as *racist* about how their horse colors equal their breeds, as they are about their fellow humans. The sorrel horse is a Western American term and signifies a beautiful red horse with no black points and maybe a blaze or a star. The Spanish equivalent for what is sorrel in the West, the word *alazán* is used. In both cases, the original meaning of either word refers to vegetation. *Alazán* refers to the color of a safflower plant at its different stages of color as it withers from a yellow to a beautiful red-brown. Sorrel is an ancient Germanic word for the dry season color of certain coastal creeping grasses.

To me, a sorrel or an *alazán*, light, medium, dark or crayon red, just means a good red horse. This red color is the color that all feral horses assume when bred together for ages. Whole bands of red sorrel horses abound in the West. So sorrel mares are a veritable genetic seed bank of horse colors waiting to re-emerge when the right man finally shows up.

Spiderwebbing – wild, dark, squiggly lines along the forearms or withers of a horse's coat color, left over from early Pleistocene wild horse color.

Stallion – a sexually intact male horse or donkey who is capable of breeding mares. They are by nature very contentious, powerfully built, and a handful. It's rare to see people riding stallions without incident, but there are those that can and do.

Sunglaze – an imaginative term for a badly understood phenomena that takes place on the sleek summer coats of certain types of horses.

Seemingly holographic, this *sunglaze* is sometimes only apparent at certain angles, while others are visible in direct light, usually floating above the base color of the coat, as if the horse were emitting light.

A solid black horse may have a *red sunglaze* in dapples that floats at a certain angle of the sun, over the black. A light yellow buckskin might have an *orange sunglaze* at a certain angle, kind of opal like. A *blue sunglaze* on a roan will reflect the sky and give out an amazing, magical blue roan.

Old-time Native/Spanish/Mesta Barbs are famous for their opalescent sunglaze. Some people confuse this with the sunfade, which can be similar, but is only the bleaching of the tips of a dark horse's hair by the intense sun, giving a kind of *frosted* effect.

Taboon (Russian) – used to describe the Central Asian and nomad custom of raising horses in large mare-and-foal herds with a single stallion in wide-open, unfenced territory. In taboon style, only geldings are ridden, and few stallions kept, and all mares are free to make more babies, and to be milked to make *kumiss* or fermented-milk liquor.

Ta'á Diné – see *Diné*.

Tie down (American cowboy English) – a leather strap that clips to the base of a noseband, to a ring on the breast collar, or front cinch, that is adjusted so a horse can't toss his head or swing it about. I don't like tie downs. A lot of people use them.

Victorio – the non-Indian name of a very heroic and amazing Warm Springs Apache leader in the late 19th century, whose attempted friendship with whites in Southern New Mexico landed him and all his people, simultaneously, at war with both the US army and the Mexican army. The accounts of Victorio's multiple escapes from captivity on horseback are legendary throughout the Southwest. With a couple of his brave partisans he was killed in a rearguard, decoy-action between both armies, in a strategy that allowed the last remnants of his particular band to escape into a mountain of Northern Mexico, where they vaporized from view, but where everyone says they are living still, suspended in a happy, magical, aboriginal dimension.

Acknowledgments

While this entire trilogy is my attempt to toast and acknowledge all the horses, one by one, whose companionship have always given me the life and vitality of the "wide open ride", it would be remiss not to remember all those people, places, and animals who made the series *Stories of My Horses* possible.

Firstly, of course, a great blessing and thanks to the mystic soul of the open land, the fabulous skies, varied terrain, plants, and animals of my native New Mexico—whose Native peoples, Spanish speaking peoples, and select Anglo ranchers and cowboys were the parent cultures that made me and the horses what we became—and where all the events revealed in the text took place.

Next, I would like to thank the spirits of all the horses themselves, both dead and still living, whose accounts appear in these three books. Without them there would have been nothing to tell.

But...

I would like to thank even more those horses both dead and alive, whose stories do not appear in these books and to apologize to those horses whose stories did for those descriptions of equally dramatic episodes of their lives that I chose to leave out.

For old wisdom insists that it is never a good idea to empty out your sack of life's hard-earned memories all the way. Because good powerful memories are special: like sourdough bread starter, where from every batch you have to keep back a fistful of dough to make the next down the line. In the same way, worthy memories retained re-start the next section of one's life, leavening the dull grind of the present into a life fully lived from where the sack of stories worth remembering is re-stocked! Always good to keep back just a pinch for the next round.

Next, I'd like to send a big, two-person *abrazo* for Liz Dwyer and Curtis Weinrich of North Star Press for their courage, love of beautiful books, love of story, and unique willingness to bring forth the three volumes of the *Stories of My Horses* in such a friendly, professional way. The literary freedom that this willingness has afforded me, allowing me to write and publish books so dear to my life with my unique language use still intact and outside the assigned genre slots where all my previous books are forced to reside, is like letting my "herd of words" out for a good delicious gallop across the forgotten soul of the American West after years of being corralled and contained in the tiny neurotic pens of east coast urban categories.

Then for my typist Susannah Hall in the UK, in honor of the most well-done, patient typing of my hand-written manuscripts, I would like to send a ride in the Queen's carriage (without the Queen, unless of course she insists on coming along) filled to the roof with the best organic butter, with bars of gold, and crates of freshly baked crumpets, tea, and a samovar strapped on top, driven by Hugh and Kayode, to the best of times and a picnic on a revived English eel river to kiss the elvers with their poetry!

Like everything else I endorse, my books are written by hand, with a pen on real paper. But this handwriting of mine is extremely idiosyncratic and hard to decipher to say the least, so it takes a special talent to read my initial screed, then type it, as written, into a program, have me rewrite on a hard copy, scan it and return it to Britain to retype, adding all my amplifications, going back and forth in this way for as many as seven rounds, for every chapter, whilst the manuscript grows into a bigger and bigger, newer and different manifestation over the months, until Ms. Hall discovers that she's been actually typing four books that I'm working on simultaneously!

I know Ms. Hall has a magnifying glass and some other manual aids for deciphering my scrawl, but no doubt she's been blessed by some supernatural to magically pull it off.

In short,

Her typing has been indispensable.

The author as illustrator would like to thank and acknowledge the late Hoke Denetsosie. In the 1930's and 40's this Diné artist developed a black and white, crow-quill pen style of illustrating the most beautiful editions of what were intended as bilingual Navajo/English primers for Native school children to learn to write both Diné and English. The most unlikely publisher for these forgotten books was the Department of Education, in the Bureau of Indian Affairs, Department of Interior, in short the US Government! In a momentary flash of intelligent vision and good-heartedness the government simultaneously put out similar bilingual language books in other Native languages throughout the country, illustrated by artists of the corresponding tribes.

Though Denetsosie's work later became associated with cartoonists and other less worthy endeavors, his illustrations for the *Na'nilkaadi Yazhi* (*Little Herder*) series was more than a brilliant achievement and has never been equaled in originality. Like everything else after WWII, the government numbed up, and anxious in the cold war lost the thread, and what began as an amazing hopeful trend was utterly forgotten. A lot of amazing artists of all types emerged from this trend but most melted away, swept back under the carpet of the craze of technological progress.

But to me the original solutions Hoke Denetsosie came up with on his own, without coaching, or tutoring to illustrate the land and his people of those times were not only so subtly ingenious, but always an inspiration to me, more so because his drawings correspond very well with some of the territory and the moods of the land in which *Stories of My Horses* takes place. He was great, lived to be a very old Native rancher, well loved by his people, but largely overlooked as an artist. I had to say something, for as I drew I always thought about him.

And now I want to say thank you to my little family,

To my beautiful eight-year-old boy Gobi, who loves our

Mesteños as much as I do, who writes stories and edits as much as I do. To my wondrous eleven-year-old star-nebula loving daughter Altai, who also writes and edits as much as I do. And to their incredibly inspired teacher and beautiful determined mother, my wife, Johanna Keller Prechtel, who using our special secret recipe of charred plants, mare, foal, and stallion-manure compost has succeeded in growing a six-foot high broccoli thicket in December when even coyotes freeze solid like statues! (Old time horses are good for lots of things besides riding!).

For their love for me and their patience with my barrage of humor and their tolerance of the overly fierce delivery of my vision regarding the need for a more substantial and beautiful culture that permeates my every word and action cannot be adequately rewarded with any words I could ever conjure.

And to you gentle reader, for your love of the *wild open ride* over the wild open land and your willingness to eschew modern cynicism and ride with me in words, in ways and into places, where hardly any go anymore these days. But if we're not spiritually lazy, things can always change for the better and often do.

All blessings.

About the Author and Illustrator

As an avid student of indigenous eloquence, innovative language and thought, Martín Prechtel is a writer, artist, and teacher who, through his work both written and spoken, hopes to promote the subtlety, irony, and premodern vitality hidden in any living language. A half-blood Native American with a Pueblo Indian upbringing, he left New Mexico to live in the village of Santiago Atitlán, Guatemala, eventually becoming a full member of the Tzutujil Mayan community there. For many years he served as a principal in that body of village leaders responsible for piloting the young people through the meanings of their ancient stories in the rituals of adult rites of passage.

Once again, residing in his beloved New Mexico, Prechtel teaches at his international school, Bolad's Kitchen. Through an immersion into the world's lost seeds and sacred farming, forgotten music, magical architecture, ancient textile making, metalsmithing, the making and using of tools, musical instruments and food and the deeper meanings of the origins of all these things in the older stories, in ancient texts and by teaching through the traditional use of riddles, Prechtel hopes to inspire people of every mind and way to regrow and revitalize real culture and to find their own sense of place in the sacredness of a newly found daily existence in love with the natural world. Prechtel lives with his family and their Native *Mesta* horses in Northern New Mexico.

Martín Prechtel's previous works include: *Secrets of the Talking Jaguar*; *Long Life, Honey in the Heart*; *The Disobedience of the Daughter of the Sun*; *Stealing Benefacio's Roses*; *The Unlikely Peace at Cuchumaquic*; *The Smell of Rain on Dust: Grief and Praise*; *Rescuing the Light;* and *The Mare and the Mouse*.

Cover Painting, *Rewa Dreaming,* by Martín Prechtel.